Lands and Peoples

THE WORLD IN COLOR

VOLUME IV

THE GROLIER SOCIETY

NEW YORK   TORONTO

P

Volume IV

TABLE OF CONTENTS

PAGE

ARID AFGHANISTAN—*A Nation of Highland Warriors*
5 Pages in Full Color 4

THE REPUBLIC OF INDIA—*From the Himalayas to the Indian Ocean*
26 Pages in Full Color 19

PAKISTAN—*The Birth and Growth of a Moslem Nation*
7 Pages in Full Color 70

KASHMIR IN THE HIMALAYAS—*The Loveliest State in India*
2 Pages in Full Color 101

THROUGH THREE FORBIDDEN LANDS—*In Tibet, Nepal and Bhutan*
8 Pages in Full Color 119

BURMA ON THE BAY OF BENGAL—*A Land Where Women are Independent* .. 149

CEYLON THE ISLE OF JEWELS—*Its People and Its Jungle-buried Cities*
8 Pages in Full Color 165

CITY AND JUNGLE IN MALAYA—*Wealthy Eastern Lands and Indolent People* 185

LAND OF THE WHITE ELEPHANT—*The Independent Siamese and Their Country*
6 Pages in Full Color 197

ANCIENT RIVALS OF THE FAR EAST—*Jungles and Rice Fields of Indo-China*
2 Pages in Full Color 213

FORMOSA, CHINA'S ISLAND PROVINCE—*Its Tribes, Once Savage Head-Hunters* 233

THE LAND OF THE DRAGON—*Some Glimpses of China and Manchuria*
16 Pages in Full Color 249

IN UNKNOWN SINKIANG—*Life in China's Westernmost Province* 289

WHERE A LIVING BUDDHA REIGNED—*Desert and Grassland of Mongolia* .. 303

A PEEP AT PEKING (PEIPING)—*Once the Paris of the Orient*
2 Pages in Full Color 317

THE CHRYSANTHEMUM ISLANDS—*Japan—from Kyushu to Hokkaido*
14 Pages in Full Color 333

TOKYO, THE PHOENIX CITY—*Capital of a Beauty-loving People* 365

THE LAND OF THE MORNING CALM—*Korea, One of the Oldest Kingdoms* .. 373

COLOR PLATES IN VOLUME IV 384

HILLS AND MOUNTAINS divide Afghanistan into high plains on which lonely shepherds wander with their flocks. Sheep and goats provide the chief source of wealth in Afghanistan.

4

ARID AFGHANISTAN

A Nation of Highland Warriors

Laced by the principal trade routes of central Asia, Afghanistan sprawls atop a plateau between Iran and Pakistan. The dominating feature of the land, the Hindu Kush range, stretches its knobby fingers from the north far into the lower-lying deserts of the southern frontier. Valleys and high plains between the fingers are fertile. There is little rain and much snow, with fierce winds that race down from the north. The people of this bleak highland are today emerging from a pastoral way of life. New roads, dams, canals, schools and popular elections have brought with them the social ferment that marks all of Asia.

ASIA is the world's largest continent. It has mothered the wonderful civilizations of India and China, with which the travelers of the Middle Ages made us acquainted at the period of their decline. From west to east the continent stretches from the Suez Canal for 6,700 miles to Bering Strait, and from north to south it reaches from Cape Cheliuskin (Severo) for 5,300 miles to, approximately, Singapore. Its climate varies from the arctic to the tropical, and barring the islands off its shores, the continent presents a solid parallelogram scalloped with the peninsulas of Arabia, India, Indochina and Kamchatka. The Japanese archipelago is the largest of various offshore islands.

The northern Temperate Zone extends along southern Siberia, while fertile grasslands creep along the valley of the Amur and on to the Pacific. Central Asia is, however, an elevated tableland ranging from ten to seventeen thousand feet in altitude, which extends from the Pamir to the Gobi Desert with the Himalayas for its southern boundary. (The Gobi is only four thousand feet above the level of the sea.) This central tableland has lakes of salt. It shows evidences of having been visited by devastating sandstorms. Of what the sand may at the same time have destroyed and preserved, further reference will be made. The Himalayas, "the Abode of Snow," which contain the highest peaks on earth, are the dividing wall between the north and the south. To the north the climate is often unkind, and in some parts the people have been pinned to the seeking of the bare means to existence. To the south abundance of food and ease of finding shelter have permitted the development of a high degree of civilization. Of rivers, China possesses in the Yangtse Kiang the longest on the continent. It is navigable for fifteen hundred miles. India's Brahmaputra, the Ganges with its tributaries and the Indus are among the great rivers of the world. The Irawadi is hardly less important. Of mountains and rivers Asia has a lion's share. She has not, however, many lakes.

Afghanistan is strategically one of the most important states in Moslem Asia. Though a Persian word for highlander may explain the term "Afghans," Afghan chroniclers call these people Beni-Israel and claim descent from King Saul through his grandson Afghana. The country borders on Iran, the Soviet Union, Kashmir, and the Northwest Frontier Provinces and Baluchistan of Pakistan. The land rises gradually from the stony deserts in the south to the Hindu Kush in the north, a continuation of the Himalayan system called the Roof of the World. The isolation of the people is due in part to the fact that the northern spurs of these mountains present impassable barriers; some peaks reach skyward twenty-four thousand feet and even some passes present the traveler with glaciers, nineteen thousand feet above the sea. This causes the climate to vary sharply not only from season to season but from noon to night. In summer the temperature sometimes rises as high as 100 degrees, but in winter the cold is correspondingly intense; an icy wind

GRACE AND DELICACY LAVISHED ON A TOWER FOR DEFENSE

The fort has long since been deserted, and the exquisite tower stands desolate. Afghanistan is scattered with ancient forts. It was the Bactria of Alexander the Great; Tamerlane swept over it; and the old silk route between Europe and the Far East led through the perilous mountains. Sometimes caravans returned with the rose-red balas rubies of Badakhshan (part of Bactria).

MERCHANTS PRAY IN THE BAZAAR

The Mohammedan religion requires its followers to worship five times daily: at dawn, after noon, before the sun sets, after it has set and after the day has ended. The worshipers face in the direction of Mecca and prostrate themselves on their prayer rugs. Friday is the "day of the assembly," when the people gather in their mosques to unite in prayer.

blows down from the snow-covered mountains and whistles through the narrow valleys, while the thermometer falls below zero.

Except for the military road through Khyber Pass between Peshawar and Kabul, the traveler must follow the valleys and climb the passes by the few rough trails that exist. Much of the region has seen few outsiders since Alexander the Great marched through the country in 326 B.C. on his way to India; and traveling is rarely undertaken even by the natives save in huge camel caravans well armed against brigands.

Deep canyons gash the central highlands. There is one defile between Kabul and Herat, ninety feet in width, that is bordered on each side by fifteen-hundred-foot limestone cliffs; for the same volcanic action that upheaved the Himalayas raised this region, fold on fold of sedimentary rock. In the mountains west of Kabul there are also great boulder bed terraces left by retreating glaciers.

The Afghans have been skillful in irrigating the narrow valleys, especially in the north where the villages are half hidden in spring by the blossoms of the orchard trees. The vineyards are famous throughout Asia, and the valley of the Herat is noted for its melons. From Kandahar great caravans take fruit down to Quetta, fortified town in Baluchistan that controls the Bolan Pass. All kinds of ordinary fruits are grown, besides mangoes and pomegranates. In both the south and east two harvests are gathered; the spring crop consists of wheat, barley and lentils, the autumn crop of rice, millet, corn and tobacco. Two other products of value are asafetida and castor-oil.

Afghanistan is comparatively rich in minerals, among which are gold, silver, coal, iron and lead, while the northern part contains copper. However, no organized attempt has been made to develop these resources.

Armed caravans with cattle, horses, and pack animals laden with fruit, silk, carpets, drugs, the wool and skins of the fat-tailed sheep and articles made of camels' and goats' hair make their way to Peshawar, Lahore, Quetta and Bokhara. They bring back tea, sugar, indigo and cotton goods—if the caravan is not plundered along the way by untamed hillmen.

The highlanders do not call themselves Afghans. Certain of the tribes speak

Persian, others Pushtoo, a Persian language to which a number of words from other languages have been added. The most important tribes are the Durani, a people of Persian origin, who have ruled Afghanistan since 1747; the Ghilzais, a race famous for their swordsmanship, who occupy the land between Kabul and Kandahar; the Hazaras, the descendants of Tatars who came from Mongolia and who are more trustworthy than the other Afghans, as some of them enlisted in the Indian Army as sappers; the Turkish Tajiks and Uzbegs of Afghan Turkestan, the former of which are sometimes employed as domestic servants and in other subordinate positions; the Aïmaks, also of Turkish extraction, who are found on the plains of the Oxus; and the strange Kafirs of Kafiristan in the Hindu Kush. The Kafirs are the descendants of the people who claimed to be compatriots of the Greeks and who gave Alexander and his army a royal welcome.

All of these tribes, save alone the Kafirs, who are ancestor worshipers, are Mohammedans and have in common certain customs, such as blood feuds, and reprisals; but they hate and distrust one another. Though there is a king, who is aided by a Parliament, his word is law only where it is supported by the bayonets of his soldiers. The Afghans are primarily a nation of horsemen. They also breed horses and annually send hundreds to India.

As a race the Afghans are tall, with hooked noses. Their long black hair is greasy. It is said that an Afghan is washed twice—at birth and just before burial. Their religion teaches them hospitality to the guest who has eaten with them; but an expert can steal a blanket from under a sleeping man without awakening him.

The Afghans, however, have no equals at guerrilla warfare. In a country where every man carries his life in his hands naturally everyone is a soldier, though discipline, even in the regular army, is extremely bad, according to Western standards.

The national costume consists of baggy, dirty-white, pajama-like trousers, a shirt worn outside them and a waistcoat, often elaborately embroidered, over which is sometimes worn a voluminous cloak. On the head is a kullah, or skull-cap, around which is wound a turban with ends falling down the back. The poor wear nothing on their feet or sometimes grass sandals,

BLACK STAR

CLOTHES MAKE THE AFGHAN MAN

While all Afghan children are well cared for, boys are especially cherished. A wealth of colorful embroidery decorates this good-looking youngster's turban and vest. He has probably already learned to ride horseback.

8

A GLACIER of the Chitral border shows with unusual distinctness the deep trough cut by a wide river of ice moving forward only a few feet a day. Valuable timber is obtained from pine woods that cover the lower slopes of many of these high mountains. In some parts wild gooseberries, hawthorns and roses are met with at altitudes up to nine thousand feet.

CATTLE VACCINATION—ONE STEP IN A GOOD HEALTH PROGRAM

Afghanistan's public-health program, started in 1943, was put on a sound basis in 1950 by UN advisers. Healthy cows mean germ-free milk, butter, cheese and meat.

THE WIDENED MAIN STREET IN KABUL IS COATED WITH ASPHALT

The once narrow, dark streets in Kabul have been transformed. They are now great, wide boulevards which gleam white and eerie at night under newly installed electric lights.

10

A TAILORED COAT OR A HOMESPUN ROBE SHUTS OUT CHILL WINDS

It was once said that to step across the disputed border from Pakistan into Afghanistan was to step back a century. Western overcoats are one of the many signs of modernization today.

11

FRUIT FROM KANDAHAR is sent all over Afghanistan, and even to the bazaars of Quetta, Baluchistan. The soil of Afghanistan is fertile but rainfall is scanty, so that irrigation is necessary in most parts. Each of these men wears a turban, the appearance of which is somewhat rope-like, wound around a skull-cap which is called a "kullah." This is the usual fashion among the tribes of the Afghanistan-Pakistan border. The fruit exposed for sale includes grapes, pomegranates, sugar melons and dates. The dates, however, come from Iraq, once called Mesopotamia.

12

EDWARDES

AFGHAN WOMEN work very hard, and in consequence they lose their good looks at an early age. One of the hardest tasks that falls to the lot of a poor woman is that of collecting wood. Many miles of rough ground must have been covered by this woman before she gathered the unwieldy load that she bears upon her back, for the land except in the valleys is barren.

A STREET IN KABUL, CAPITAL OF LITTLE-KNOWN AFGHANISTAN

Kabul, in the fertile valley of the Kabul River in the eastern part of the Asiatic country, is hemmed in by mountains known as the Hindu Kush. Only 125 miles to the east is the historic Khyber Pass through which ancient hordes invaded India. The plains around the city are watered each spring by melting mountain snows, but winters are severely cold.

FOOD COOKED WHILE YOU WAIT IN KABUL, AFGHANISTAN

Where the summers are warm and dry and the pace is unhurried, a passer-by has time to pause and purchase food from an accommodating vendor. Afghanistan as a whole is still quite backward and undeveloped, and the only modernization that has been accomplished is in the city of Kabul. Since the turn of the century some industries have been established.

ADULTS LEARN TO READ, THE EASY WAY, IN KABUL

Word charts (the script is Arabic) with pictures are a visual aid to the teaching of reading. Until recent years, most of the Afghans, a wandering people, could neither read nor write. To overcome this handicap, there are schools for adults as well as children. Some classes are in modern buildings; others are held on hillsides for the shepherds and their families.

but the wealthier classes affect richly worked leather slippers.

Outside the towns, such as Kabul, Kandahar, Herat and Ghazni, the Afghans live in fortified villages, with the local khan's, or chief's, house, which usually has a high tower at one corner as the citadel and rallying point. The ordinary house is a single-story structure built of mud bricks, with a flat roof on which the family sleeps during the summer. The windows are without glass and have thick wooden shutters. The door is of rough timber and is secured at night by a heavy beam thrust through staples. No carpets cover the mud floor: a string bed or two and a pestle and mortar for grinding grain comprise the furniture. The kitchen is outdoors in a walled courtyard at the back and consists of a mud oven, a pot for boiling meat and a sheet of iron on which thin cakes of bread are baked.

Like nearly all Eastern races, the Afghans are kind to their children, of whom the boys are the more prized by the parents. Perhaps this is only natural in a land where every man is wanted for raiding or for protection against raiders and where the son must carry on the blood feuds of the father. Though elementary

15

education is compulsory and colleges have been founded at Kabul, the only education received by a large majority of the boys is instruction in the Koran from the village mullah, or priest.

Afghanistan is the region that dominates India's overland communications with Europe; its southeastern border is on the frontier of Pakistan. Actually there are two lines, the political boundary which is shown on maps, and an "administrative boundary" which runs irregularly about thirty miles east of the political boundary. The area between is known as tribal territory; it is governed by the tribes themselves. This has proved to be a convenient arrangement as Afghans are extremely sensitive about trespassing on their territory and the British can thus deal with raiding tribes without entering Afghanistan proper. The country is little developed as Afghans are suspicious of change. In their resistance to Western reforms, it was possible to remove Europeans from

Kabul by airplane, over forested ravines and precipices and snow-filled defiles, which have always made it easy for the Afghan mountaineers to maintain their independent ways against the inroads of civilization. In the meantime, it seems a matter for manslaughter to the Afghan Moslem who glories in his beard to be ordered to shave, while the substitution of the Western hat and trousers for the fez and the loose nether garments in which he is accustomed to sit cross-legged on the ground is an infringement of his ancient rights to which he will not be easily converted. The unveiling of his womenfolk, the forbidding of the court officials to have many wives, and the sight of his queen in Parisian short skirts was a shock ill calculated to bridge a gulf of thousands of years of conservatism in this regard. Manhood suffrage was, however, adopted as one step toward progress.

AFGHANISTAN: FACTS AND FIGURES

THE COUNTRY

Bounded on the north by the Turkmen Socialist Soviet Republic of the U.S.S.R., on the east and south by western Pakistan and on the west by Iran (Persia). The area is 250,000 square miles. The population, according to the latest Afghan estimate, is about 11,000,000.

GOVERNMENT

Since 1922, the government has been a constitutional monarchy with legislative power vested in a Parliament which consists of a king, a Senate and an Assembly. The Senate is made up of a maximum of 50 members nominated for life by the king; the Assembly of 171 members who are elected. The country is divided into 7 major and 3 minor provinces, each of which is under a governor. In 1926, the title of King instead of Amir was adopted.

COMMERCE AND INDUSTRIES

Most of the country is mountainous, but the fertile plains yield well with the assistance of irrigation. Two crops a year are harvested, one in autumn consisting of rice, millet and corn and the other in spring consisting of wheat, barley, peas and beans. Fruit and vegetables are abundant. Fat-tailed sheep furnish the chief meat diet. The fat of the

tail is used as a substitute for butter, and the wool is the principal export. Horses, camels and goats are raised also. Minerals include copper, lead, iron, coal, gold and lapis lazuli. The chief industries are manufactures of silk, felts, carpets and articles from camels' and goats' hair. Exports, chiefly to India and Pakistan, are raw wool, manufactured woolen piece goods, fruits, vegetables, asafetida and other drugs, spices, cattle and hides, and the imports are cotton goods, indigo and dyeing material, sugar, tea, hardware and leather.

COMMUNICATIONS

There are no railways in the country, and there are practically no navigable rivers. Merchandise is carried by camel and pony on government trade routes. In the larger towns, there is telephone and telegraph service.

RELIGION AND EDUCATION

Nearly all of the people are Sunni Mohammedans. Elementary education is free and there are various special schools for higher education. Kabul has a university.

CHIEF TOWNS

Populations (estimated): Kabul, the capital, 206,208; Kandahar, 77,186; Herat, 75,632; Mazar-i-Sharif, 41,960; Jalalabad, 14,756.

THE REPUBLIC OF INDIA

From the Himalayas to the Indian Ocean

With the birth of the Republic of India there began one of the greatest adventures in democracy the world has yet seen. For until then the Indian people had had little experience in governing themselves but were ruled by kings, emperors, princes or viceroys. For centuries India has been a melting pot of many groups, so that even today a variety of languages are spoken and there is a host of different customs. To weld all these groups together, to teach them the ways of democracy and to raise their standard of living are the great tasks of the young Republic. Confident of success, India optimistically faces the future.

THE ancient land of India is today like a land reborn. Not until 1947 did it become free and independent, after years of British rule. Since that time many changes have taken place. These changes affect every one of its millions, from the poor villager plodding down a dusty bullock track to the university-educated Indian hurrying through a city street to his law office.

In a few years, more than 550 princely states, large and small, disappeared from India's map. The rajahs who ruled these states under the British are today rajahs in name only; their domains belong to the people. In the place of British provinces and princely states are twenty-eight orderly states in which many people for the first time have the right to choose their own leaders. War has been declared against poverty and its by-products, illiteracy and ignorance. Indian farmers, who had been using the same time-worn methods as their fathers and grandfathers before them, are learning new ways of increasing crop production. Land is being reclaimed from the desert, jungle growth and weeds. Scores of dams are being built to harness rivers and to irrigate the land. New industries are being founded; and millions, adults as well as children, are being taught to take their place in changing India.

On January 26, 1950, India officially became a sovereign democratic republic. To Indians this day is as important as the Fourth of July is to Americans or Dominion Day to Canadians, and Republic Day is celebrated every year with great parades. India's constitution guarantees to all its people, regardless of race, caste, color or creed, religious and political freedom.

Mahatma Gandhi is regarded as the father of India. This shy, saintly little man, working with the Indian National Congress, brought about through nonviolent resistance and civil disobedience India's political freedom. Preaching Moslem, Hindu and Christian doctrines alike, he was deeply touched by the inequalities imposed on India's untouchables, the lowest of the old Hindu castes. Today, renamed by him *Harijans,* meaning children of God, they are taking their place in a new and free India where caste discrimination is forbidden by law. Jawaharlal Nehru, no less active in India's fight for independence, followed Gandhi as India's popular hero and became its prime minister in 1947.

As a republic, India is one of the youngest states to take its place among the nations of the world. Paraphrasing the Britisher who claims "there has always been an England," the Indian can claim that there has always been an India. More than five thousand years ago there were flourishing cities on the banks of the Indus (now in Pakistan). Few Westerners realize what we owe to the ancient civilization of India. The Arabic numerals and the idea of zero, without which our scientists would be helpless, were discovered by Indian mathematicians and used in India for many centuries before they found their way to Europe. Indians were solving complicated geometrical problems

THE PEARL PALACE built by the Maharajah Sindhia of Gwalior stands in the middle of a beautiful park known as the Phul Bagh, which means the Garden of Flowers. The princely state of Gwalior became part of Madhya Bharat, a constituent state of the Indian Republic, in 1948. Massive buildings, pavilions, pleasure grounds and ornamental lakes fill the grounds of the palace, where the former rulers of Gwalior lived. The photograph was taken from the huge fortress that, perched on its high rock, frowns over and offers protection to the town of Gwalior.

THE FORTRESS OF DAULATABAD stands in Hyderabad, a constituent state of the Republic of India. The fort was built in the thirteenth century, and then it could not be breached. It crowns an isolated granite rock, the sides of which rise straight up to a height of a hundred feet all around. On the encircling plain beneath are six lines of stone walls, and the bridge over the great moat leads to a passage cut through the rock. On the summit stands a pavilion and the citadel, which is reached by climbing a steep flight of exactly one hundred steps.

21

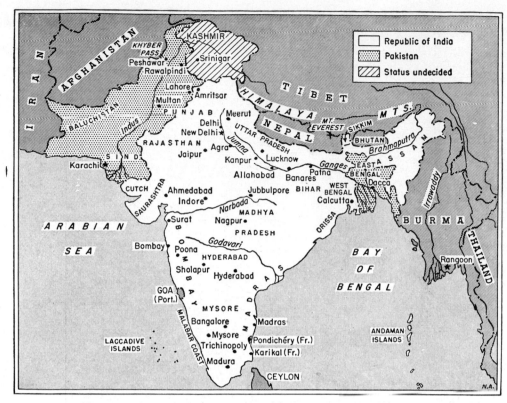

THE POLITICAL DIVISIONS OF THE INDIAN SUBCONTINENT

long before the rest of the world was able to do so. Even Aesop's fables, with which children everywhere are familiar, had their origin in India.

Not all the Indian land that had been formerly under British rule was united under the Republic. When the British recognized the right of India to its independence in 1947, they granted to every province and princely state the right to determine its own status. The Moslem leaders of some northwestern provinces in which Moslems were a majority and those in East Bengal felt that they should form a separate nation. Today the northwestern provinces form Western Pakistan. On the peninsula's northeast coast, separated by eight hundred miles of Indian territory, is Eastern Pakistan. On India's east and west coasts are some small colonies of France and Portugal. India's other neighbors are Nepal, Tibet, Bhutan and China in the north, and Burma in the east.

India is still a large country. In terms of population its 357,000,000 people make it second only to China. One out of seven people in the world is an Indian. As a democracy, India has the largest number of voters in the world.

From its tip in the tropics, at Cape Comorin, India stretches two thousand miles north, spreading in the shape of a giant triangle to the majestic heights of the perpetually snow-clad Himalayas. South of India's three-thousand-mile frontier the land varies from some of the world's highest mountains and broadest river valleys to great plains and high plateaus fringed by dense forests and uncut jungle. At its northeast end, in the state of Assam, the little village of Cherrapunji receives the world's heaviest rainfall, as much as five hundred inches in one season. In the northwest, years pass without the parched soil of some parts of Rajasthan receiving a drop.

On either side of south India, two mountain ranges, the Eastern and Western Ghats, roughly follow its coasts for

A HUGE IMAGE, of *papier-mâché* and wood, is a feature of a *puja*, or religious festival, at which the adventures of Rama are dramatized.   The *Ramayana* is a famous Indian epic poem.

SPLENDID SOLDIERS, such as these Marathas or Mahrattas of central and western India, in the seventeenth and eighteenth centuries conquered a number of states later under British rule. They were defeated by the British in 1803 and again in the war of 1816-18. The Marathas are a handsome group of Hindus and number around twelve million.

24

about a thousand miles. These ranges are the rims of the great central plateau of southern India, the Deccan. Between the Ghats and the sea are two fertile coastal strips. The Malabar Coast on the west and the heavily wooded crags of the Western Ghats are the first area to receive the moisture-laden winds known as monsoons, which bring nearly all of India's rain in one season. From June to September the monsoon travels diagonally across the peninsula, showering great curtains of rain as it goes. The impenetrable wall of the Himalayas then sends them reeling back over northern India.

The Roar of Mighty Rivers

In remote caverns and icy reaches of the towering Himalayas is the origin of India's mightiest rivers, the Ganges and the Brahmaputra. Starting from many little tributaries, which go thundering down through steep gorges cut by centuries of flowing water, the two rivers flow far apart. North of Assam the Brahmaputra makes a U-turn, flows down through the hills and jungles of Assam to mingle its waters with that of the Ganges in numerous smaller rivers of the Ganges Delta before emptying in the Bay of Bengal.

For most of India there are only three seasons, the monsoon or rainy season from June to September, when the air is bracing and pleasant, a mild winter season, and a very hot season from March to June. The south of India maintains its tropical climate all year round, but December and January in central and northern India have hot days followed by cold nights, sometimes producing frost.

Nature Lends Her Blessings

Nature has been bountiful to India. It has forests of deodar, teak, sal, ebony, blackwood, lac and bamboo, many rare, brilliantly hued orchids and the hundred-petaled lotus. Its southern coasts are fringed with groves of coconut, banana and mango trees, and almost every kind of fruit is found in the land. Its banyan trees are giants, little forests in themselves. With branches dropping shoots to the ground, they attain enormous proportions. In the Botanical gardens of Calcutta there is a banyan tree more than 170 years old and more than 1,000 feet in circumference.

The coming of the monsoon is a miracle to behold. Within a week, shriveled grass, brittle brush and brown landscape are transformed into thick, luxuriant greenness. Where one had an unobstructed view of a field a week before, the land is now covered by all manner of growth which seems to have mushroomed under one's very eyes. No wonder that a famous German scholar of Indian culture, Max Müller, once said, "If I were to look over the whole world to find the country most richly endowed with all the wealth, power and beauty that nature could bestow—in some places a very paradise on earth—I should point to India."

Costumes and Customs

Even more striking than the land are India's colorful people. No more fascinating variety in human types, costumes and customs can be found anywhere in the world. Gay, multicolored and graceful saris are worn by the majority of women. Wide gypsylike skirts and jackets mark the women of Rajputana, and bright satin trousers and velvet jackets the hillwomen. A village woman is likely to be dressed in a skirt, short blouse and duppatta scarf thrown over her shoulder. Bearded Sikhs and Rajputs are proudly turbanned and attired in dignified close-fitting coats and loose white trousers. The peasant in his loin cloth, the student with his shirt hanging out over loose cotton pants and wearing a Gandhi cap, the ash-covered and painted ascetic who has renounced the world to seek spiritual truth—all and more are to be found in this storied land.

In race, Indians are mainly a blend of two peoples, the Aryans and the Dravidians. No one is sure from where either of these peoples came, but the Dravidians, a dark-skinned city-dwelling people, were in possession of the land when the Aryans descended on the river valleys of north India about four thousand years ago. The Aryans were a light-skinned

THE PEARL MOSQUE at Delhi was built in the seventeenth century as a private chapel for the Emperor Aurangzeb, third son of Shah Jehan, who usurped the throne in 1658, after murdering two brothers and imprisoning his father. The mosque is of marble wonderfully carved, and decorated with colored designs. It lies within the walls of the fortress-palace.

AN EXECUTIONER of a maharaja's court in the days when the princes of India had absolute power of life and death over their subjects. This giant of a man must have been a terrifying figure, his bulk made even greater by armor studded with sharp spikes. His shield and curved sword must also have been wielded mightily in hand-to-hand combat.

people who probably came from central Asia or Europe and sprang from the same stock as do most Europeans. They were proud warriors and drove furiously into battle on chariots, chasing the Dravidians southward.

Although, as the centuries passed, the two peoples intermingled, the Dravidians predominate in the south and the descendants of the Aryans in the north. Through the caste system, which separated people into groups according to hereditary occupations, many high-born Indians have maintained their Aryan features. A Brahmin teacher or a Rajput noble of the north is likely to be light-complexioned, sometimes with blue or gray eyes, and in features quite like a European. In the south the Dravidian's descendant of Madras is dark, wavy-haired and thin-faced.

Though these are the two peoples from which Indians are mainly descended, many others invaded India. Persians, Greeks, Huns, Scythians, Arabs, Turks, Afghans and Mongols poured through India's mountain passes in search of plunder or land and added their strains to the population. Some of these mixtures have produced distinct types still existing today. On the Malabar Coast are Semitic-looking peoples, probably the descendants of Arab traders who settled there generations ago. In north Bombay State the brown, stalwart Marathas, India's last great conquering people, are believed to be a mixture of Scythian, Aryan and Dravidian. In the mountainous north and in Bengal, the Indians are likely to have a slightly Oriental cast to their eyes, showing the influence of long-forgotten invasions of Mongoloid peoples.

Outside of Indian civilization, but perhaps the original inhabitants of the land, are primitive tribes living in inaccessible

PHILIP GENDREAU

THE CANALS OF ALLEPPY, a town in the southwestern state of Travancore, extend many miles inland. They serve as a means of communication with the inhabitants of the interior.

THE HIRAKUD DAM under construction on the Mahanadi River. Through an irrigation and flood-control program, India hopes to increase her annual food supply by 8,000,000 tons.

A CARVED BANANA TREE frames the entrance of a Hindu temple in the city of Jaipur. The temple is located in the heart of the city on the grounds of the Palace of Amber.

A SADHU lying on a bed of thorns attracts a crowd in Banaras. Sadhus, or holy men, live in poverty, depending upon alms as they wander throughout India performing marvelous feats.

THE HAUNTING TONES played by an Indian snake charmer entrance a deadly hooded cobra. The man sits with complete confidence, knowing that his music will hold the snake at bay.

THE JAMA MASJID at Ahmadabad, a city that was once the greatest in western India, is one of the loveliest mosques in the East. It was built by Shah Ahmed in the fifteenth century. The pointed arches and the elaborate decoration that covers every visible surface are typical of this period of architecture, which flowered in India during the reign of the Mogul emperors. Christians are allowed to enter mosques, but before entering one they must take off their shoes and leave them outside, as do the Mohammedans themselves.

THE KEEPER OF A SHRINE sits before an open-air temple, tolling a bell throughout the day. The bell calls passers-by to come to prayer. Imposing masks, one black and one white, crowned with exotic headdresses, represent the gods. Spread before them are offerings of food, some of it served to the deities in brightly polished copper pots and dishes.

RADIAL ROADS extend in all directions from Connaught Place, the commercial center of New Delhi. Founded in 1912, the city was laid out in a symmetrical design by its architects.

THE ALL INDIA RADIO BUILDING, located a short distance from Connaught Place, stands as one of the finest examples of contemporary Indian architecture in the city of New Delhi.

COTTON MILLS provide the chief source of employment for the citizens of Bombay and the surrounding districts. Above, two workers at the Spring Mills are baling the spun cloth.

© E. N. A.

DELHI'S GREAT MOSQUE, the Jama Masjid, is one of the largest mosques in all the Islamic world. Three domes of white marble rise from the roof. The two minarets are 130 feet in height, and from them a wonderful view of the entire city can be obtained. In days long ago, the huge doors of the main gateway were opened only to admit the Mogul emperors, and they are used now only on state occasions and by personages of great prestige; other visitors may enter only by the wicket. The mosque was built by Shah Jehan in the seventeenth century.

A MONUMENT erected at Alwar in memory of a former maharajah stands beside the still waters of a pool. Children sit upon the steps leading down to the pool, while their elders gossip in the shade of one of the pavilions. Founded by the Rajput chieftain Pretap Singh in the latter half of the eighteenth century, Alwar has many fine palaces and temples.

areas of the Western Ghats and other parts of south India. They are Negroid in feature and often less than five feet in height. It is thought that they were driven into the hills by more powerful peoples before the dawn of history. Their life has changed little from ancient times. The bow and arrow are still their principal weapons. They are so shy and fearful of their more civilized neighbors that even few Indians have seen them. In central India are other primitive tribes called the Gonds, perhaps the remnants of other ancient race movements. In the northeast are Mongoloid tribes, scarcely less primitive, such as the Nagas. They are a peaceful people today, but not so many years ago they were head-hunters.

The Oldest Book of Man

The ancient Aryans were a zestful, energetic folk who loved life and their freedom. The nature of India, with its rushing rivers, storm clouds and jungles, inspired them to joyous outbursts of song and poetry, and they loved to amuse themselves with chariot races and archery contests. Yet they had a serious side. They pondered deeply over the meaning of life and afterlife. Eventually their poetry and ponderings were written down and form the VEDAS, mankind's oldest book. From these and later writings came the religion and philosophy of Hinduism.

Hinduism is difficult to define. It has no set creed and has been described as a way of life permitting many paths to realization of oneself with God. It has many levels and sects. One of its most lofty conceptions of God occurs in the ancient VEDAS and says of Him *neti, neti, neti, neti* and means "not this, not that, not even that, and not that either!" On other levels Hindus have many gods and goddesses. One belief Hindus have in common is that of rebirth. A Hindu believes that by his good behavior in this life he will reach a higher level in the next life and so on until he reaches a perfect state and his soul blends with the divine.

More than 250,000,000 of India's people follow the Hindu religion. India's second largest group are the Moslems, who number about 43,000,000, making India the third country in the world in terms of Moslem population.

Other Religious Groups

Since the first century of the Christian Era, India has been home to Nestorian Christians, located mainly in Madras State. According to old accounts, they are converts of the Apostle Thomas who settled in India after wandering about the world. Today Indian Christians of all denominations number about 5,000,000. The Sikhs, a group whose religion is based on Hinduism with Moslem influences, number about 5,000,000. In Bombay State is a community of Parsis, descendants of Persians who follow a belief called Zoroastrianism. The Parsis are important in the commercial and industrial life of Bombay. Jains (a Hindu sect) and Buddhists are some of the other important religious groups.

Holy Days Are Gay Days

Religious ceremony plays an important part in Indian life. There are twenty-six official religious holidays in India including Moslem, Sikh, Jain, Christian and Hindu. Most of these holidays are occasions for festivities rather than religious rites. Dussera or Durgapuja is a harvest festival lasting ten days, which commemorates the victory of the Indian epic hero Rama over Ravana, king of demons, who carried Rama's beautiful consort, Sita, off to Ceylon. On one of the festival days there are grand parades. The processions are headed by tall, nervous camels clad in bright green cloth etched with gold, atop of which sit mustached members of India's proud camel corps. Then come elephants clad in beautiful golden robes almost reaching to the ground, with tassels hanging from their ears, their trunks painted a gaudy mixture of yellow, green and blue, and a big circle painted around each eye. The elephants are followed by richly caparisoned horses, palanquins, silver coaches and standard-bearers with silken banners, flanked by tall guards carrying sharply pointed spears.

On another of the festival evenings, In-

THE DANCING GIRLS execute intricate movements without apparent effort, but the smooth flow of the steps is really the result of long training. The dances are usually in a slow rhythm and every gesture has a meaning, even the flick of a single finger. One performance is supposed to represent incidents in the life of Krishna, considered by the Hindus as the incarnation of God and worshiped as invincible in war and love. With his worship are associated brilliant color, the perfume of flowers, milk and honey and all things joyous.

SWAMPLANDS, where malaria once bred, have been sprayed so they can be plowed for food.

SCIENTISTS, working in the paddies, carry on their tests for improving the rice crop.

dians all over the country re-enact Rama's victory over Ravana. The play is usually held in an open court, and hundreds of spectators crowd the aisles, stand on the side lines and even perch on the flat stone roofs of nearby buildings. The brilliant green, blue and saffron of women's draped saris glow jewel-like in the lights of the court. The actors are often boys, and no one seems to mind too much when King Sugriva, the king of monkeys, played by a boy dressed in a red shirt, a tail and a monkey mask, forgets his lines. King Sugriva was Rama's ally, and with his aid Rama leaped over to Ceylon, conquered Ravana, the demon king, and rescued his beautiful Sita. On the last night of the festival gigantic wood and *papier-mâché* images of the demon Ravana and his confederates are paraded through the streets amid jeers, and then dramatically burned.

As soon as you leave one of India's cities you are almost immediately in the country. The roads are often little more than bullock tracks, deeply rutted and, in the dry season, covered with inches of siltlike dust. Looking over the fields, the land seems to be sparsely settled. Only occasionally does one see a lonely figure working in the field, outlined against the sun, almost lost against the horizon.

Yet on a country road leading to a city the driver of an automobile is hindered in his progress by every manner of obstacle. There are caravans of goats, herds of cattle, bullocks, slow-moving and nervous camels, tongas and ekkas, the rural taxis of India, all going to market. Drivers of automobiles sound their horns constantly. At the blast of a horn, a camel may take fright and try to bolt away while its attendant shouts or cajoles, and everyone stops to watch.

Soon one sees tribes of monkeys which swarm the country. Bold fellows, they cross roads, sit on houses, even jump into the crawling carts for some object that catches their fancy. There is a strong taboo against taking their lives among most Indians, even though the animals do great harm to crops. However, some farmers are gradually being persuaded to shoot at the monkeys that swarm over their fields.

Great flocks of chattering and quarreling parrots take wing. As they move together across the sun from one tree to another, their wings glisten. Off in the distance one of India's many varieties of vultures hovers, intent on some dead or

THE PEDAL THRESHING MACHINE helps the farmers of India to winnow rice more quickly. Intensive studies are being made to find ways of increasing the production of rice.

A TAILOR drowses outside his shop in Simla. Located on a ridge of the outer Kumaun Himalayas, 7,100 feet above sea level, Simla has long been a popular hill resort in India.

EAST AND WEST blend together in Bombay, even in the architecture. Oriental domes and Gothic-looking towers harmonize pleasantly on buildings that house the city government.

dying animal below. Occasionally one spies a beautiful partridge or a brilliantly hued pheasant. At night, traffic ceases and again the land looks lonely. Far-off hills are dimly outlined in the moonlight, and now and then the shriek of a hyena or the howl of a pariah, India's wild dog, pierces the silence.

Among the most interesting sights to a visitor in India are the annual fairs held in many rural areas. Some of these fairs cover as much as fifty acres of land. People come from many miles around, and the streets leading to the fair are jammed with farmers, herders, merchants, fakirs (holy men), women, landed gentlemen, many walking, some riding in the curious small ekkas. A few honking automobiles can be heard above the din. Costumes of all kinds greet the eye. Brilliant saris adorn the women, whose little feet and palms are stained with henna. Bracelets

tinkle on their graceful ankles. Some look almost like gypsies, with jewelry on ankles, wrists, arms and ears, and a little ring in the nose. Sadhus (holy men), naked except for a loin cloth, their bodies smeared with yellow ochre, and farmers in vests and loose cotton dhotis mingle with the crowd.

Alongside the road are buffaloes and cows, and the tents and huts of those who plan to stay a few days. Over all is wafted the smell of thousands of little cooking fires. Merchants yell their wares of cakes, sweetmeats and stacks of chapatties, a thin fried wheatcake which forms the staple food for most of India. Curried vegetables are placed in the center of the chapatties, or an Indian may break off an end and pick up some vegetables with it.

The livestock section of the fair is breath-taking. As far as the eye can see are rows upon rows of camels, bullocks,

47

THE ADHIL SHAHI SULTANS made Bijapur their capital during the great days of the Deccan kingdom in the sixteenth and seventeenth centuries. After the Mogul Emperor Aurangzeb of Hindustan captured the town in 1686, the buildings fell into picturesque ruin. At the height of the Deccan kingdom, Bijapur was known as the City of Victory. The walls

enclosing the town are about six miles in length, and inside these is the citadel. On some of the bastions are huge old guns. One, called Lord of the Battle Plain, is fourteen feet long. The hall of Gol Gumbaz, the magnificent tomb built for the Mahomed Adhil Shahi, contains the largest domed space in the world. The gigantic dome is 124 feet in diameter.

THE DIAMONDS AND EMERALDS in the turban of this Rajput bridegroom cost $300,000.

buffaloes, cows and calves, and hundreds upon hundreds of horses. Attendants stay close to the animals and point out their good qualities to sharp-eyed merchants. The immensity of the camp makes one think that this is what the camp of Harsha must have looked like. Harsha was a great Hindu king of the seventh century. Starting from a small principality, he conquered nearly all of the north in an attempt to put all India under one umbrella. He had thousands of elephants and cavalry, and for six years his army had no rest but moved on from conquest to conquest.

There are side shows, movies in tents, beautifully dressed dancing girls, jugglers, freaks. Competing with the side shows are snake charmers with their baskets of cobras and their little reedlike pipes for charming the snakes out of the baskets. Others have a cobra in one basket and its mortal enemy, the little mongoose, in another. For a price the mongoose is taken out and then the cobra. The quick little mongoose darts at the snake and grips it just below its ugly spreading hood. Before the mongoose can kill, however, an attendant separates the two mortal enemies.

About 70 per cent of India's people are engaged in agriculture. Rice is grown extensively in the Ganges Valley and in wet regions such as Assam and the Malabar and Coromandel coasts. Wheat and sugar crops are important in Uttar Pradesh and the Punjab, and cotton in the Deccan. India is a leading producer of tea. Plantations are found in various parts of India, though mainly in Assam and the Western Ghats. Here also are plantations of coffee, rubber and spices, including cardamom.

Although India ranks high among nations as a food producer, its output is far from sufficient for its needs. Almost every decade there has been a famine somewhere in India. Every time the monsoon rains fail, thousands of people perish. In 1943, a terrible famine broke out in Bengal and thousands died of starvation. Even in good years many people have little more than a bare minimum to keep them alive. For centuries the villagers of India were left to themselves, knowing little of the causes of their meager supply of food or

A RAJPUT. Originally the name of a governing caste, Rajput today means a landowner.

AN OLD TEMPLE in Jaipur that looks like new because of the replanning program that the city undertook. Streets and buildings were renovated, cleaned up and made more beautiful.

of the diseases that plagued them.

Since achieving independence in 1947, the Indian Government has taken giant strides to make India agriculturally self-sufficient. Under a five-year plan begun in 1951, India was spending $3,500,000,-000 on one of the biggest development programs ever undertaken in the world. For a country where the average income per person is only $52 a year, this was a stupendous amount. One hundred and thirty-two river projects for the purposes of irrigation, food control and power de-velopment were under way. The Damo-dar Valley development in Bihar and West Bengal is among the largest and is mod-eled after America's TVA. The United States Bureau of Reclamation furnished advice for these projects which eventually will increase India's 49,000,000 irrigated acreage by 16,000,000, enough, it is hoped, to make India self-sufficient at least in its minimum requirements.

The United States also furnished $50,-000,000 in technical assistance for com-munity-development projects. Fifty-five

51

THE MALL—the main street—in Simla, lined with shops. In the Himalayan foothills, the town is delightfully cool in summer. Visitors flock there to escape the heat farther south.

areas, each with about three hundred villages, were selected under this program. The pilot Etawah project in Uttar Pradesh was a remarkable success. Shy Indian peasants were taught crop rotation and the use of improved implements and better seeds. Indians who had seldom seen a motor car were taught how to drive tractors and how to service them. The people of Etawah proved that their ignorance and backwardness were the result of isolation and neglect. By 1953 they had already increased production by 40 per cent.

The construction at Sindri, in Bihar State, of the largest fertilizer plant in Asia will help solve one of India's most vexing problems. Because fuel is scarce in India, the people dry and burn cow dung as fuel instead of putting it back to fertilize the impoverished soil. The Central Tractor organization, originally formed with 180 tractors obtained from the United States Army after it built the Ledo Road in World War II, plays an important role in clearing land of the dreaded kans weed, which grows fourteen inches into the soil. In other ways too, all over India, the newly awakened people are dedicating themselves to raising their standard of living.

India is in many ways a paradox—a believe-it-or-not country. In spite of being mainly an agricultural country, it has many large modern cities and industries. It is one of the world's largest producers of manganese and supplies about three-quarters of the world's mica. Its steel works at Jamshedpur, in Bihar, are the largest in Asia and cover several acres of what was once jungle. A surprise to North Americans is that, after the United States, India is the world's largest producer of movies. India's largest industry, however, is textiles. The cities of Bombay, Ahmadabad and Coimbatore hum with the activities of its huge cotton mills.

NEAR SIMLA, the outer ridges of the Himalayas reach up to the clouds. Houses cling to the sides of the hills and a narrow road makes its winding way up the tree-covered slopes.

IN THE DAYS OF BRITISH INDIA, Gurkha women would come down from the hills of Nepal with their husbands, who enlisted in the Indian army. The women and children lived in special quarters inside the lines of the Gurkha regiments. Famous for their soldierly qualities, the Gurkhas furnished some of the best infantrymen in the colonial army.

THE HINDU TEMPLE in Gujarat was built in the eleventh century. The elaborate carvings that decorate its entrance are a superb example of Hindu craftsmanship. The temple is dedicated to Surya, the sun-god, the personification of sunlight and the vivifier of man. Representations of Surya show him riding in a splendid chariot pulled by seven fiery steeds.

A KETTLE BOY from a mill canteen pours tea into brass cups for some women workers during their noon recess. Their lunch lies on the two round plates on the ground before them.

Silk is produced at Banaras and in Mysore. In West Bengal is the world's largest concentration of jute mills.

Many new industries have been added in recent years. At Bangalore, the capital of Mysore State, is a modern airplane-manufacturing plant. In 1949, the first Indian-built ocean-going ship was launched; and a few years later the first locomotive steamed out of an Indian factory. With the addition of automobile, locomotive, steam-roller and machine-tool plants, India is entering upon a new era of industrial progress.

In spite of its many industries, nevertheless, India is dependent on imports of heavy machinery, such as tractors, automobiles, locomotives and various other metal products. Since World War II, when Indians became acquainted with Western goods and equipment, about 20 per cent of India's imports have come from the United States. India's main exports are jute, tea, manganese, mica, tobacco, coffee and spices.

Calcutta, Bombay and Madras are India's main ports as well as largest cities. Bombay, the gateway to India, has a beautiful harbor studded with hilly islands and ringed with a palm-fringed shore. As India's cities go, it is young, dating back to its acquisition by Portugal from the Sultan of Gujarat in 1534. Calcutta, too, is a young city. Although it is fifty miles up the Hooghly River, it is India's busiest port. Along its world-famous Chowringhi Road, lined with hotels, restaurants, clubs and government buildings, is Maidan Park which is bordered by the Hooghly River.

Unlike many Western farmers, farmers in India do not live on the land they till. Since ancient times it has been the custom to group dwellings together in villages for safety against wild life and conquering peoples. There are more than one half million such villages scattered over India, and three-quarters of the population live in little villages or small towns. The farm communities are poor, rarely more than a collection of mud huts and adobe houses clustered along a narrow, dusty street. Whether a village is in the plains of the Deccan or in a river valley of the Uttar Pradesh, it is much the same. There are no electric lights or utilities of any kind. In a town of any size, goldsmiths occupy one street, potters another, grain dealers still another and so on according to trade or profession.

The chorus of clinking hammers on metal, the whir of potters' wheels are pleasant sounds. In the morning children run to the village tank to wash; others are already leading bullocks or goats to pasture. A cloud of dust rises, which mingles with the acrid blue smoke from cow-dung fires cooking the morning cup of tea. Women pass on their way to the village well, moving gracefully with earthen jars on their heads.

Again at dusk the acrid, but not unpleasant-smelling, smoke of cooking fires and the dust of returning cows and bullocks swirl in the purplish light of a dimming sun. Children run about and play as children do the world over. In front of tiny shops lights flicker and above the shouts of children and the whir of insects one sometimes hears the lonely tinkle of the temple bell.

Men Against Animals

The farmer's day is long, from daybreak to sunset, and, in some parts of India around harvest time, he must remain out in the fields all night. On platforms built on stilts the farmers yell, wave their arms and beat tin cans to keep hungry deer and jackals from ruining their crops. Occasionally a tiger follows the deer into the fields and a platform comes crashing down, a life snuffed out.

In the village life is safe, but in fields bordering on jungle and wooded tracts and in the high-grassed Terai there are many kinds of lurking danger. Snarling wolves, howling pariahs, sleek tigers and leopards, bears, shrieking hyenas and the vicious wild pig haunt the green glades. Crocodiles lurk in the muddy depths of gulleys. Graceful deer, the sharp bark of foxes, strutting peacocks, monkeys, flocks of parrots creating an incessant din, their

EWING GALLOWAY

A POTTER in Delhi makes his earthenware in the open, selling his cups to those who pass.

JAMES SAWDERS

MILKMEN, their brass jars filled with milk, ride their donkeys to the market in Jodhpur.

WALKER

BUDDH GAYA, in Bihar, is one of the most holy places of the Buddhist religion because there Gautama Buddha, the "Light of Asia," is believed to have received enlightenment. A huge pagoda marks the holy spot. The terrace, shown above, runs around the temple, and the strange stone ornaments on the right are shrines that have been erected by pilgrims.

KUTB MINAR, which is about eleven miles south of Delhi, is considered the most perfect tower in the world, and is one of the architectural wonders of India. It is built in five stories and rises to a height of over two hundred feet. The summit is reached by flights of steps. A cupola was added, but it was destroyed by an earthquake in 1803.

A HOUSEWIFE stirs the dough for chappaty, a thin griddle cake made without salt.

wings glittering in the sunlight, are common sights and sounds to the hunter.

During the rainy or cold season, snakes of all kinds are likely to enter village huts seeking warmth. Most of them are harmless, but the krait and cobra are deadly. Every year thousands of people die from cobra bites. Though antivenom is available, the victim often dies of shock before help can arrive. Travel over the roads is slow and the antivenom may be brought too late to be effective.

In northeast India and in the Western Ghats, wild elephants still roam the forests, now protected from extinction by law. Also protected are Asia's only lions, in the state of Saurashtra.

The isolation of villages is broken by visits of traveling actors, acrobats, jugglers and tumblers and troupes with trained animals. India's numerous holidays also provide an excuse for merrymaking. During the festival of Diwali,

DARTING HANDS stitch an elaborate design on fine cloth. Indian craftsmen have gained world-wide fame for their skill in embroidering silk and gold threads on velvet and silk.

THE VICTORIA INSTITUTION, one of the oldest girls' schools in Bengal, has its classrooms in the former home of Kesshub-Chunder Sen, a pioneer in women's education in India.

63

THE HOLY CITY OF BANARAS, capital of Banaras District, is located along the north bank of the Ganges River for three and a half miles. The city was probably founded about 1200 B.C. Splendid temples and costly palaces are reflected in the waters, as sacred to the Hindus as the Jordan is to Christians. Thousands of pilgrims come here each year to undergo

CANDLER

the rites of purification from sin. At intervals along the bank there are flights of steps by which pilgrims may go down to bathe in the water. The Hindus believe that to die in Banaras and have one's ashes scattered upon the Ganges is to be certain of gaining salvation. The city is a maze of alleys, many lined by temples and shrines.

BRITISH INFORMATION SERVICES

A FOREST OF WIRES in the generating station of a hydroelectric plant. Great efforts are being made to harness water-power resources, to provide electricity for factories and homes.

when the cities are ablaze with myriads of lights, the villagers have bonfires and torchlight parades. The spring festival of Holi is an especially joyous occasion to young children and prank-loving grown-ups. Holi is a festival of colors, and no one is spared, not even the animals, from being smeared with pink, the favorite color, or other hues. Using bamboo syringes, children leap out of hiding places to daub each other and their elders. By sunset everyone is a gaudy pink from head to foot. At night there is a huge bonfire, for which children have gathered the fuel. Their peak moment comes when a village elder applies the torch.

Formerly the only visitor from the government was the tax-collector. Today government caravans, portable hospitals and educational units are visiting many villages. Wherever a caravan stops, it draws people from hamlets over a wide area. Mothers with wide-eyed children on their hips, old men and young, await the beckoning of the doctor to have their injuries and diseases treated. The doctors of the traveling Gandhi eye clinic perform as many as fifty cataract operations in one day. It is a pathetic sight to see children, old men and women, lying on charpoys inside the tents, which are the hospitals of rural India, understanding little of their ills and putting all their faith in the doctor. They are grateful for and proud of what their government is doing for them.

The Republic of India has set for itself the task of bringing free and compulsory education to all children up to the age of fourteen. It will be many years before the program reaches all of India's 60,000,-000 children, but already the results show. The literacy rate jumped from 13.5 per cent in 1947 to 20 per cent in 1953.

Village schools are usually in the open, often under a big tree such as a pipal. From forty to sixty students are gathered in rows according to their grades. Each child has a homemade slate made by his father. He takes a smooth board, trims it into shape and then rubs it with grease and soot until it is permanently black. The child is taught to mix white clay with water until it reaches the consistency of white ink. A small brush, also made at home, completes the child's equipment.

Adults are being taught to read and write, and even government personnel are being taught Hindi, the national language. Hindi was chosen from among twenty-six languages spoken in the country. These languages for the most part fall into two groups—those deriving from Dravidian-speaking peoples such as Tamil and Telugu—and those of the Aryans—Bengali, Punjabi, Hindi and so on. Because many people do not yet know Hindi, English is still in official government use. Most government employees are familiar with English. Hindi is not expected to replace English as the official language of the Indian Government before 1960.

In the field of higher education, India has long had adequate universities. The University of Calcutta is one of the oldest, dating from 1858. At present India has 28 universities and more than 750 colleges. Several new research institutes and technical schools are being built to increase the desperate need for technicians of every kind. Thousands more are training in universities abroad. More than 1,200 Indian students are enrolled in North American universities alone.

It is in the hands of these young Indians that the future of their country lies. They are still too few but they are working hard, dreaming of accomplishing in a few years what it has taken most countries generations to do. Though few nations have ever had to face such great obstacles, the millions of India are moving forward slowly and in a democratic manner.

BY PETER WELGOS

THE REPUBLIC OF INDIA: FACTS AND FIGURES

THE COUNTRY

The Republic of India was formerly a part of British India. It achieved self-governing Dominion status in the Commonwealth of Nations in 1947. In January 1950 it became a sovereign democratic republic. It is bounded on the north by China, Tibet, Bhutan and Nepal, on the east by Burma and the Bay of Bengal, on the south by the Indian Ocean, on the west by the Arabian Sea and Pakistan. The area is 1,138,-814 square miles; population, 356,891,624. The Andaman and Nicobar islands are included in the Republic.

GOVERNMENT

The Government is composed of a president, two houses of Parliament—(upper) the Council of States and (lower) the House of the People—and a number of advisory ministers. The president is elected by members of Parliament and the various state legislatures and serves for five years. He may be re-elected. Members of the Council are elected by the members of the state legislatures, and members of the lower house are directly elected by the people on the basis of adult suffrage.

COMMERCE AND INDUSTRIES

Agriculture is the chief occupation. India has more acres (over 50 million) under irrigation than any other country. To further increase agricultural output, the Government is supporting a number of new large reservoir and irrigation projects. The principal crops include millet, rice, corn, wheat, barley, tea, sugar cane, cotton, jute and rubber. Chief industries are the weaving of cotton cloth, production of tea, jute, steel and cement, metalworking and silk raising. The most important minerals are coal, petroleum, chromite, copper, iron, mica, magnesite and manganese. Leading exports: raw jute and cotton, tea, spices, textiles, hides. Chief imports: manufactured cotton, metals, machinery, grain.

COMMUNICATIONS

Railroad mileage, about 35,000, mostly government-owned. There are some 90,000 miles of surfaced roads. Length of telegraph lines is 113,500 miles. Air service is maintained within and beyond India.

RELIGION AND EDUCATION

About 80% of the population are Hindus. However, the constitution guarantees complete religious freedom for all. A 16-year plan is under way to modernize the education systems and to introduce free and compulsory schooling through the age of 14. In addition to primary and secondary schools, there are 28 universities and more than 750 colleges. There are also numerous technical and vocational schools.

CHIEF TOWNS

Population: Delhi (including New Delhi, capital, and suburbs), 695,686; Calcutta, 2,610,-256; Bombay, 1,489,883; Madras, 777,481; Hyderabad, 739,159; Ahmedabad, 595,210; Kanpur, 487,324; Amritsar, 391,010; Lucknow, 387,177; Nagpur, 301,957.

© E.N.A.

THREE GATEWAYS give access to the courtyard of the Jama Masjid, and a long flight of steps leads up to each. Sometimes bazaars are held on these stairways and the merchants sell such wares as rugs, shawls and embroidered muslins, gold and silver filigree work, jewelry and carved ivory. It was on the site of the mosque that the Persian raider Nadir Shah watched while his army cut off over a thousand human heads. Nearby Chandni Chauk, the Silver Street of Delhi, seventy-four feet wide, is lined with warehouses and shops dealing in gold and silver work.

CANDLER

AMRITSAR'S GOLDEN TEMPLE is the sacred place of the Sikhs. It stands in the center of the Pool of Immortality. The four doors are of silver, and white marble forms the lower portions of the walls, gilded copper the upper stories. Verses from the Granth, the scriptures of the Sikhs, are inscribed on the walls of the richly gilded and painted interior. A white marble causeway fully two hundred feet long, with ornate painted and gilded lamps on either side, leads to the temple. Foreign visitors may enter the building only through a north door.

A KARACHI MERCHANT displays his treasures of the deep. His wares are gathered from the waters of the Arabian Sea, which abound in shells of all sizes, shapes and colors.

PAKISTAN

The Birth and Growth of a Moslem Nation

Though West and East Pakistan are separated, each has at least one great natural advantage. West Pakistan includes practically all of the valley of the Indus River, one of the subcontinent's great waterways, and has a long coast on the Arabian Sea. East Pakistan is where the waters of the Ganges and Brahmaputra rivers merge and form a vast delta before they reach the Bay of Bengal. As the prosperity of Pakistan is partly dependent on international trade, this access to the sea helps to overcome the handicap of division.

IMAGINE what sort of country Canada or the United States would be if the eastern part were separated from the western part by another country. To go by train or road from one section to the other, you would have to get permission to pass through the nation in the center. Otherwise you would have to fly or go the long way around by ship. Pakistan is in just this troublesome geographic position, for it is divided into two parts with the Republic of India in between. The situation is satisfactory neither to India nor to Pakistan; but the people of Pakistan preferred partition, or division, to union with India.

Most Pakistani are Moslems, followers of the prophet Mohammed, who lived some 1,300 years ago. The people of India are largely Hindus, having a religion that dates from before the birth of Christ. So different are the ways of life imposed by these two faiths that it was never possible to weave their peoples into a single pattern.

In the years after the death of Mohammed, Islam (Mohammedanism) spread both to the west across Africa and to the east across Asia. Islam teaches that there is only one God, that faithful followers of Mohammed should worship only this God and live according to certain rules laid down in their holy book, the Koran.

Under the zealous leaders of the faith, Islam became not only the chief religion for millions of people in North Africa and Asia but also became the guide in lawmaking, government and business. Laws on marriage and divorce and even land ownership and inheritance developed under Islam. Religious as well as political power was concentrated in the hands of kings and other rulers. In Canada and the United States, we believe in a separation of church and state, but in the Moslem world the church and the state are one. The laws that the courts uphold are the laws of Islam. Frequently the ruler is the spiritual head of the people.

Though the Hindu religion is based on a faith in one supreme God, there are a number of lesser gods, differing in rank. A basic Hindu belief is the transmigration of souls—that is, when a person dies, his soul passes on or is reborn in another person or even an animal. Therefore, stanch Hindus will not kill any animal lest it be the murder of a soul, and so it follows that they do not eat meat. The differences between the Hindu and Islamic philosophies also extend into such matters as marriage, burial and inheritance. So you can see the difficulties that would arise in trying to set up one government for both Moslems and Hindus.

Under British rule, there was a gradual education of the Indian people. A few of the most brilliant students went to English universities. Out of the most highly educated group came the leaders in the struggle for independence. Hindus worked through the Congress Party, under the leadership of Mohandas K. Gandhi; and Moslems worked through the Moslem League, under Mohammed Ali Jinnah.

However, these parties really agreed on only one point: that the British must get

A RAINBOW OF COLOR, some girls perform a folk dance in the streets of a village. They slap their sticks and jangle their golden bracelets to keep the rhythm of the dance. The flashing metal, the bright hues of their dress and the flowing of their gauze-like head-coverings add grace and gaiety to their stylized motions. In dancing, they move only their arms and the upper part of their bodies, so that they stand, like tossing flowers, in one place.

72

out of India. On almost every other matter there was fundamental disagreement, arising mainly from the religious differences of which we have spoken.

The Moslems Press for Partition

In the old India there were about 90,-000,000 Moslems and 300,000,000 Hindus. Because of their religious teachings, many Moslems refused to attend the schools set up by the British or to allow their children to do so. The result was that the Hindus, besides outnumbering the Moslems, were better educated. Consequently, the Moslem group greatly feared that in a free, united India the Hindus with their superior schooling would hold the most influential government positions. This possibility seemed even worse to the Moslems than British rule. This is why the Moslems pressed for a separate country. On the other hand, the Congress Party leaders were strongly opposed to splitting the subcontinent.

During World War II, Japan threatened to extend its conquest into India. To maintain a base for supplies and the movement of troops in Asia, Britain needed the co-operation of India. This situation seemed to give both the Congress Party and the Moslem League an opening. In 1940 the Moslem League resolved officially to press for an independent country, which they called Pakistan. Also in 1940, after rejecting an offer by the British Governor General to appoint a War Advisory Council of Indian representatives, the Congress Party started a campaign of nonviolent demonstrations against the war. As a result, several thousand Congress Party leaders were arrested. Moslem leaders were more co-operative in the war effort and this eventually helped them to achieve a separate nation.

A Plan for Independence Rejected

The Japanese captured Rangoon, Burma, in March of 1942, not many miles from the Indian border. Almost immediately the British Government sent Sir Stafford Cripps to meet with Indian leaders. Cripps had the authority to promise that at the close of the war India would be allowed independence, either within or without the Commonwealth of Nations. Both parties rejected the offer. The Moslem League did so because there was as yet no guarantee of the formation of Pakistan. The Congress Party rejected the offer because it did not forbid partition and also because it did not provide for enough Indians to take part in the wartime Government. Thus the Cripps mission failed. In August 1942, the Government again arrested Congress Party leaders for civil disobedience. The last of these were not released until the war ended, in 1945.

After further unsuccessful negotiations in 1946, widespread rioting broke out between Hindus and Moslems in Calcutta and in East Bengal. About ten thousand persons were killed, and East Bengal had an influx of fifty thousand homeless refugees. These tragic clashes stirred the British Government into action. In February 1947, Prime Minister Clement Attlee announced that the Government would grant full self-government to India, in any form that seemed most suitable, by June of 1948 at the very latest. Lord Mountbatten was appointed governor general; and when he arrived in India, he helped to work out the plan by which the subcontinent was divided into two nations. The division took place on August 15, 1947. Provinces voted as to whether they would join Pakistan or India. The Constituent Assembly for Pakistan met in Karachi on August 11, and Mohammed Jinnah became governor general. (Sadly, Jinnah died only a few months later.) The secretary of the Moslem League, Liaquat Ali Khan, became prime minister.

Troubles of a New-Born Nation

Vexing problems remained, however, and some may not be completely solved for years. The boundary line between West Pakistan and India is well agreed upon for most of its extent. Kashmir, in the north, has caused the most trouble. The state lies astride the headwaters of the Indus River system so necessary for irrigation water in Pakistan. Its people are in large part Moslems, but there is a considerable number of Hindus. Under the British the ruling family was Hindu; and this family lined up on the side of India when partition came. However, Pakistan refused to recognize Kashmir as being part of India. Finally, in 1953, Pakistan and India agreed to let the people of Kashmir vote on which country they wished to join.

The first major penetration of what is now Pakistan by the Moslems came in 712 A.D. Then the Sind, in the southern Indus Valley, was conquered and its people were converted to the Islamic faith by an expedition from Mesopotamia (present-day Iraq). At about this same time Moslem Arab traders entered Bengal (East Pakistan). A second great wave of Mohammedans descended from Afghanistan around 1000 A.D., and Moslem rule was extended along the Ganges to include Bengal. Many of the lower Hindu castes were converted to Islam then, for it gave them a sense of dignity that was lacking before.

Just after 1500 there was another invasion, this time by the Moguls, a Turco-Mongolian people from central Asia. The

Mogul rulers extended their power widely throughout the Indian Peninsula. Akbar (1556–1605), the most outstanding of the Great Moguls, placed the empire on a sound economic basis and gained the support of much of the Hindu population by his tolerant attitude. Toward the end of his life, Akbar attempted to start a new religion combining aspects of Islam, Christianity and Hinduism.

Aurangzeb, the ruler who followed, reverted to a more severe Moslem doctrine and fought many battles with Hindu princes in the southern part of the Indian Peninsula. When he died, the empire broke up into individual states, many with Moslem rulers and Hindu residents. Much of the conflict between Moslems and Hindus has stemmed from the fact that the Hindu majority was conquered and ruled by a Moslem minority.

In the 1700's, Europeans began to establish trading posts along the coast, and ultimately Great Britain came into control of most of the subcontinent. Some states were annexed directly. In others, the authority of the ruling family (usually Mos-

PHILIP GENDREAU

THE WARLIKE QUALITIES of his people are not apparent in this young Pathan as he peacefully tends his small bullocks on the Ghakhi Plains of the North-West Frontier.

74

THROUGH KHYBER PASS runs the road that leads to the Pakistan-Afghanistan frontier. Since time immemorial, the narrow pass has been a highway used by caravans and armies.

lem) was upheld, but their foreign affairs were subject to British regulation. This political pattern of the old India was not broken until 1947, when the boundaries of Pakistan were established so as to enclose only those areas in which there were distinctly Moslem majorities. However, partition led to a tremendous exchange of peoples. The large Moslem minority in the new nation of India (about 6,500,000 people) migrated to Pakistan; and the Hindus in Pakistan (about 5,000,000) moved in the other direction to India. It was an upheaval that caused considerable suffering and hardship. Fanatics on both sides used it as a signal to incite rioting, bloodshed and terror.

Not only are the two halves of Pakistan separated by hundreds of miles; they are also far apart in regard to such matters as climate, the shape of the land surface.

East Pakistan, also known as Bengal, lies at the mouth of the Ganges and Brahmaputra rivers and faces on the Bay of Bengal. It is a flat lowland area, consisting mainly of the delta of the two great rivers. Being so level, the delta receives the full force of the summer monsoons, winds that bring rain in deluges. They begin in April, and during the summer months they cause more than a hundred inches of rain to fall on parts of the coast. The whole of Bengal receives more than ten inches of rain in the one month of July. Summer days in Bengal are hot and muggy indeed. In September, when the force of the monsoons begins to lessen, a gentle northeast wind blows over the Bay of Bengal. The most pleasant month is apt to be January, when less than an inch of rain falls and the weather is sunny and relatively cool.

West Pakistan is about six times larger than East Pakistan and is considerably more complex in its geography and in its weather. Here, as in Bengal, a river forms the core of the area. This river, the Indus, starts in the Himalaya Mountains in Tibet to the north. By the time it reaches the heart of Pakistan, it is swollen with the water from four branches. In addition to the river lowlands, there are

THE CITY'S BUSY LIFE flows past the building of the Karachi Municipal Corporation. Along the sidewalk, Moslem merchants have set up their booths in true Eastern fashion.

lofty mountains and rugged highlands. In contrast to humid Bengal, West Pakistan includes one of the driest deserts in the world. Very little of West Pakistan gets more than twenty inches of rain all year, and much of it receives less than five inches. Such rain as does come in the south falls in the summer months. In the north the rain is more evenly distributed throughout the year.

On the east side of the Indus River is a low, rolling desert; in some places sand dunes stretch for miles. To the west of the Indus the upland surface of Baluchistan rises in places to more than five thousand feet above sea level. This plateau is separated from the wide Indus Valley by the Kirthar Range in the south and the Sulaiman Range in the central portion. Northern Pakistan extends into the towering Hindu Kush, where peaks soar to more than 18,000 feet. In this northern area lies the famous Khyber Pass; through it runs the road that joins Pakistan with its neighbor Afghanistan. Near the Sulaiman Range is the Bolan Pass, which connects Pakistan with Iran. These passes, and especially the Khyber, have

been routes of travel since the beginning of history. Alexander the Great came through the Khyber Pass in his attempt to conquer India.

Pakistan is chiefly an agricultural nation, as most countries of Asia are. However, it differs from a number of the others in that it produces several commodities that sell readily in the world market. Bengal supplies about 98 per cent of the globe's jute. On the shores of the Lakshya River, in East Pakistan, one of the largest jute mills in the world was opened in 1954. Jute is a canelike plant from which a coarse brown fiber, used in making burlap cloth and rope, is obtained. Burlap bags carry much of the world's rough, bulky products, particularly potatoes. The hot, wet climate of Bengal is well suited to the jute plant, and the quality of Bengal's jute is high. Rice is grown on the largest portion of the land in Bengal, however, though this crop is consumed mostly at home.

In West Pakistan, cotton is the main crop in terms of international trade. The Indus River, like the Nile in Egypt, supplies irrigation water to thousands of acres

PAKISTAN EMBASSY INFORMATION DIVISION

ON MANORA ISLAND, near Karachi, a jagged mass of rocks is known as Land's End. If one were to sail due south from here, he would not sight land until he reached Antarctica.

THE COASTAL TOWNS of Pakistan rely on the sea for much of their food. Fishermen have no difficulty selling their ocean-fresh catch almost as fast as they can unload it.

of valley land that do not receive enough rain. The soil is fertile, nevertheless, and cotton of medium to high quality grows exceedingly well. Wheat is the major grain crop of West Pakistan, and it occupies most of the cultivated land. In the Punjab, since about 1920, irrigation has made hundreds of acres of land available for growing wheat. The yield is high, and normally wheat is exported, mostly to Great Britain. Millet, barley and corn, important in the diet of the Pakistanis, are also grown in West Pakistan.

Although the export crops are raised on large farms, those that fill the country's own needs are usually very small plots, hardly more than gardens. They are tilled with the crudest of implements; and in times of drought and crop failure, the farmers and their families are haunted by the specter of starvation. One of Pakistan's gravest problems arises from the fact that the majority of the farmers do not own the land they work. Landlords take a large portion of the annual crops for rent payments, leaving the farmers with barely enough to exist until the next year's harvest.

There are no widely separated farmsteads, such as those of North America. Instead, the farm folk live in small vil-

PAKISTAN EMBASSY INFORMATION DIVISION

THE SEA has weathered the face of this old fisherman from Chittagong in East Pakistan.

lages, usually little more than a collection of dirt and straw huts, huddled together in the middle of their fields. The village is the basic unit of government and social life; and unless disaster strikes, the people do not travel far beyond. Each little community has its well, its mosque and its elders, who guide the affairs of the village. About the only contacts between many of these villages and the central Government are the payment of taxes and the supply of men for the army.

Of the 114,000,000 acres of land in Pakistan, less than half is farmed, and about half of this land must be irrigated. There is practically no agriculture in the highlands west of the Indus River, and here nomads make their living herding sheep.

In recent years the abundant fisheries of Pakistan have taken on new importance. Shrimp is the most valuable catch, and huge quantities are frozen and shipped abroad. There are extensive oyster beds, and sharks are caught for their vitamin-rich oil. In 1953 the haul of all fish and seafood amounted to about 365,000,000 pounds; and it was estimated that there

AVA HAMILTON

AN OLD-FASHIONED WOMAN of Pakistan screens herself from view in public.

A MOTLEY THRONG crowds the street of Anarkali bazaar in Lahore. The bazaar, a busy market place of many small shops, is one of the characteristic features of an Eastern city.

was an international market for 300 times as much.

Heavy industry as carried on in Western nations depends upon large supplies of coal and iron ore. On this score, Pakistan stands small chance of becoming a major industrial nation. Many manufactured products must be imported. Cotton cloth makes up about 20 per cent of the imports; and yarn, machinery and vehicles make up another 25 per cent. Most of this trade is carried on with Great Britain and Japan and, to a lesser extent, with the United States. Nevertheless, industry is being encouraged in Pakistan, to help bring about a better balance in the country's economy.

Although the Government of Pakistan controls such industries as munitions, hydroelectric development, transportation and communications, there are a number of private enterprises. Many textile and cotton-processing mills have been opened in West Pakistan and others are under way both here and in Bengal. In the mid-1950's, much cotton and jute were being sent to India for processing, an arrange-

ment that was satisfactory to neither country because of the tension between them.

In Baluchistan and on the western frontier, wool production is the main source of income of the pastoral tribesmen. The wool is exported mostly to Great Britain, though woolen mills are being built that will be able to make use of some of this production. In Sialkot, in the Punjab, high-grade tennis rackets and other sporting goods are made to sell to Great Britain, Australia and the United States.

There is considerable manufacturing in homes. These cottage industries supply a large portion of the villagers' needs. Weaving is still carried on by housewives as part of the daily tasks. Skilled wood-carvings, metalware and leather goods show an artistry not found in factory-produced articles. Bengal is noted for its ivory carvings.

Much of Pakistan's mineral wealth is found in the western part. Here is one of the world's greatest deposits of chromite. The metal is used in making chrome steel, which is extremely hard and strong. Gypsum, valuable for plaster manufacture,

BENGALI WOMEN of East Pakistan, swathed from head to foot in loose, flowing robes of cotton, carry home their water supply from the village well in great earthenware pots.

THE FLIMSY SHACKS of a Sind village are built of matting over a framework of poles. The people who dwell in such humble homes know little or nothing about modern sanitation.

and salt are also found in large workable deposits. Normally Pakistan imports coal from India and other nations. No doubt it will continue to do so, though the country has some coal of its own and a few mines are in operation. There are also some oil wells—more oil is being searched for and small amounts of iron ore.

Transportation in Pakistan varies from the most modern of airplanes to the most ancient kind of two-wheeled oxcart. The country inherited from the British about 7,000 miles of railroads and about the same mileage of hard-surfaced roads, as well as more than 50,000 miles of improved dirt roads. Railroads and highways reach most parts of the country. The only rail line connecting the Indian Peninsula with Iran runs through the Bolan Pass. Boats, an inexpensive way of traveling, ply the rivers in the interior of Bengal as well as the Ganges, the Brahmaputra and their branches. Airlines join the main cities. Karachi, a stopping point for all flights to the East and the West, has one of the finest airports in the whole of Asia.

As the transportation system was built by the British when they controlled India, the highways and railroads, of course, connect Pakistan and the Republic of India.

East Pakistan is one of the most densely populated areas in the world, with about 780 people to the square mile. In West Pakistan there are more than 250 people per square mile for much of the area, and along the Indus River there are more than 125. In contrast, the desert to the east and the mountains to the west and north are sparsely populated. From these figures, however, you can see that Pakistan must farm as much land as possible.

Pakistanis belong, racially, to the Caucasoid family as distinct from Mongolians and Negroes. Yet, because the subcontinent was settled over a long period of time by peoples migrating from the north and west, there is considerable variation in their appearance from one area to another. The northern and western people have light tan skin coloring. The western borderland of Baluchistan is home to a group who resemble the Iranians and the Afghanistans. Those in the east of West Pakistan are quite dark, generally with black, wavy hair. In Bengal, which is very close to China, there has been a considerable intermixture of Mongoloid peoples with the ancient Dravidian group of India.

Language differences in the nation are extreme. Even though the various tongues stem from the same source, the Indo-European family, to which our own language belongs, the dialects may be as different as French is from Spanish. In the west, Urdu, Punjabi, Baluchi and Pashtu are the main tongues. In the east, Bengali is most widely spoken. However,

NOT CHARACTERS from the Arabian Nights, but turbaned and bearded Pakistani masons. The Government of the Moslem nation is working to better the lot of its laboring class.

83

A SECTION of Multan's colorful bazaar, in the shadows of the city's Municipal Building. Multan, in the Punjab, is one of the province's major road and rail junctions.

because modern education developed under the British, English is spoken by the highly educated minority. More than 80 per cent of the Pakistanis can neither read nor write the language they speak.

The continued existence of several languages is understandable in view of the fact that the various groups have been isolated. Until this century, transportation remained very primitive and even yet most of the people are too poor to travel except in case of dire need.

Although Hindu literature, including drama, is old and fluent, Moslem literature is relatively recent. Nevertheless, much delicate and beautiful poetry has been written by Moslem poets. Through both verse and prose works there runs a strain of Persian influence.

The Mogul emperors erected some of the most dazzling architecture the world has yet seen. At that time the center of political power was in and around Delhi, so that the more famous examples of Moslem design are in India. The Mohammedans built three kinds of structures, in the main: mosques, forts and tombs. The Taj Mahal, probably the most celebrated building in the world, near Agra, was erected by the Shah Jehan as a tomb for his wife. Under the next ruler, Aurangzeb, when Mogul power was beginning to decline, there was considerable building in what is now West Pakistan. The most notable example is the Moti Masjid (Pearl Mosque) in Lahore. Many cities in Pakistan, however, have beautiful, domed mosques with slender minarets.

It was also under the Moguls that Persian miniature painting was introduced.

AT KOTRI, on the Indus River, the great weir of the Sind Barrage (dam) nears completion. By it, the river waters will be diverted into canals to irrigate the surrounding country.

CONVENIENT SHOPPING for a Pakistani housewife. In the cities, merchants often sell their wares from door to door, just as this turbaned dealer in cotton goods is doing.

MASTER WEAVERS of Pakistan produce fine rugs that follow traditional Oriental patterns. The delicate designs have changed but little in many hundreds of years.

A FACTORY WORKER counts and packs thousands of little brass bangles. They will become elements in costume jewelry to be exported to countries far removed from Pakistan.

RICE FIELDS on the low-lying delta of the Ganges and Brahmaputra rivers must be protected from the devastating force of the monsoon's wind and rain by a covering of straw.

THE HOT, MOIST CLIMATE of East Pakistan is ideal for the growing of many tropical products. Here a group of pickers are examining baskets of nuts harvested at Areca.

THE STATE UNIVERSITY at Karachi is one of five universities furnishing higher education to the young men and women who will one day be Pakistan's leaders in many fields.

Usually the subjects were historical scenes or portraits. Geometric design, appearing on wood and leather, is, however, most characteristic of Moslem art. This is because it is against the teachings of Islam to represent any living thing.

Of Pakistan's cities, Karachi, the capital, is most important. It is just north of the mouth of the Indus River. From about 1935 to the mid-1950's, it grew from a moderate-sized town to a metropolis of more than a million people. Because of the great influx of refugees from India and the establishment of government departments there, Karachi looks something like a boom town, in spite of its great age. Government buildings show the signs of hasty construction and housing facilities are extremely crowded. Karachi has long been of great importance as a port and, like other ports where ships from all over the world dock, it has a cosmopolitan atmosphere surrounding it.

Lahore, Pakistan's second largest city, is the capital of the Punjab state. It presents a great contrast to the bustle of Karachi, for Lahore keeps the charm of ages past. Baber, the first Mogul conqueror, lived in Lahore. There are several tombs and mosques, built by the Emperor Akbar, that are breath-taking in their magnificence. The city is an important railway-repair center; and cotton gins and mills, brick kilns, a glass factory and bookbinding establishments make it fairly important industrially. Nearby are the market cities of Lyallpur, Sialkot and Multan. The rich agricultural area surrounding all these cities has received an overflow of the immigration from India; and the population of Lahore itself has increased tremendously.

Other large cities in West Pakistan are Hyderabad on the Indus (as distinguished

92

EXCEPT FOR THE DRESS of teacher and pupils, this schoolroom resembles classes in some other parts of the world. New schools are being founded to help fight illiteracy.

ENGLISH AND ARABIC are the written languages in Pakistan. Here the sure hand and steady brush of an expert calligrapher produce pages of graceful, flowing Arabic script.

MUSIC IN PAKISTAN has remained practically unchanged over the past three thousand years. Almost none of the music is written. It is passed down from generation to generation by ear, and each performance differs to some extent from every other. The music may be called folk music for it all represents the continuation of a national tradition. Musicians may perform on specific occasions or they may be retained by wealthy sponsors, but they rarely hold public concerts. The musicians also act in plays with religious meaning, a way of teaching their beliefs.

THE MEMBERS OF THE SIKH RELIGION follow the teachings of Guru Nanak, who attempted to combine the Moslem and Hindu beliefs into one faith at the start of the sixteenth century. Throughout the years they have developed into a strong military, as well as religious, organization. Among the first reforms of the Sikhs was the abolition of the caste system.

THE ONLY DECK is the sun-deck on this ferryboat across a fast-moving river in East Pakistan. Transportation in many parts of the nation is often by way of small river craft.

from another Hyderabad in India), Rawalpindi in the north and Peshawar at the entrance to the Khyber Pass. When normal caravan trade flows to and from Afghanistan, the Peshawar bazaar opens for two days a week. It is a noisy affair, splashed with color and pervaded with a thousand odors. Trade is brisk in raw silk, textiles, gold and silver lace and thread, sugar, tea and fruits.

Dacca is both the largest city of Bengal and its capital. An ancient city, it is passing through a period of great change. Modern city-planning procedures are zoning off residential districts and industrial sites. The University of Dacca is also being enlarged. Bengal's main port is Chittagong, replacing Calcutta (in India) as East Pakistan's port.

The Indus Valley was the site of one of the oldest civilizations. A highly organized city folk dwelt here in about the same period as the Babylonians and ancient Egyptians. Diggings near Karachi have uncovered ruins of an ancient city called Mohenjo-Daro, dating from around 3000 B.C. and built on a still older city. The people living here had two-story brick houses with outside stairways and tile bathrooms, as well as a community swimming pool and underground drainage tunnels. Many of these were improvements that remained unknown to Europe until as late as the eighteenth century. The Indus Valley people also had systems of counting, writing, measuring and weighing. No one yet knows how or why they vanished.

About twenty miles west of Rawalpindi are the ruins of Taxila, a city with a record extending over a thousand years, from 500 B.C. to 500 A.D. In the third century B.C. it was the residence of Asoka, a Buddhist sovereign. Here are imposing round, cupola-topped buildings erected as Buddhist shrines. A famous Buddhist university was located here in the seventh century.

Of the more than six million Moslems who moved to Pakistan from India, most came from the East Punjab. Many of the immigrants were farmers, and farmland had to be provided for them. The cities of Pakistan also had to absorb large numbers of weavers, potters, shoemakers and other artisans, which severely taxed the country's economy. Gradually resettlement projects were organized, and the newcomers have achieved a modest amount of security.

After winning its freedom, Pakistan chose to stay within the Commonwealth of Nations. Up until the end of 1953 Pakistan still had no written constitution. One was being planned, however, outlining a republican form of government. Meanwhile, Pakistan was governed according to the parliamentary system used in England. Considerable authority is retained by the state governments. The area bordering on Afghanistan, the North-West Frontier Province, is administered as a territory. Its capital is Peshawar. Mountain tribes, Pathans, are dealt with on an individual basis by the central Government.

The Pathans have long had a reputation as rough and ready fighters and, like most mountain people, they are freedom-loving. There was some resistance among them to the Pakistan Government, along with an effort to form their own state, to be called Pathanistan. Though there was disorder for a time, the Pathans are beginning to see the advantages of being part of Pakistan. Several projects were begun in the area in 1953. Pathan tribesmen laid down their rifles to help build a tremendous electric generator, deep in a mountain off the shores of the Kabul River near Peshawar. In time the station will provide power for a number of industries being started near the city and also will bring electric light to thousands of homes. Besides this, a twenty-four-mile-long reservoir, stretching from the Afghanistan border, will supply a tremendous amount of water for irrigation purposes. Dams will make the Kabul River navigable, thus offering an alternative trade route to the Khyber Pass.

Fabulous as this project is for a country the size of Pakistan, it is only one of many that eventually will transform not only the North-West Frontier but the whole nation. For, with energy and enterprise, Pakistan is striving to overcome centuries of underdevelopment and to bring prosperity to its people.

By JOHN R. DUNKLE

WADING THROUGH SALT in a lake near Karachi. Running waters carry sodium to the lake, which has no outlet. Evaporation is great in this dry region, and large salt beds form.

A PESHAWAR FRUIT-SELLER sits cross-legged amidst his shop's profusion of fruit. Peshawar, a caravan city at the entrance of the Khyber Pass, is famous for its bazaar.

PAKISTAN: FACTS AND FIGURES

THE COUNTRY

Formerly a part of British India, Pakistan became an independent nation in the Commonwealth of Nations in July 1947, as a result of the Indian Independence Act of the same year. Pakistan consists of two separated areas in the northwestern and northeastern parts of the Indian subcontinent. Western Pakistan includes four provinces, Baluchistan, the Punjab, the North-West Frontier and Sind. Eastern Pakistan includes East Bengal and most of Sylhet, a former district of Assam. A few native states have acceded to Pakistan. The total area is 364,737 square miles; the estimated population is 75,842,165.

GOVERNMENT

Following partition, a Constituent Assembly was formed to govern the new nation. Its members were elected by the legislatures of the provinces. The assembly planned to draft a republican constitution which, when ratified, will provide for two legislative houses, with members elected to serve 5 years. The head of state will be elected jointly by both houses. He will be advised by a council of ministers headed by the prime minister. The principal officers of the present government are the governor general and prime minister.

COMMERCE AND INDUSTRY

Pakistan is principally an agricultural country and one of the greatest grain producers in the Far East. Rice and wheat are the main food crops; jute, cotton, tea and oil seeds are also produced in large quantities. There are rich but largely undeveloped deposits of sulfur, petroleum, chromite and coal; salt, lime, antimony, asbestos and gypsum are also found. Industries include cotton spinning and weaving, flour milling and other food processing. In the western zone there are large railway shops and iron and steel foundries.

COMMUNICATIONS

Railway mileage totals about 8,000. Not all of the more than 58,000 miles of roads are suitable for all-weather travel. There are telephone, telegraph and air services.

RELIGION AND EDUCATION

Moslems comprise 85% of the country's population. The rest are Hindus, Christians and Parsis. To do away with high illiteracy, the central and provincial governments are planning to make schooling compulsory in the primary grades. Punjab University in Lahore and Sind University in Karachi are among the institutions of higher learning. There are also a number of technical and industrial schools.

CHIEF TOWNS (*Populations*)

Karachi, capital, 1,126,417; Lahore, 849,476; Dacca, 276,033; Hyderabad, 241,801.

KASHMIR IN THE HIMALAYAS

The Loveliest State in India

If India may be described as irregularly diamond-shaped, Kashmir lies in the northern peak of the diamond, walled in by the highest mountains in the world. The lovely land of Kashmir is not only one of the most important states of India, possessed of a semi-independence under a separate ruler, but it has the finest climate, and part of its people—the Brahmans and the Rajputs—are of Aryan blood. The richness of this country has through the centuries attracted to it such conquering races as the Moguls, the Pathans and the Sikhs. Every summer large numbers of European officials, merchants and others go there to escape from the heat of the Indian plains.

WE can get the best idea of Kashmir, which lies to the north of the sun-scorched Punjab, by thinking of it as three parallel strips lying northwest and southeast. First comes the range of the Pir Panjal, the barrier that separates the happy valley, as the land has been called, from India; then the valley itself, the plain of Kashmir, which is called the nearest approach on earth to the Garden of Eden; and last, the chain of sheltering hills which rise in tiers of extraordinary grandeur up to the mountain wall on the north.

Kashmir has been likened to an emerald set in pearls, for the valley is always green, and during nine months of the year the inner circle of hills that rings it about is white. Farther north lie the eternal snows. Nanga Parbat, 26,620 feet, is visible from certain points in the valley, and K2, or Mount Godwin-Austen, 28,278 feet, the second highest mountain in the world, can be seen from a spot only a day's journey distant.

The Pir Panjal, the southern wall, through the passes of which Kashmir is entered from the plains of India, is the most delightful playground in the Himalayas. In it there are open spaces, where we can gallop over downs of short turf and through forest glades. We can look down into the green valley over meadows dotted with clumps of birch, maple and pine, and as we walk along we crush the flowers which grow so thickly.

But it is not the flowers alone that make the land so beautiful. Nearly every mountain range in a temperate climate, given

sufficient rain, is more or less a garden. It is the position of the garden that gives the Pir Panjal its unusual beauty. To say that it commands a wide view of the plains is to convey little.

From most Indian hill-stations or their neighborhood one gets an extensive view of the plains. But the plain on which we look down from Gulmarg, in the Pir Panjal, is a mountain plain, another garden under the rock garden, quite different from the sunburnt expanse of the plains of the Punjab. The green and golden valley of Kashmir is over eighty miles long and from twenty to twenty-five in breadth. It lies at an elevation of some six thousand feet above the sea. In it are all the fruits of the earth and there is no corner of it which is not beautiful.

From the Pir Panjal the traveler does not look out over an endless stretch of country as he does from the southern slopes of the Himalayas. The Vale of Kashmir owes most of its loveliness to the fact that it is not very large. If a mist hid the lakes and mountain buttresses, it would still make a picture of unforgettable beauty and mystery. But when the mist lifts and we can see all, we understand then why the valley with its encircling hills is famous as the most wonderful natural garden in the world.

The visitor to Kashmir seldom sees the Pir Panjal in spring. Up to the end of the second or third week of April, Gulmarg, a favorite resort, is uninhabited. All through the winter the huts lie deep in snow. It is only in July and August when the valley grows hot and mosquitoes be-

© E. N. A.

KASHMIRI WOMEN, whether rich or poor, display in their costumes a fine sense of color harmony. In India one can generally tell from an individual's dress not only her social standing, but her native place and her religion, while one is informed of her race from her mode of hair dressing. These women are obviously high-caste ladies of leisure.

CHILDREN OF NORTH KASHMIR, with their delicate features, are charming in their bright, gold embroidered clothing. Most Hindu children go bareheaded, but as this brother and sister are dressed in their best clothes, the little girl wears a light shawl on her head and the boy has a magnificent turban. The Hindus of North Kashmir are a fine race.

103

A TIMBERED VILLAGE NESTLES AT THE FOOT OF A LOFTY PEAK

The rough-hewn cabins that house the villagers of tiny Dawar, near Gurais, are clustered in
the shadow of Mount Habkhaton which rises to a height of more than 13,000 feet. Like other
inhabitants of Kashmir, the people of Dawar live out the simple pattern of their existence within
a mountainous terrain that is famous throughout the world for its breath-taking scenery.

come a nuisance that folk flock to this upland town. The place is nothing more than a huge inn—a collection of tents and huts, the Maharaja's palace, the Residency, where the prime minister and his government work for the season.

We might leave Kashmir without setting foot in the Pir Panjal and still think of it as the most delightful country in the world. The road from the railway at Rawalpindi, in the Punjab, to Srinagar drops into the Jhelum Valley below Murree and follows the bank of the river, cut into the edge of the cliff, until it comes to

Baramula under its cedar forest and enters the Vale of Kashmir.

In the last few miles before Baramula the torrent becomes a wide, placid stream; the valley broadens out into rich cornfields and pastureland; walnut, willow and elm enfold snug villages. At Baramula the Jhelum becomes navigable.

Baramula is the gateway of Kashmir, and the visitor can leave the road and continue his journey to Srinagar, the City of the Sun, in a houseboat. He will be poled and towed to the Wular Lakes and Manasbal with their mountain background.

UNATIONS

KASHMIRI WOMEN EXAMINING SILK COCOONS IN SRINAGAR

Long noted for their fine shawls, the people of Kashmir are now turning their attention to the weaving of silk, as industrialization advances on the Indian continent. Srinagar, in a valley surrounded by the snow-covered Himalayan Mountains, is the summer capital of Kashmir. Over the countryside around the city grow the mulberry shrubs on which the silkworms feed.

BLACK STAR

THE HEAD OF A TRIBE OF WANDERING MUSICIANS

The people of Kashmir enjoy folk music and dancing, and tribes of wandering musicians, called Bhands, help to keep the old tunes and steps alive. Usually they roam from village to village after the harvest is over, for then the people have more leisure. This man, the leader of a Bhand, plays an instrument that looks something like a modern oboe.

NOT TIME BUT MAN DESTROYED THIS LOVELY TEMPLE

The beautifully carved structure was built at Martand some time in the eighth century A.D. and dedicated to a Hindu sun-god. At that time most of the people were Hindus. By the fourteenth century, Mohammedan rulers had gained the upper hand. It was by the orders of one of the most fanatic of these Moslems that the lovely building was demolished.

MOHAMMEDANS AT PRAYER IN THE COURT OF A SRINAGAR MOSQUE

Today about three-fourths of the people of Kashmir follow the Mohammedan faith, though for many years the rulers have been Hindus—a situation that has caused friction and has kept old grievances alive. In 1952, however, the monarchy was abolished. This action was passed by a convention meeting in Srinagar, presided over by a Mohammedan prime minister.

A LATTICED DOOR PROVIDES A SETTING FOR A KASHMIRI BEAUTY

Over the girl's ears, suspended from the headdress, are shieldlike ornaments. The loose coat, with several slits, is worn over voluminous trousers. Slippers and shawl are embroidered.

A LADEN BARGE ON THE JHELUM RIVER AT SRINAGAR

The river is not very wide as it passes through the city, so bridge construction is simple. There are seven wooden bridges like this. In Kashmir, the Jhelum is called the Veth River.

EWING GALLOWAY

A TURBANED SIKH WEAVER DISPLAYS HIS FINE WARES

The world's finest shawls are produced in Kashmir as are also some high quality carpets. The shawls for which Kashmir is so famous are woven of silk as well as of wool spun from the fleece of goats bred for this purpose. The merchant is demonstrating the exceptionally fine quality of the fabric he is holding by pulling it through a small ring.

Women and children crowd the balconies and river steps. They wear a long garment in bright colors with loose, turned-up sleeves. The Kashmiri women are pretty and the children are often beautiful, with regular features, fair complexion and large, bright, black eyes. Their hair is worn in long plaits, bound with coarse woolen threads and tassels. Their lives are hard, however, and they soon lose their good looks.

Srinagar lies between two hills. On the top of the one to the north is the straggling, yellow fort of Hari Parbat; that to the east is the Takht-i-Suleiman, or "Throne of Solomon," rising a thousand feet above

the plain. The Dal Lake washes the bases of both hills, and both are reflected in its clear waters. It is a spring-fed lake and the water is as clear as crystal. The surface, five miles in length and two and a half in breadth, is broken by belts of gigantic reeds, bulrushes, floating gardens and islands.

There are gardens of cockscombs in the dry patches between the dykes, a rich warm glow of color, and fields of bright marigolds, which the true Hindu plucks daily to strew on the altars of the god Siva. At every turn in these creeks there is a new glimpse of the hills. The Nishat, Shalimar and Nasim gardens,

© Underwood & Underwood

THE WINDING JHELUM SEEN FROM THE "THRONE OF SOLOMON"

Srinagar lies between two hills, one called the "Throne of Solomon," on the east, and one the Hari Parbat on the north. On the Throne of Solomon is a magnificent temple of stone, said to have been founded in extremely ancient times, although the present buildings are probably not more than four hundred years old

THE GREEN VALLEY of Kashmir is a natural garden in which nearly all the fruits of the earth grow bountifully. Here oxen are seen dragging a primitive plow in a rice paddy.

on the shores of the lake were made by the Moguls, who were the rulers of India for over two hundred years. The Nasim, or garden of breezes, is famous for its "chenars," or plane trees, planted by the Mogul emperor Akbar in the sixteenth century. All these gardens are built on the same plan. A spring-fed canal runs down the centre, dropping from terrace to terrace by a series of cascades into reservoirs in which fountains play. The walls of the canal are of marble or old limestone, and have niches for lights, which glisten on nights of festival behind the falling water.

The Nishat Garden is finer than the Shalimar. Its terraces slope down from the steep rocks behind it to the green shores of the lake, so that the last pavilion, covered with roses and jasmine, overlooks a bed of lotuses. The Pir Panjal, twenty miles beyond the opposite shore, forms the southern screen.

From Bandipur on the Wular Lake, we may climb the zigzag path to Tragbal over the Burzil and Kamri passes to Gilgit and the Pamirs. Ten days out of Srinagar, camp can be pitched under the Tarshing Glacier at the foot of Nanga Parbat. Or a visit may be paid to the cave of Amarnath, the natural temple of Siva under the snow. According to Hindu mythology, Siva is a god who forms the supreme Trinity with Brahma and Vishnu. Siva is the destroyer of this life or the re-creator of a new form of life.

Or leaving the houseboat at Ganderbal, after seven days' march one crosses Zoji-la, which is 11,300 feet high, the lowest pass in the northern wall, and is well on the road to Leh in Ladakh a province of Kashmir which makes an ideal contrast to the barrenness left behind. Some of the pleasantest haunts of the side valleys may be reached in a morning's walk from the houseboat.

Islamabad, at the eastern end of the valley, where the Jhelum ceases to be navigable, is a favorite camping ground. Within a circle of a few miles lie the blue springs of Bawan, the Mogul Garden of Achibal, the rock caves of Bomtzu, the monastery of Eishmakam, and Martand, the ruined Temple of the Sun.

The valley is strewn with ancient temples. Martand is believed to date from about the eighth century A.D., during the period of early Hindu civilization in Kashmir. The ruins are of a bluish-gray stone with a tinge of pink.

The temple stands on one of the flat ridges peculiar to the plain. In the valley on either side a river appears and dis-appears among villages set in poplar clumps and groves of walnut and willow, and one can look down on a well-irrigated plateau, where fields of purple amaranth and the green and chocolate colored rice crops stretch away to the yellow hills. The glittering waters run underneath the road, feeding the rice fields and turning little mills. Such is the valley in spring. In summer Dal Lake is ablaze with tall pink lotuses, acres of them, through which a channel is with difficulty preserved for navigation. By July or August most of the visitors will have gone to the upland plateaus, either to Gulmarg or to the

AN EARLY-MORNING VIEW OF THE RIVERSIDE AT SRINAGAR

Later in the day the placid Jhelum River, which divides the city in two, is the scene of considerable boat traffic, and the seven low wooden bridges are crowded with pedestrians.

ETERNAL SNOW ON THE LOFTY MOUNTAIN PEAKS THAT RING THE LOVELY VALE OF KASHMIR

The Jhelum River valley is hemmed in by the Himalayas and the Hindu Kush. Snow covers the awesome ranges nine months of the year, and on the highest slopes it never melts. The valley is six thousand feet above sea level, while the mountains tower four miles above the plain.

114

COZY HOUSEBOATS AFLOAT ON THE JHELUM RIVER IN THE VALE

The custom of living on houseboats in the Vale of Kashmir was begun by English visitors from India many years ago.   At that time no foreigners were permitted to erect houses in the vale.

VARIETY OF DWELLINGS ALONG THE RIVER BANK AT SRINAGAR

In contrast to the homes in the picture above, these houses seem ramshackle.   In fact, the vale has so many lovely lakes and waterways that houseboats are the preferred dwellings.

and orchards of apples, quinces and cheeries are reflected in the lake.

It is interesting to watch the sheep being washed at the autumn shearing in Islamabad. They are dragged out of the stream and their hind legs are held up while the relentless wooden scoop scours their fleeces. Fine cloth is woven from this sheep wool.

However, the once famous Cashmere shawls are made from the wool found beneath the hair of the Kashmir goats. Some of these shawls, which many people treasure today as family heirlooms, have an embroidered border. This kind of needlework is a specialty of the region around Srinagar.

Both industry and agriculture are on a small scale. Most of the Kashmiri own or rent tiny farms on which they raise rice, wheat and other cereals for their own use. Some fruit is grown for export and canning. The chief industry is sericulture—raising silkworms—which dates back to the fifteenth century. Wool and silk are spun and woven at home.

Srinagar is a center for wood-carving, carpet weaving, silver and copper articles and papier-mâché, as well as the embroidery mentioned above.

There are no railroads in Kashmir itself, but the Jammu-Pathankot motor highway links the state with the railroad system of India. The Banihal cart road, about two hundred miles long, connects Srinagar, which is the summer capital, with Jammu, the winter capital.

Kashmir was once part of the Mogul Empire; and in the late 1700's it came under the rule of Afghans. In 1846 the former state of Jammu and Kashmir was created when a Jammu chieftain, Gu-

UNATIONS

A PAUSE IN THE DAY'S OCCUPATION. A shepherd leans on his staff and watches his flock, in the hills.

camping grounds in the valleys of the northern tributaries of the Jhelum, where wild goats, bears and deer still haunt the silences. By October the air is nipping,

116

lab Singh, a Hindu, acquired the Vale of Kashmir. The dynasty founded by Gulab was a benevolent one, and the people gained a measure of freedom. Nevertheless, as a large majority of the Kashmiri are Mohammedans, they have never been altogether happy under Hindu maharajas. Discontent became more vocal during the 1920's and 1930's. One popular demand at that time was for a government by legislature rather than by royal decree.

Thus Kashmir, with a Hindu ruling house and a Mohammedan people, became a disputed area in August 1947 when the subcontinent was divided, largely along religious lines, and the two new countries of Pakistan and India were created. The Maharaja was free to join Kashmir with either country. At first he hesitated, but in October 1947, as armed tribesmen poured into Kashmir from Pakistan, he hastily acceded his state to India. Immediately the Indian Army took over the defense of Kashmir and troops were flown in. India placed the dispute before the United Nations in January 1948, but all during that year Kashmir was the scene of bitter strife between Indian and Pakistani divisions. In January 1949, a United Nations commission finally succeeded in bringing the undeclared war to a halt. Four years later, in 1953, India and Pakistan at last reached agreement on the conditions by which the Kashmiri people themselves could decide their own fate by popular vote.

BLACK STAR

RECESS IN SRINAGAR. A pole-pushed ferry takes a group of school children on a favorite outing, a cruise to the floating gardens of Dal Lake. Lotus thrives in the limpid waters.

A TIBETAN FASHION PLATE. The striped silk apron indicates that the lady is married. Her wooden patruk (headdress) is decorated with coral. The necklaces are coral and turquoise.

THROUGH THREE FORBIDDEN LANDS

Man and Nature in Tibet, Nepal and Bhutan

In this chapter, we are to read about three countries, which all lie close together, where few travelers have been welcome. If we look at a map of Asia,
we find that India and Pakistan are shut off on the north by the Himalaya
Mountains, beyond which lies an immense and little-known territory called
Tibet. For many years it was really an independent country, with a government by priests, although nominally it remained an outer dependency of
China's. However, in 1951, the Chinese Communists marched in and made it Chinese
territory in fact. The smaller independent mountain states of Nepal and Bhutan
stand between Tibet and the Indian subcontinent and are separated from each
other by the even smaller Indian state of Sikkim.

A PREHISTORIC sea, the Middle Ocean, once separated China and Northeast Asia from the Deccan of India. (Salt water fossils have been found at what are now altitudes of four thousand feet.) In time a gigantic mountain ridge, the Himalayan, was built up by geologic upheavals. Now peaks from three to five and a half miles high, with level valleys high between the ridges, drop abruptly on the south to the plains of India. On the northern side we have the plateau of Tibet, a land of mystery high under the shining snow peaks. A land dry and barren but affording pasturage for the flocks of the fiercely independent Mongolian tribes who dwell there. Their religion is Lamaism, a faith reminiscent of Buddhism, in which the Dalai Lama is believed to be a reincarnation of Buddha.

The Lamas for years permitted none but the Chinese to enter the capital, Lhasa. Explorers were turned back at the rude forts along the route, or were murdered, and China prevented any trade with India. In 1904 the government of India succeeded in sending a mission to Lhasa to establish trade relations directly with Tibet; the Dalai Lama fled, and three Tibetan marts for Indian goods, Gartok, Yatung and Gyantse were agreed upon. Thereafter caravans of pack-sheep and of yaks crossed with Indian cattle began winding over the fourteen- to eighteen-thousand-foot passes, usually to a point near Darjeeling, to exchange raw wool for cotton piece goods and other com-modities. By 1908 Tibet further agreed

that it would consent to no foreign inter-ference without the consent of the British. When, in 1910, the Chinese sought to re-invade this hidden land, the British ex-tended their protection, and the Dalai Lama sought refuge in India. He re-turned to Tibet in 1913, declared its in-dependence of China and established an arsenal at Lhase. Nonetheless Tibet re-mained a nominal dependency of China's.

Chinese Communists marched into the outskirts of Tibet in 1950; and in May 1951, they announced the "peaceful lib-eration" of Tibet through a political set-tlement. Thus the Red flag was planted on the "roof of the world" and the Com-munist conquest of the Chinese mainland was completed. There were promises that the position of the Dalai Lama would be maintained and that religious freedom would be protected. At the same time the Communists called for a return of the rival, pro-Communist Panchen Lama, who had been in exile in China.

Between Sikkim and the Yatung Val-ley of Tibet there is a gap in the mountain wall. A trip through it to Tibet is like stepping back into the fifteenth century. High above the plain of Lhasa, the capi-tal, towers the Potala, a fortress-palace. Tibet is a land of praying wheels. These are turned by wind or water and contain strips of thin paper on which is printed the Buddhist mystical prayer "Om Mani Padme Om!" (Ah, the jewel in the lotus, ah.) As these wheels revolve, the prayer is thus thought to be repeated countless millions of times. Small prayer wheels are carried in the hand by nearly everyone, and one passes long rows of them attached to the walls of houses and monasteries.

Another device for the easy production of prayer is the pole twenty or thirty feet high with thin strips of muslin nailed to it which flutter in the breeze, and upon which is written the same sacred text. These are the praying flags, or "horses of the wind."

The "chorten"—a pyramidical shrine for offerings, often built over the relics of some Buddhist saint—and the "mendangs"—long walls in the middle of the road, built for the most part of stones on which is inscribed the same Buddhist prayer—are so common that one comes to look on them as natural features of the country.

Flowery Valley and Bleak Waste

In May the Yatung valley is beautiful; on the sides of the mountains the red blooms of the rhododendrons can be seen among the pine trees; the rocks in the stream are covered with moss, which forms a bed for gentian and anemones, celandines, wood sorrel and irises. But a few miles beyond Gautsa, near the meeting place of the sources of the Ammo-Chu River, one passes the last tree, at an elevation of thirteen thousand feet. Beyond there is nothing but desolation.

The Chumbi valley leads into the higher tableland, where you first see typical Tibetan scenery. The climate for the greater part of the year is terribly severe and the shaggy-haired Tibetan yak is the only beast. A numbing, grit-laden wind blows over the high plains and in January the thermometer falls to 25 degrees below zero. The traveler goes for sixty miles through this wasteland before he sees the first solitary willow in the valley of the Paina-Chu.

Rare Pieces of Cultivated Land

In the valley of the Paina-Chu the traveler comes upon the first of the plains where the ground can be cultivated. There are very few of these in Southern Tibet, but every bit of them is used to grow food for men and beasts. After three days' traveling one again enters the treeless region, and on the fourth night camp is pitched in the snowy range of Noijin Kang Sang, nearly one thousand feet higher than the top of Mont Blanc. The Karo-la or Karo Pass, over sixteen thousand feet in altitude, lies under the summit of the range twenty-four thousand feet and magnificent glaciers come down to within five hundred feet of the track. Then the road descends to the basin of the great Yamdok Tso, the Turquoise Lake, a wild and beautiful stretch of water, with arms winding into the mysterious crannies of hills which perhaps no white man has ever trod. The road to Lhasa runs along the edge of the water for a long way and then goes up the ridge to the north to the Khamba-la, twelve hundred feet above the lake level.

The Great River of Tibet

The path makes a sudden turn, and the traveler looks down into the great trough where the Tsang-po river cuts through the bleak hills and desert tablelands of Tibet from west to east. This is no detached oasis, but a continuous strip of rich vegetation. The Tsang-po and its tributaries have drawn to them half the population and the greater part of the merchandise of Tibet. A mysterious river, in parts unexplored, it was only recently discovered to be a part of the Brahmaputra, which flows through Assam.

The river is crossed by a ferry at Chaksam, where it flows so swiftly that it is dangerous for boats; yet the Tibetans in their light craft made of hides can go up or down the river for a distance of one hundred miles. It is the main way for traffic in the country and is crowded with boatloads of pilgrims in seasons of festivals. A hundred miles upstream the Tashi Lama of Tashi Lunpo holds court. He is the "Great Precious Teacher," the second of the Grand Lamas of Tibet, considered even holier than the Dalai Lama himself, whose power is political.

Lhasa, the City of Mystery, blessed by

EDMUND CANDLER

A DEVIL DANCER who takes part in one of these religious dances makes himself look as dreadful as he possibly can. With the grotesque mask and head-dress that he is wearing, the lama, as monks are called in Tibet, is here supposed to represent the sort of fiend that Tibetans will meet in the next world if they do not lead righteous lives in this one.

121

the Buddha, and the Potala, the palace in which lives the Dalai Lama, lie three days' hard travel beyond Chaksam. Lhasa is hidden from sight until one has a view, at about seven miles distance, of the Potala, which seems to be a golden dome standing out on a steep rock in the center of the valley. To the south the Chagpo-ri, another such rock, rising from the banks of the Kyi Chu, is crowned by a yellow fort and the Lamas' Medical College. The narrow ridge between this rock and the Dalai Lama's palace is bridged by the Pargo Kaling, a typical Tibetan chorten, through which is cut the main gateway into Lhasa.

The city of Lhasa is circular in shape. Its streets, unpaved and undrained, are often little more than muddy tracks.

However, there are several spacious parks. The finest, Norbu Linga (Jewel Park), is on a small lake to the west.

To an outsider there is little splendor in Lhasa except for the Potala, rising high above the huts at its foot. The palace catches the eye at once. It is not a palace on a hill, but a hill that is also a palace. The rock is merely the foundation stone. It is difficult to discover where the rock ends and the building begins. High above the causeway one face flashes white in the sun, a stretch of nine hundred feet of bare wall without a break, then at the height of a church steeple row upon row of windows, thousands of them, oblong openings which look like dominoes. On top, in the center of this massive block of rock and brick,

BLACK STAR

THE INDIAN EMBASSY is one of the imposing buildings of Katmandu, capital of Nepal Crouching stone animals guard the pillared entrance, which faces well-tended lawns.

A POLICEMAN halts the visitor at the Nepal border. Travelers make the difficult trip to the Valley of Katmandu by narrow-gauge railway, a stretch of road and a mountain trail.

123

THE MARKET SQUARE of Patan, close to the capital of Nepal, is crowded with interesting examples of Oriental architecture. The building with three roofs is typically Nepalese.

A FEARSOME FACE DECORATES THE TOWER OF A BUDDHIST TEMPLE

There are some 2,700 shrines in the Khatmandu Valley and thousands of priests of both Hindu and Buddhist faiths. The Buddhist temples here, unlike those elsewhere, do not house relics of Buddha. Instead they are apt to have five shrines to the Dhanibuddhas, the five saints below Buddha. Most of the temples have dome-shaped roofs with lofty spires.

THE DHARM RÂJÂ is a king without power, as the real ruler is the Maharaja. But when acting as the temporary head of the Buddhists, as shown here, he appears gorgeous in yellow brocade, while behind him and before hang gorgeous banners worked with fabulous beasts. On the table are the drum, bell and vessels of silver and gold used in Buddhist services.

stands the Phodang-marpo, the red palace of the priest-king, in tiers of bright crimson. The present Dalai Lama is a child born in western China in 1935. The Tibetans firmly believe that he is the fourteenth incarnation of Buddha. Until he is eighteen a regent will rule.

The outskirts of Lhasa make up for the dirt and unsightliness of its streets. It is a waterlogged city approached from the west by a stone road raised over a marsh. The visitor passes beautiful spots in the Tsang-po valley and lower down the Kyi Chu, but these are only patches of fertility and he does not expect to see the wide belt of green by which Lhasa is encircled—willow groves divided by clear running streams, swaying poplars, walled-in parks with palaces and fish ponds, marshes where the wild ducks, left undisturbed, have become bold, and barley fields stretching away to the hills.

Warrens of Tibetan Lamaseries

The lamaseries outside the city are almost hidden by trees and their golden pagoda-shaped roofs have a green background formed by the base of the mountains. Each is a little town in itself. In design the Tibetan lamaseries are all much alike, a warren of monastic buildings, temples and narrow streets, perched in white tiers on stone terraces built out from the rocky sides of the hill, honeycombed with passages, halls, chapels and cells. In the dark and grimy recesses of the temples loom the great gilded Buddhas, life size, covered with precious stones, especially turquoises. The smell of the butter lamps before the altar is almost suffocating; their smoke has hidden the showy paintings on the wall. It is a relief to look through the dark pillars to the cloistered courtyard and quadrangle outside, where the sun is shining and flowers bloom in the garden. The truth is that Lamaism has sunk back into the worship of spirits supposed to live in all manner of objects. Every rock and cavern is marked with superstitious emblems.

There are happier sides to the picture. Most travelers in Tibet will remember being entertained by jolly abbots in the Rongbuk valley, where the Everest Expedition discovered that the mountain sheep, tamed by the hermits, would come to feed out of their hands.

An Inhospitable Land

The only Tibet known to travelers over the Indian frontier is but a narrow strip of green country at the beginning of a mountainous desert. Central and Northern Tibet form a vast and cheerless tableland. From the passes north of Lhasa there is a view of mountains stretching away in endless ridges. This is only the beginning of the wilderness, which continues to the borders of Mongolia and Chinese Turkestan.

At the eastern end of the Himalayas, north of India, is the mountainous state of Bhutan which likewise is closed to the traveler. The land consists of range after range of mountains between which lie narrow valleys watered by fast flowing streams. The best idea of Bhutan can be had by imagining it to be a gigantic stairway leading from the humid plains of Bengal to the chill tableland of Tibet.

Bamboos and tree ferns are found in the lower valleys and oaks and rhododendrons cover the sides of the mountains up to a height of eight thousand feet, at which point they are replaced by dark forests of pines and firs. Unfortunately for the traveler, owing to the damp atmosphere, a leech is waiting on nearly every leaf that overhangs the path, ready to attach itself to any living creature that passes. Besides these pests, there are many kinds of stinging and biting insects in this every way inhospitable land. High up on the sides of the mountains can be seen the great Buddhist monasteries.

Guarding many of the passes, especially those leading to Tibet, are great fortresses, each of which contains a central citadel occupied by the governor and his family. Both the monasteries and forts have overhanging eaves to shed the snow and wooden galleries like those of Switzerland.

A Tortuous Approach

Bhutan is usually entered from Buxa, Bengal, whence the road bends and twists

A SENSITIVE BEGGAR of a Tibetan frontier town. He conceals his face behind a be-whiskered mask so that he will not be embarrassed as he pleads for alms from door to door.

PIX

FREQUENT LANDSLIDES block the single road that winds its way through the Himalayas
to the heart of Tibet. Laborers must then clear the fallen rock to keep the route open.

THE BHOTIAS have never welcomed strangers to their almost inaccessible country. A dzong, one of many such mountain fortresses, protects the rugged countryside of Bhutan from invaders.

like all Himalayan trails until it reaches Punakha, the seat of government. There is another way into the country up the valley of the Manas River, which rises in the Tibetan lake, Yamdok Tso, and flows across Bhutan from north to south; but as yet practically nothing is known about the northern and eastern borderlands.

The Bhotias, as the inhabitants of Bhutan are called, have built their little villages chiefly in sheltered spots where they can grow wheat, barley, millet, mustard and chillies. Owing to the steep nature of the country they make their fields in series of terraces, each of which is supported by a stone embankment, which may be as much as twenty feet in height. The farmers cultivate no more land than is absolutely necessary, because when there is anything left over to sell,

it is likely to be taken from them by the lamas of the nearest monastery or by the governor of any fort in the neighborhood.

The government of the country was originally in the hands of the Dharm Raja or spiritual head and the Deb Raja or temporal ruler. Today the Dharm Raja has little authority save in matters of religion. A hereditary maharaja is the executive. The country's foreign relations are largely governed by India.

Until the end of the last century there was no real form of government, the strongest governor making war on the weaker ones and acting as a king in his own district, while the poor people were robbed and oppressed by everyone. The first maharaja was Sir Ugyen Wangchuk, who was elected in 1907. He had to fight hard to make the governors recognize his authority.

140

Although their political influence is a thing of the past, the lamas of Bhutan's huge monasteries still wield tremendous force through their hold on the superstitions of the common people. Since the Buddhism that they represent has largely degenerated into devil worship and sacrifice to appease evil spirits, the lamas are looked upon with dread by the Bhotias, who believe that they have supernatural powers.

The inhabitants of western Bhutan are like the Tibetans in appearance, and equally suspicious of strangers. They have to work hard in their terraced fields, which are sometimes swept away down the hillsides by the terrible storms that break over the mountains. Since the officials receive no regular salary, they take what they can get from the people of the district, who can do nothing to protect their property. Eastern Bhutan is practically unexplored.

The independent state of Nepal lies to the west of Bhutan and is separated from it only by Sikkim. Nepal stretches along the Himalayas for a distance of five hundred miles. The whole country is a wild tangle of mountains, the only flat space being the valley of Nepal, in which the capital, Katmandu, is located. Outside this valley there are no cities and almost no towns or large villages.

For many years Nepal has been ruled

THE PEOPLE OF THE HIMALAYAS rely upon the shaggy yak for food, clothing and transportation. Yak caravans make difficult journeys along narrow trails across the mountains.

IN KATMANDU, THE OUT-OF-DOORS MAKES A HANDY SCHOOLROOM

Instead of using paper, both teacher and pupil do their writing on crude wooden tablets that can be wiped clean at the end of the lesson and used over again. The alphabet of Hindustani, the language of Nepal, consists of many complicated symbols that are difficult to master, and the teacher must have a great deal of patience with his young student.

NEPALESE WOMEN WHO BELIEVE YOU ARE WORTH WHAT YOU WEAR

The inhabitants of Nepal are known in general as Paharis, or "dwellers in the cliffs." They are divided into various tribes such as the Bhotias, the Gurungs and the Magars. The Bhotias are a nomadic tribe and their women, as shown above, adorn themselves with ornate jewelry made of coins. The size of the family fortune may often be gauged by the decorative display.

143

PANNIERED DONKEYS AND A CHORTEN IN A TIBETAN VILLAGE

A chorten is a Buddhist shrine with a chamber that houses a relic. A spire or an umbrella may
surmount it. This old chorten has been made into a gate, a rather unusual use.

144

SPREADING EAVES AND A PRAYING STATUE IN KATMANDU

The capital of Nepal is a city of temples—most of them dedicated to Siva, one of the Hindu
trinity. The architectural design is unique and is called Newar, or Mongoloid Nepalese.

EMIL REYNOLDS FROM COMBINE

OUTSIDE A TEMPLE a Nepalese tribesman holds aloft a Buddhist prayer wheel. His rough outer garments help to protect him against the icy winds that blow through the mountains.

by a member of the Sah family, who has held the title of maharajdhiraja, or king. An attempt at parliamentary government did not succeed. Until recently, few white men had ever seen the mountain fastness outside the valley which so nearly constitutes the state itself. This valley was originally the bed of a lake 4,500 feet above sea level; and a legend relates that when the lake drained away, its waters were released by the god Manjusri, who cleft the rim of mountains with his sword. The chasm thus made is alleged to be the Kot-bar or Sword Cut, and much of the ancient art of the region represents Manjusri, the patron saint of Nepal, with uplifted sword. Geologists offer the theory that the lake burst its boundaries during some violent earthquake and escaped into what is now the Baghmati river. A ropeway was made in 1927 to carry goods to the valley from Raxaul.

There is a narrow strip of cultivated land where the foothills of the Himalayas slope down to the plains of northern India. Beyond lies a belt of jungle twenty miles wide known as the Terai, one of the finest regions for big-game hunting in the world. After passing through the Terai the traveler is faced by a succession of mountain ranges that extend clear to Tibet, the highest peak being Mount Everest, more than 29,000 feet. It stands on the frontier between the two countries. This highest known summit in the world was never attempted by climbers until 1912, and it defeated them all until the Sir John Hunt expedition of 1953.

COMBINE

SPEEDY DAK RUNNERS, working in relays, carry the mail over narrow mountain passes in Nepal. Roads and railways are few and far between; and the only airport is at Katmandu.

HEAPED CLOUDS AND JAGGED MOUNTAIN MASSES IN TIBET

The forbidding aspect of the "roof of the world" can be seen even at this comparatively low level. Yet the mystery and solitude of the country continue to challenge the imagination of man and have lured him to some of his boldest ventures. The crude little boat on the river is made of wood covered with the skin of the yak, the animal of a hundred uses in Tibet.

TIBET, NEPAL AND BHUTAN: FACTS AND FIGURES

TIBET

Though nominally an outer dependency of China for many years, Tibet was considered an independent country for all practical purposes. All this changed, however, when the Communists gained control in China. Red Chinese troops marched into the outlying reaches of Tibet in 1950; and in May 1951, the Chinese Communists announced that the theocratic (by priests) government of Tibet had surrendered. The country is bounded on the north by Singkiang, on the northeast by Tsinghai, on the east by Sikang, on the south by Bhutan, Nepal and India, and on the west by India. The frontiers are not definitely established; but the estimated area is 469,294 square miles; and the population is about 3,700,000. The capital is Lhasa, which has a population of about 50,000. The prevailing religion is Lamaism, a variant form of Buddhism. Some agriculture is carried on, and barley and other cereals, vegetables and fruits are grown. Minerals include gold, borax and salt. In the pastoral regions sheep and yak, buffaloes, pigs and camels are raised. The most common industries are wool-spinning, weaving and knitting, and the making of images and other decorations for religious use.

NEPAL

An independent kingdom in the Himalayas, bounded on the north by Tibet, on the east by Sikkim, on the south and the west by the Republic of India. The estimated area is 54,000 square miles, the population about 7,000,000. The capital, Katmandu, has a population of about 108,805. Most of the people are Hindus.

The government, nominally under the Maharaja, is actually a military oligarchy. All power is in the hands of the Prime Minister.

The chief products are rice, ginger, sugar, tobacco, potatoes, fruits, cattle, hides, gums, oil seeds, jute, timber and saltpetre. There are valuable forests in the southern part. Chief exports are cattle, hides and skins, opium and other drugs and the imports are cotton, silk and woolen piece goods, leather, brass, iron and copper wares. There are two railways, totaling 58 miles in length.

BHUTAN

A state in the eastern Himalayas, bounded on the north and east by Tibet, on the west by the Tibetan district of Chumbi and Sikkim, on the south by the Republic of India. The area is about 18,000 square miles, the population about 300,000. The religion is a Tibetan form of Buddhism. The government is under a hereditary Maharaja. Chief products are rice, corn, millet, lac, wax, different kinds of cloth, musk, elephants, ponies and silk. There are valuable forests. Muzzle-loading guns and swords of highly tempered steel are manufactured. Other manufactures, including woven cloth and wooden bowls, are for home use.

BURMA ON THE BAY OF BENGAL

A Land Where Women Are Independent

Burma, formerly a part of the Indian Empire and later a British Crown Colony, since the end of the second World War has become the republic of the Union of Burma. It is a land where the women occupy an unusually privileged position. They dress like men, smoke cheroots, conduct shops and forego chaperonage. Burma is a land in which the means to a livelihood is easily procured and people devote much time to the building of their Buddhist temples. "The temple bells are ringing," sang Kipling of Mandalay, " . . . An' the dawn comes up like thunder outer China 'crost the Bay." Here, too, elephants are used in the hills as beasts of burden. Burma is also the home of the Padaungs of the colder north, the Lihsaws who live just across the frontier from Yun-nan, and the Akhas of the Shan States.

BURMA, formerly an important province of the Indian Empire, lies on the Bay of Bengal, between Assam, Tibet and China, Indo-China, Siam and Malaya. Ranges of hills running south from the rim of the Tibet plateau make traveling wearisome in the eastern portion of the country. Anyone who wishes to cross these hills must continually descend into deep valleys, then ascend four thousand feet or more.

Burma proper lies in the valley and basin of the Irawadi, one of the world's great rivers. Its basin forms one of the three natural divisions of Burma, of which the other two are the Arakan with the Chin hills, and Tenasserim with the basin of the Salween. The Irawadi is navigable for about nine hundred miles. After a journey of a thousand miles it carries down so much silt that it yellows the Bay of Bengal. It has an average breadth of a mile and a half, but below Rangoon it sometimes reaches for several miles from shore to shore. Its swift currents then prevent ships from anchoring and people must go ashore in small boats. Indeed, when it overflows, at the rainy season, it becomes ten miles wide at certain points. Up and down this great highway passes a large portion of the commerce of the country, notwithstanding that a railway runs more or less parallel to it for much of the way. All the wealth of Burma comes down the Irawadi—teak, oil, rice, indigo, ground nuts, jade, amber, rubies, silver and, not least valuable, rubber. Upstream go manufactured goods, foodstuffs, milled rice and other of the necessities of life for the Burmese and also the European inhabitants. There is a large local trade in silk, "ngapi" (pickled fish) and "let-pet" (pickled tea).

The only towns of importance are Rangoon, Moulmein and Mandalay. Rangoon, situated in the delta of the Irawadi, was the British capital and chief port. It boasts a model jail, which can accommodate three thousand. Moulmein across the Gulf of Martaban, was the first British capital. The old native capital of Upper Burma is Mandalay.

Burma is rich in forests. Reserved forests alone, maintained principally for timber, cover 31,637 square miles. Her extraordinary fertility is due in part to her more than abundant rainfall. That of the Arakan along her upper coastline and Tenasserim, the coastal strip that depends from the south of Burma between the Gulf of Siam and the Indian Ocean, averages two hundred inches in a year—nearly five times, that of, say, New York—while there is ninety inches in the Irawadi delta. In the mountains of the extreme north, however, lies a zone as dry as California.

Unlike the Hindus, the Burmese are generally supposed to have migrated from Western China to the headwaters of the Irawadi, as did the people of Tibet. Their language is monosyllabic, though it depends a very great deal less than the Chinese on intonation. The alphabet, on the other hand, shows evidence of having been borrowed from the Aryan Sanskrit

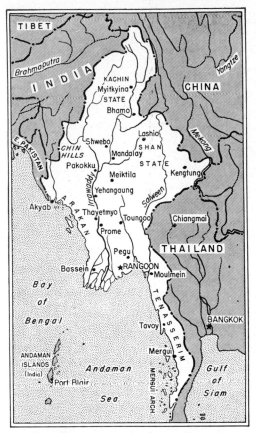

HOMELAND OF THE BURMESE

of India, and it is true that the Buddhist scriptures of Burma came from Southern India and Ceylon.

Protected by hilly walls, the Burmese maintained their independence for centuries. Then during the nineteenth century wars were fought with the British which resulted in making Burma India's largest province. It really began with a dispute over the Arakan and Chittagong, which generated such ill feeling in Burma that she eventually made preparations to invade Bengal by way of Manipur. This invasion the British prevented by occupying the strategic port of Rangoon in 1824 and advancing up the Irrawaddy. As a consequence, the disputed Arakan came under British administration, together with Assam in the north, and Tenasserim in the south. Further territory in Lower Burma was acquired in 1852. The third

change came in 1886, when Upper Burma was annexed. Burma became a Governor's Province of India in 1923. In 1937 it was separated from India and became a Crown Colony of the British Empire. Burma was conquered by the Japanese in 1942 after a brief campaign.

After the Japanese surrender in 1945, agitation for independence grew. Conferences in London between Burmese independence leaders and British government officials led to the formation of a Constituent Assembly and finally, in January of 1948, complete independence.

Burma is chiefly agricultural and its prime export is rice. The tourist will enjoy visiting the ricemills, the teak sawmills and lumber yards in which elephant labor is employed, and perhaps the petroleum refineries, which represent a third important industry. Just below Rangoon, at Pazundaung, on the Irrawaddy, stands a ricemill so vast that it turns out tons of rice a day. To it float barges loaded with the "paddy" (unhusked rice) which has been garnered with a hand-sickle, often by coolies from Hindustan. From the barges, heavy basketloads are carried on the head or shoulders to the mill. The paddy is first run over sieves and shakers to remove dirt and grit, then passed between grinders which remove its outer husks and leave a brown "natural" rice more wholesome than polished, where rice is the mainstay of the diet. This brown rice is run through pearlers to remove the clinging inner husks, then through sieves to grade it for the storage warehouses.

The humming teak sawmills at Rangoon employ hundreds of elephants, for teak is heavy. The hard wood preferred for Oriental temples and carved furniture is so heavy that in the green state it will not float. It grows in the hills amid bamboo brush, and elephants are used first to drag the logs downhill through the heavy undergrowth. Young bulls rounded up from the wild herds of the North Burma forests are chiefly used for this work because first it is easier to train the young animals, then because their tusks are useful as levers for picking up logs and for carrying them about the lumber yards. The great beasts appear to have almost human intelligence as they kneel before a log, thrust their tusks beneath it midway, then steady it with their trunks as they move it. When the rivers are deep, they can swim about, pushing the logs to place as directed by the drivers who sit on their heads. When the creeks are as "sludgy, squdgy," as Kipling's poem describes them to be, the elephants can go into mud knee-deep to float the logs in what water there is. In return for this labor, which would be impossible to any other living creature, the pachyderms must be kept scrubbed and curried, fed on tons of hay and bran, with perhaps rice and molasses for dessert, and given frequent holidays. The wild herds of the jungle are conserved by a commissioner of elephants who corresponds in importance to the forest supervisors of other countries.

Burma is one of the important oil producers of the world and supplies a good proportion of the lamps of Asia. The Burma Oil Company has huge refineries at Syriam and elsewhere, and its own fleet of oil tank steamers. Burma also has some of the finest and largest jade mines in the world and sells quantities of the costly transparent jade to wealthy Chinese for jewelry.

In Rangoon, natives of India, Chinese, Malays and Europeans jostle one another. White men find it too hot to walk, and unless they have their own automobiles, patronize the "gharries" (pony cabs) or street cars, which have second-class compartments. A few natives ride bicycles; others draw carts in competition with humped cattle. The city is a religious center because it contains the famous Shwe Dagon pagoda.

In the country districts, the houses are built of bamboo, with palm leaves to thatch the roofs and matting to paper the walls. Rice flourishes in the fields and delicious fruits grow wild. There is thus little inducement to thrift. When a man becomes wealthy, he buys jewelry for his wife and daughters, gives feasts to his neighbors or builds a pagoda that he may acquire merit for a future existence.

AVA HAMILTON

A WOMAN of the Southern Shan States.

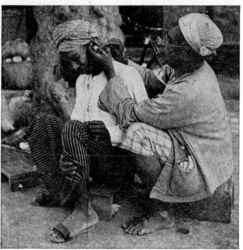

DUNGAN-PIX

HEALERS practice in the streets of Mandalay.

Notwithstanding, the women are exceptionally capable and energetic. In Rangoon certain of them have even been appointed to the Rangoon judicial court. Every Burmese woman is a born shopkeeper: every girl wants to manage a stall in the bazaar. Once she has gained her desire, she will sit there above huge baskets of grain or lengths of colored silks, smoking a cheroot as long as a school ruler. This business capacity of the women is the more surprising in that, until recent years, there was no education pro-

NIMBLE FINGERS AND POTTERY PLATES

The worker above is turning out Burmese pottery which, while sturdy and durable, is not as artistic as many of the other native wares. The people of Burma are highly skilled as weavers, sculptors and gold and silver smiths, and they also produce interesting brass and lacquer work. They like to adorn their houses and boats with their own ornate wood carvings.

vided for girls. If the husband is idle or ailing, the wife can divorce him. But he may claim his freedom if the wife gives him no sons.

In most of the out-of-the-way villages there may be a "pongyi kyaung," or monks' house, and the drone of voices coming from it will lead us to the schoolroom, where a dozen boys are shouting out the letters of the Burmese alphabet.

When Burma attained its independence, the school system came under state control. It includes primary, middle and high school grades. Primary education is free. In secondary schools, Burmese is the language of instruction, with English required as a second language. Rangoon is the seat of the University of Rangoon as well as of the University for Adult Education for those who do not qual-

WHERE THE MARK OF BEAUTY IS A VERY LONG NECK

The principal adornments of the women of the Padaung tribe are brass rings or coils worn around their necks, arms and legs. They start with one ring of the collar when they are very little girls, and add to this as they grow older until the later ones rest upon their shoulders. The practice results in grotesquely elongated necks, regarded as a sign of great beauty.

153

A SPIRED PAGODA ON THE TOP OF A HILL NEAR LASHIO

Burma is often called "the land of pagodas," for the charming structures dot the countryside. They are not temples, but reminders of Buddha, erected to gain merit for the builders.

A SERENE LANDSCAPE OF ROLLING HILLS IN UPPER BURMA

Northern Burma is plateau, though it is not a perfectly level one but rises as high as five thousand feet above sea level. The little-known Padaung people inhabit this region.

ify for the former. The Intermediate College at Mandalay now confers degrees and is due to become a university.

In Burma every name has a special meaning, and some of them are very quaint. A boy, for instance, may be Mr. Grandfather Elephant or Mr. Crooked and even Mr. Like-his-Father; and a girl may be called Miss Dog's Bone, Miss Naughty, Miss Rabbit or Miss Affection. A custom, however, decrees that the children must have names beginning with the initial letter of the day on which they were born. This rule is considered im-

BLACK STAR

DANCERS AT A PWE—THE MOST POPULAR FORM OF AMUSEMENT

There are several kinds of *pwè*, which may include acting and singing as well as dancing. These dancers are wearing exquisite *longyis*—draped skirts using five yards of cloth.

IN THE STEEP HILLS of Burma, elephants do the heavy work, such as hauling timber.

portant, because boys and girls born on certain days may marry only those born on other days.

The days of the week are each connected with a particular animal. The children thus have birth animals as people have birthstones. Monday is represented by a tiger, Tuesday by a lion, Wednesday by an elephant, Thursday by a rat, Friday by a guinea-pig, Saturday by a dragon and Sunday by a fabulous creature, half bird and half beast.

When a girl reaches the age of eleven or thereabouts her ears are pierced with great ceremony. The friends of the family are invited to a feast by the customary method of sending around packets of pickled tea. It is the girl's début. She may scream when the silver wires pierce her lobes, but the process will not have ended until—perhaps a week later—the holes are large enough for the insertion of larger jewels.

The corresponding ordeal for the boy is even more painful, for he is tattooed. All Burmese have their legs tattooed from knee to thigh in such a way that, from a short distance, it looks as if they were wearing dark blue tights. The process is so agonizing that only a part can be undergone at a time, and a boy has to show his manhood by bravely enduring the pain. Anyone who shirked would be a coward.

Every boy also has to go into a Buddhist monastery for some time before he can assume the status of a man. He puts on a yellow robe like those worn by the monks, and conforms to the rules of the monastery while he is there. This does not mean that he will become a monk, though many do so. There are thousands of monks in Burma, supported by the community.

Men and women dress so much alike that at first it is difficult to distinguish between them. Both wear cotton or silk skirts and little white jackets, but the men's skirts for ordinary wear are shorter and more sack-like. Their skirts, or *putsos,* for gala days, however, are made of many yards of the richest silk. The women's gala dress, which reaches to the ground, is tightly girt about the body. The great distinction in the dress of the two sexes is that the men are never seen without their headdresses, or "gaung-baungs" while the women wear nothing on their heads. Their glossy black hair is coiled on top, with an orchid or some other blossom hanging down over the right ear. The men wear their hair long also, but a Burman with a beard is unknown, and very few of them have even a moustache.

The best way to see the Burmese in their fine clothes is to go up to one of the great pagodas on a festival day, for then men, women and children give themselves up to devotion and merrymaking.

The chief place of worship is the great Shwe Dagon, or Golden Pagoda, of Rangoon. It stands on raised ground, and long flights of steps lead up to it on four sides. At the foot of the main steps two enormous white beasts with glistening red eyes and mouths ever stand on guard.

Placed at the sides of the steps are stalls with wax tapers, lotus, frangipani and jasmine, gold leaf and sweetmeats. These are bought by the people flocking to the shrines. Each flight leads up to a platform (larger than a city block) from the center of which rises the golden spire of the pagoda. On its top rests a gilded cage set with jewels and hung with hundreds of pure golden and silver bells, which tinkle in the breeze.

All around the base and at the edges of the platform are shrines, some of them decorated with teakwood carvings. Others are covered with a mosaic of bits of colored glass which glitter in the sun; others still are gilded over. There are posts topped by the sacred goose, there are almost life-size carved elephants, and there are bells which swing between two posts. As a Burman passes one of these bells, he will pick up a deer's horn from the pavement and strike a note to let the good spirits know he is there.

The whole scene is gay beyond description. Here a fortune-teller cries out that he will tell your fortune by a cast of the dice. There, in the shadows before a gleaming alabaster or brass figure of the Buddha, are wax tapers stuck on the ground and piles of flowers, and before them men and women crouch devoutly.

Mandalay is a Mecca for Buddhists. It must have hundreds of pagodas, of which the seven-roofed Arakan is considered the holiest. It contains an image of Buddha said to be the only one ever made during his lifetime. The larger sections of the heavy brass figure proved so difficult for the workmen to handle that, it is related, Buddha himself came to their aid. This revered statue was brought to the capital city in 1784.

Only two meals a day are eaten by the people of Burma, except by the monks, who may not eat after midday. Boiled rice is put on a large platter from which all help themselves, and little saucers of such condiments as curry, onions or chil-

FISHING NETS LIKE HUGE MEGAPHONES ON LAKE INLE

Swooping one of these nets through the water, the fisherman can haul up a good catch. The lake, which teems with finny creatures, is in Upper (or northern) Burma on the Shan Plateau.

BLACK STAR

A YELLOW-ROBED PRIEST AND SHWE DAGON PAGODA, RANGOON

The most sacred shrine of the Buddhist world is a solid stupa (mound) of brick—built over a relic chamber—covered with gold leaf. The place of worship is the surrounding terrace.

PIX

A GIGANTIC SITTING BUDDHA IN A SHRINE NEAR RANGOON

Rangoon is famous for its numerous shrines dedicated to Buddha, the most famous being the Shwe Dagon shrine that dominates the city. Hundreds of Buddhas are grouped about its spire.

IN RANGOON: AN OFFICE BUILDING THAT LOOKS LIKE A PALACE

Rangoon is one of the most modern cities in the Far East. Among its many fine buildings, some are as Oriental-looking as one would expect but others show Western influence.

A BURMESE VARIATION OF A GONDOLA IN RANGOON HARBOR

The water taxi, with upcurved bow and stern, is somewhat like a Venetian gondola. Rangoon has another feature in common with Venice; it is built largely on filled-in swamp.

A DRUGGIST'S STALL IN A CROWDED BAZAAR OF RANGOON

Looking for all the world like someone ready for baking, a Rangoon druggist studies the passing scene from his ovenlike stall, a cubicle at the entrance to a market building.

AVA HAMILTON

A HUGE HEAD of Buddha, apparently growing out of the hill, is the chief indication that the buildings are those of a religious order. Most of the Burmese people are Buddhists.

lies are served with it. The Burmese eat with their fingers. They roll a ball of rice neatly between finger and thumb, take a little condiment and then place the morsel in the mouth. When everyone has finished, each in turn goes to the waterbutt by the door to drink.

One of the most popular forms of entertainment is the plays, or "pwes." These take place as often as not out of doors. They are free, for they are given by some wealthy man for the entertainment of his friends and of anyone else who cares to come. They are very long, sometimes lasting more than one day, and the spectators come and go as they please. The plays are usually legendary tales about princes and princesses. The actors wear

old-fashioned court costumes and make long speeches, but there is always a clown to relieve the tedium and, judging by the laughter, he is really funny. Sometimes performances are given by marionettes cleverly worked by strings.

The people of the hill country are quite distinct from the Burmese. The Shans, a fair, sturdy race, are the largest tribe, but the Karens, who are divided into Red and White Karens, are nearly as numerous. There are also many other tribes, of which the best known are the Padaungs and Palaungs, the Akha, Lihsaw, Lahu and, in the north, the Kachins. Many of the Kachins live in districts which lie beyond the jurisdiction of the government, and they have so-called slaves, who are

EXPERT ARTISANS carve and paint countless images of Buddha in a shop near the Arakan Pagoda, southwest of Mandalay. In the city itself there are said to be 730 pagodas.

really domestic servants and are quite well treated by their masters.

The hill country, which lies between Burma proper and China, has recently been given back to the tribal chiefs, who rule independently within their own states.

Of all the odd customs observed by these hill races, none is more strange than this: when a Padaung girl reaches the age of seven her neck is encircled by a brass coil, which is extended from time to time. These coils are never removed, and as the girl grows older her neck is naturally stretched by the rings until she looks like a Jack-in-the-box, with the lid permanently drawn back. The more rings a Padaung woman carries, the more fashionable she is considered to be. The limit is somewhere in the neighborhood of twenty-seven. The last rings are larger than the others and they rest on the shoulders. Coils of brass similar to those worn on the neck are also worn on the arms and legs. This custom of adorning the body with metal rings is common to many of the tribes of Burma's hill country. Among some of these tribes (among the White Karens, for example) rattan rings replace the brass ones.

The costumes of these races are very picturesque. They weave and dye their own cloths. Reds and blues and trimming made of white strips or of seeds are enhanced by all kinds of strange and often very effective ornaments made from the silver that is found in the hills.

The peoples of Burma believe in good and bad spirits. Much of their lives is passed in endeavoring to propitiate the bad spirits, and in most of the villages in the hill country may be found tall spirit-posts, at which sacrifices are frequently made. It was formerly believed that photography had been devised as a magic method of capturing them. But so great has been the appeal of the beads, hand mirrors, tobacco tins and other bribes that to-day the difficulty is to keep the entire village from crowding before the camera.

BURMA: FACTS AND FIGURES

THE COUNTRY

Bounded on the north by China and Assam; on the east by China and Siam; on the south by the Bay of Bengal; and on the west by Assam and Pakistan. The area, including the Shan States, is 261,757 square miles. The total population of Burma is estimated to be about 18,674,000.

The present republic of the Union of Burma included the six northern and 28 southern Shan States. Britain retains rights of defense of the republic.

GOVERNMENT

The Union of Burma gained its independence on January 4, 1948. Burma had been under British rule since the first Burma War of 1826, and was administered jointly with India until 1937. In June 1947 Burma's Constituent Assembly voted for the establishment of a republic, and a treaty agreeing to this was ratified in London in October, 1947.

COMMERCE AND INDUSTRIES

Essentially an agricultural country, about 85% of the people living on the land. Rice is one of the most important crops. In the dry zone, sesamum, millet, peanuts, cotton and beans are cultivated. Some rubber is produced. The most important mineral product is petroleum. Valuable jade mines are worked. Other minerals are tin, tungsten ore and silver. Teak forests provide teakwood which is exported. Other exports are rice, silver and petroleum.

COMMUNICATIONS

Length of metalled roads, 3,760 miles; unmetalled roads, 6,770 miles. There are 60 miles of navigable canals. Railway mileage, 1,777.

RELIGION AND EDUCATION

Most of the people are Buddhists with 843 people out of every 1,000 following this religion.

Primary education is free in state schools. Secondary education is not free, although many allowances and free places are provided. A state teachers college was opened in 1947. The University of Rangoon was constituted in 1920. There is an intermediate college at Mandalay. A forest school, an agricultural college and research institute and a technical institute and veterinary college provide special education.

CHIEF TOWNS

Rangoon, capital, population, 500,800; Mandalay, 163,243; Moulmein, 71,181.

CEYLON THE ISLE OF JEWELS

Its People and Its Jungle-buried Cities

This fragrant island off the southeastern tip of India is a land of tea and rubber plantations, coconut palms, mines of precious stones and jungle-hidden ruins of mighty cities that flourished long ago. These cities were deserted by their inhabitants when the Tamils invaded the island more than a thousand years ago. Two of the most important are frequently visited by tourists.

THE ancestors of the now dominant Sinhalese race in Ceylon came from Bengal. Later, Tamil invaders arrived from southern India and for centuries held the upper hand by force of arms. Finally the Sinhalese abandoned the northern part of the island to the Tamils, who remain today. In 1505 Portuguese invaders appeared on the west coast and established a chain of fortified settlements. A hundred and fifty years later the Dutch ousted the Portuguese, but in 1796 were themselves ousted by the English. After becoming a crown colony in 1802, Ceylon progressed through various stages of self-government. Finally in 1948 it assumed full sovereignty and became a member state within the British Commonwealth of Nations.

In Colombo, its capital, the island has one of the finest harbors in the East. It is not a natural harbor, but has been made one at great cost and labor. The best natural harbor is Trincomalee up the northeast coast. Ceylon has low-lying shores, sandy and palm-fringed; but in the interior Mount Pedro, the highest peak, rises to over eight thousand feet. Near it is the health resort of Nuwara Eliya (pronounced Nuraylia), a settlement over six thousand feet above the sea to which white people who live in Ceylon go when the low country gets too hot. The tourist will find it interesting to visit the tea and rubber plantations.

Flowers bloom the year around. When we land at Colombo, it is the color that first attracts attention. The emerald water of the harbor contrasts with the figures of the men in pink or yellow garments lounging along the wharf. One old man in snowy garments, who looks like a priest, is a Sinhalese gentleman. Be-

tween the shafts of a rickshaw is a little man in a loin cloth with fuzzy hair sticking out from under a red fez. These two men are of quite different races and beliefs. The Sinhalese, who are Buddhists, ruled the island before the Hindu Tamils came from India; but even before them were wild men called Veddas. There are still a few Veddas, but they live hidden away in the jungles of eastern Ceylon. The population is largely Sinhalese, but there are also Mohammedan Moormen, the descendants of Arab traders, and a mixed population with Portuguese and Dutch blood in their veins, as well as Europeans.

The Tamils are sturdy, hard-working people. It is they who run in the rickshaws. This is a calling that descends from father to son. We may sometimes see a brown tot who staggers uncertainly as he runs, following his father as the man dodges this way and that. He is training to be a rickshaw coolie.

The open-front shops of Colombo are filled with colored silks and fine embroideries, copper and brass and ivory, to say nothing of jewels like those that dazzled the eyes of Aladdin. Here are stones which have been discovered in the island. They lie in gleaming piles. There are moonstones, which are found chiefly in Ceylon; there are rubies, topazes, beryls, cats'-eyes, zircons and jacinths; there are sapphires that gleam like the tropic sea.

But the pearls of Ceylon are the finest of her jewels. The odd thing is that the fishing season lasts only from one to two months in the early spring. The main pearl fisheries were formerly over on the east side by Trincomalee, but the pearl oyster is changeable in its ways, and year by year the catch declined in value until

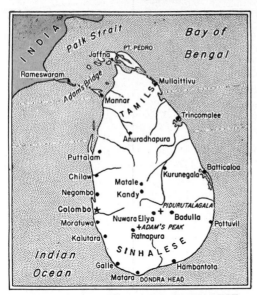

HOME OF TAMILS AND SINHALESE

it dropped to nothing at all. At the same time this particular kind of oyster appeared, as once before, on the west side, in the sand of the Gulf of Manaar, close under the shelter of the chain of islets known as Adam's Bridge, which links Ceylon to India. A valuable pearl bank has also been discovered at Twynam Paar. In 1925 the government opened a pearl fishery, and many Tamils and Moormen earn enough as divers during the short season to keep them the year around. There is, of course, a risk of injury to the lungs, as they dive without apparatus. The Tamil merely holds his nose; the Arab uses a nose clip.

The Ceylon pearl oyster, unlike that of the South Pacific, is hardly two inches in length and has a shell that one may crush between the fingers. The bags of oysters are sealed by a government inspector and taken ashore, where they are counted, the government taking two-thirds and the men one-third of the catch.

Ceylon devil-dancers are well known to everyone who has been in the East. Their costumes and antics were, in the old days, claimed to heal the sick by driving out devils, but now their performance is merely for money. To tempt money from the pockets of visitors, jugglers also do incredible feats, but the snake-charmers are always the greatest attraction. These men train their pets until the snakes seem mesmerized, and do whatever they wish.

Huge cobras, seven or eight feet long, fix their flickering eyes on their master, and, rising from their coils, sway to and fro to his piping. Finally they coil around his neck and nestle against his cheek, meek and obedient. These men really have some secret power not known to everyone, and they can mysteriously call wild snakes from their holes.

We must leave Colombo and go up country. There are many ways of doing this. The railways are good as far as they go. The roads are excellent. They were begun early in the nineteenth century by a boy named Thomas Skinner, who came out when he was only fourteen as an ensign in the army. He was told by his commanding officer to go off up country and make roads. The roads, when he started work upon them, were mere jungle tracks, but he gave them such sound foundations that they have remained good ever since.

We might go about the island by native boat, for Ceylon is cut up by waterways, especially near the coast, and has many rivers. The bamboo boats, the pretty villages, the wild life on the banks make this method pleasant, though it takes a long time.

The railways are wonderfully built, running in places on terraces cut out of shelving rock. Sometimes the line doubles on itself, so that the engine passes the rear carriages on a higher level, going the opposite way.

The first thing we notice as we leave the plains is the cultivation of paddy, or rice. It is grown on terraces built up in such a way that they can be flooded. Unfortunately, Ceylon does not produce enough rice for its own needs, but has to buy from Burma and other countries.

Higher still we see the tea bushes growing in regular lines. Tea forms one of the largest exports of Ceylon. About five-sixths of it is sent to England. Women pickers wear red head-cloths, ear-

THE HARBOR OF COLOMBO is one of the liveliest in the Far East. Hundreds of fishing boats, motorboats, yachts and ocean-going liners and freighters tie up in the harbor's calm waters.

A DEEP-SEA DIVER waits to have his helmet adjusted before descending into Colombo Harbor. An artificial harbor, with four breakwaters, it is checked constantly for repairs.

A STIFF BREEZE BELLIES THE SAIL OF A FISHING CANOE

Along the coast of Ceylon sand bars are frequent, and these shallow craft can glide over them easily. Sharks lurk in the water, and they are caught for the extraction of their oil.

OXEN PULL HUGE LOADS OF FREIGHT IN CEYLON'S HARBOR CITY

Colombo, capital and leading port city of Ceylon, is a city of contrasts. Here East meets West,
the old meets the new, and modern cars ease slowly past lumbering ox-drawn carts.

169

RICE FIELDS provide the principal native food. There are only twenty-five acres to every hundred and eighty people, and Ceylon cannot grow all the rice that she needs because she does not everywhere get enough rain to feed such thirsty plants. Much of her water comes from a wonderful system of irrigation tanks installed centuries ago by a long dead civilization.

THE TEA GARDENS of Ceylon, now the island's chief source of wealth, annually provide many millions of pounds for export, chiefly to the United Kingdom. Those shown above are in the Dimbula district, near Nuwara Eliya. Coffee used to be grown on these fertile hillsides, but fungus attacked and killed the coffee plants, and the tea industry was substituted.

171

THE TEMPLE OF THE TOOTH NEAR THE CITY OF KANDY

Dalada Maligawa, the Temple of the Tooth, stands on the north shore of an artificial lake outside the city of Kandy. The temple supposedly contains a real tooth of Buddha. The original tooth was brought to Ceylon in the fourth century. It is believed that, in 1560, the Portuguese took the original from northern Ceylon to Goa, where it was destroyed.

172

rings and anklets. Tamils do this work for the main part.

With tea-growing, planters combine other things, such as rubber. On some roads we see great reddish-brown cocoa pods hanging from the trees like Chinese lanterns. Then there are the shrubs that yield pepper, spices and gingery cardamoms.

The wealth of Ceylon is, however, largely natural and not cultivated. First in importance come the palms, which fringe every sandy coast and love to send their roots clear out under the salt water.

Everywhere we see coconuts and find houses thatched with palm leaves. There is also the palmyra, which flowers but once in forty years, bursting upward in an enormous nosegay of frothy millions of tiny flowers. From this palm are made the palm-leaf books used by the priests, who write on them with a sharp point. There is the talipot palm with long leaves which fold up, so that people use them as umbrellas. A rough sort of brown sugar is made from another palm.

Every village has clumps of feathery bamboos growing alongside the houses.

AMERICAN PRESIDENT LINES

ANCIENT STONE CARVING IN THE DALADA MALIGAWA IN KANDY

A bit of discolored ivory two inches long, supposed to have been a tooth of Buddha, is kept within the Dalada Maligawa, or Temple of the Tooth. It is enshrined upon a pure gold lotus flower and seven jewel-crusted bells fit over it. The Portuguese claim to have burnt the tooth when they captured the city, but many Ceylonese believe the original was hidden.

STEVENS

THE TAMILS OF CEYLON, two of whom are shown here performing a native dance, migrated from southern India to the northern part of the island. A quarter of the population is made up of Tamils and two-thirds of Sinhalese. For hundreds of years Tamil and Sinhalese have battled, but they now live peaceably, though the former are Buddhists and the latter Hindus.

NOSE AND TOE RINGS are worn by Tamil girls who earn their living in the tea gardens of Ceylon. Small and slight, they are none the less hard workers. The Tamils are a Dravidian people who came from India where the language is still spoken by something like twenty million people. They have also spread into Burma and even into Siam.

175

The forest, carefully tended by the government Forest Department, includes such valuable woods as ebony, satinwood and teak. The last is largely used in the construction of ships, even nowadays when there are so many steel vessels.

Plenty of fruit and vegetables can be plucked by the villagers. Bananas or plantains are a staple part of their diet. There are also limes, oranges, mango-steens, custard apples, papaws (which are like melons) and jack fruit (which looks like so many pumpkins), a cattle feed growing on a small stem straight from the trunk of a tree.

Cattle form the chief beasts of burden, some drawing heavy carts and some pulling lighter two-wheeled vehicles. These latter are trotting bullocks, but they cover no more than four miles an hour, while

LIFELIKE FIGURES CROWD THE WALL OF A BUDDHIST TEMPLE
Buddha is the central figure in this temple interior. He is surrounded by worshipers in various attitudes of reverence. One shields him from the elements; another offers him sustenance.

JINRIKISHAS IN THE BUSY FORT DISTRICT OF COLOMBO

Jinrikishas—man-powered carriages—are used in many cities of the Far East, and one sees them side by side with up-to-date cars. The Fort District—the part of the city that was built within the walls of a colonial fort—is the business section of Colombo. The city is a supply stop for vessels bound to or from the Suez Canal, Cape Town or Singapore.

THE RIVERS OF CEYLON, with their banks picturesquely overgrown by palms and flowering jungle plants, are not very large and have shifting sandbanks at their mouths, so they cannot be used by ships of large tonnage. But as many of them are connected with one another by canals, they are useful for native transport. Many native boats like these, thatched to give shelter from sun and rain, drift loaded down to the ports, and toil back empty against the swift stream. The warm waters are infested with crocodiles, but men, none the less, take the risk of fording them.

AN IMAGE OF BUDDHA seated in meditation reposes deep in the jungle of Ceylon, just where it was carved more than a thousand years ago. This colossal granite figure is but one of the signs of a vanished civilization that has been discovered in Anuradhapura. Another statue, 146 feet long, of Buddha sleeping, can be seen at Polonnaruwa.

A GEM PIT IN CEYLON

Ceylon is an island of gems—sapphires yellow and blue, misty moonstones, crimson essonites and garnets, cats'-eyes, deep green alexandrites and zircons blue, green and brown. Above, workers are gathering gravel in a gem pit. The earth is brought up in baskets and stored in a pile. Later it is carefully washed and picked over in the search for precious stones.

the heavier beasts in the agricultural carts do only two.

In the deep recesses of the forests, where flying foxes play, monkeys swing from branch to branch and birds of paradise flash through the green gloom, one travels by jungle tracks that can be traversed only afoot or at best by a slow ox-wagon. Here one may still find wild elephants, leopards, buffalo, sambar deer and sloth bears, mongeese and porcupines, to say nothing of snakes, jackals, crocodiles and tortoises, which invade even the irrigation tanks.

The famous Lost Cities were built in the times of the ancient kings. After they had been deserted by the Sinhalese, who fled from the attacks of the Tamils, the jungle covered the cities with living green. There are ruins in many parts of the island, but the two cities visited by people from all parts of the world are Anuradhapura and Polonnaruwa.

The first named was the capital from about 500 B.C. to 800 A.D. Here granite blocks have been carved in quaint and interesting scenes by hands long since dust. Huge dagobas, or mounds like rounded hills composed of uncountable numbers of bricks, rise from the jungle. Granite columns fallen this way and that remain by the hundreds. One might spend days exploring. At Polonnaruwa there are also splendid temples of brick. Polonnaruwa became the royal residence after the fall of Anuradhapura in 800.

CRUDE LATEX IS ROLLED INTO SHEETS OF CREPE RUBBER

Latex is a milky fluid that oozes from some plants and natural rubber is obtained from it. Crepe rubber in this case is simply crude rubber in crinkled sheets, made by passing the hardened latex through powerful rollers. Ceylon has a number of rubber plantations and the latex is partly treated in factories on the island. Much of it is shipped overseas.

BLACK STAR

THIS DEVIL DANCER of Kandy, with his marvelous head dress of jingling brass, believes that he and others of his calling, by dancing themselves into a frenzy, can frighten away the devil that possesses a sick man. At least the Tamils used once to hold such a belief. Nowadays they often dance in the hope of collecting money from interested travelers.

. SKEEN & CO

THIS SINHALESE GIRL has the beauty typical of her race, of clear skin, regular features and large eyes. The men of Ceylon, as well as the women, dispose of their long black hair in a knot at the back of the head, and wear the loose robes suited to a hot climate. The Sinhalese also reflect in their jewelry their skill at work in gold, silver and ivory.

About midway between these two cities is to be found one of the strangest places in any country in the world. The huge rock of Sigiri, composed of red granite, thrusts itself up out of the surrounding jungle like a gigantic mushroom. This steep-sided rock is four hundred feet in height. In the fifth century A.D. King Kasyapa, after killing his father and seizing the throne, fled to this refuge from the wrath of his elder brother. For eighteen years he ruled Ceylon from the top of this rock. He had a palace constructed on the top, within which was a great red granite throne which remains to this day, though the palace lies in ruins.

At Kandy, in the center of the island, reigned the last of Ceylon's kings. His throne, supported by dragons of cut crystal with amethyst eyes, was carried to Windsor, where it remains to this day. Many of the nobles descended from the ancient royal house of Kandy are living, and on festival occasions appear in their quaint dress with flat hats and their voluminous skirts caught up by gorgeous jewel-studded belts.

The center of interest at Kandy, however, is the Temple of the Tooth. This contains a curious relic which has accompanied the royal house of Ceylon in all its changing fortunes. The original tooth (whether of Buddha or not) was brought over from India, hidden in the hair of a princess. Whether this identical tooth is still there, or, as some say, was stolen by the Portuguese and has been replaced, matters little. A tooth lies today encased in a series of caskets in charge of the Buddhist priest and once a year is carried in procession on the back of an elephant.

On Adam's Peak, to the south, is guarded a great imprint in stone said by Buddhists to be the impression of the foot of Buddha and by Mohammedans to be that of Adam. Of one thing there can be no question—it is not the impression of anything human: it is six feet long

---

CEYLON: FACTS AND FIGURES

THE COUNTRY

An island, in the Indian Ocean, which lies south of India. The area is 25,332 square miles and the population is 6,693,945.

GOVERNMENT

Formerly a British Crown Colony, Ceylon achieved dominion status in February, 1948. By special agreement, the British government retains the right of defense of the island. A constitutional government is headed by the Governor General and Prime Minister. For purposes of administration, the island is divided into 9 provinces.

COMMERCE AND INDUSTRIES

Agriculture is the occupation of about two-thirds of the people, and coconuts, rice, tea and rubber are the chief products. Cacao, tobacco, spices, areca nuts and sugar-cane are grown also. There are numerous cattle and buffaloes, swine, sheep, goats and horses. Mineral products include graphite or plumbago, gems (sapphires, rubies, moonstones, cat's-eyes and other precious and semi-precious stones), monazite and mica. The preparation for export of tea, rubber, coconut products, citronella oil, spices and rice cleaning are the principal industries. Manufacturing such as weaving, basket work, tortoise-shell boxes, earthenware, jewelry, metal work, lacquer work and carving is of minor importance. The principal exports are tea, copra, crude rubber, coconuts, coconut oil, coir, plumbago (graphite), cacao and citronella oil, and the imports are rice, cotton manufactured goods, sugar, beverages, tobacco, coal, iron and steel goods and machinery.

COMMUNICATIONS

There are about 900 miles of railway, and about 13,200 miles of telegraph line and 18,900 telephones.

RELIGION AND EDUCATION

A majority of the people are Buddhists. Hindus, Moslems and Christians rank next in number.

Education is free from the kindergarten to the university. The University of Ceylon was established in 1942 by combining the Ceylon Medical College and Ceylon University College. There is also the Ceylon Technical College with courses in science and engineering.

CHIEF TOWNS

Colombo, the capital, population 361,000; Jaffna, 63,000; Galle, 49,000; Kandy, 52,000.

REPUBLIC UNDER BRITISH PROTECTION

Maldive Islands, 400 miles southwest of Ceylon, are governed as a republic, with an elected president, a prime minister, a senate of 80 members and a lower house. The Maldives are a group of coral islets which produce coconuts, millet, fruit and edible nuts. The people, numbering about 93,000 Moslems, are great navigators and traders.

CITY AND JUNGLE IN MALAYA

Wealthy Eastern Lands and Indolent People

Singapore, Sanskrit for "the Lion City," stands at the crossroads of the East on the ocean highway between Europe and the Far East. It is the main gateway into countries whence comes much of the world's rubber and tin. It stands at the end of a long peninsula which, with a number of islands, makes up the former Straits Settlements and Malay States. The British, who secured control of Malaya in 1824, were the first to really tap the vast natural resources of the country—its tin, rubber, oil-palms and agricultural products. These resources were lost to the world during the Japanese occupation in World War II, but were restored following Japan's surrender in 1945. The Federated and Unfederated States, with two of the Straits Settlements, became the Federation of Malaya in February, 1948, under British protection.

WHEN we speak of Malaya we mean those parts of the southward pointing Malay peninsula that include the states of the former Federated and Unfederated States of Malaya, and the Crown Colony of Singapore (including the Cocos Islands and Christmas Island).

Since the end of World War II, however, the nine states and two of the former Straits Settlements have become the Federation of Malaya, a British protectorate. These are Perak, Selangor, Negri Sembilan, Pahang, Johore, Kedah, Perlis, Kelantan and Trengganu; and the former settlements of Penang and Malacca. The former settlement of Labuan is administered by the governor general of Malaya.

Although we know of these provinces as Malaya, the peninsula is still called Malacca by the peoples on the continent of Europe, after the name of its oldest town. The settlement of Malacca was founded by the Malays, who came from Sumatra as early as the twelfth century. The Portuguese, who occupied Malacca in 1511, found the interior occupied by cannibals and the coast by Malay, Chinese and Japanese spice traders. The Dutch East India Company expelled the Portuguese in 1641 and the English finally secured control in 1824.

Inland, rice, fruit and rubber trees have been planted, and their products are beginning to give the settlement new life. In the shops we can find beautiful examples of basket work. The Malayan forests are famous the world over for producing the finest materials for basket-making, and in Malacca by far the best of the baskets are made. Malays work slowly, however, and, as they take a month to make a set of baskets, the craft is of little commercial value.

As, with the coming of the Dutch, the trade of Malacca began to decline, Penang, an island at the northern entrance of the Straits of Malacca, which was the earliest British settlement, became the more important place. But no sooner was the settlement of Singapore founded than Penang began to lose its trade. Recently, with the increase of tin-mining and rubber-planting in the Malay States, it has become busy once more, and its beautiful scenery attracts large numbers of tourists. So that now it shares with Singapore the first place among Malayan ports.

We approach Singapore by steamer via the narrow red-walled straits leading to Keppel Harbor which is crowded with the shipping of seven seas. Its waterfront is lined with warehouses, oil tanks from which piers reach out in a fringe for a mile along shore. It is also an important air and naval base and the centre of air traffic from East and West.

In Commercial (or Raffles) Square east of the fort, rickshaws and gharries stand lined up like parked motor cars (though there are also electric cars), their fares fixed by the municipality. European men in white ducks and sun helmets, wealthy Chinese merchants and nearly naked water-peddlers, sailors and tourists of every nationality mingle in the in-

BRITISH INFORMATION SERVICES

CLASSIC ARCHITECTURE IN SINGAPORE

Although only about one per cent of the population of Singapore is European, sections of the city have a distinctly Western appearance. Victoria Hall, left, and the Municipal Building, right background, are in classic-revival style. They could quite suitably appear in Toronto or Philadelphia. Singapore is big, noisy and overcrowded, with a wonderful harbor,

AMERICAN PRESIDENT LINES

RICKSHAW A LA MODE

You will get the real flavor of Singapore in the Asiatic districts of the city. If you are too tired to walk, you may rent a tri-shaw, a sort of rickshaw mounted as a sidecar on a bicycle. The open air shops display all sorts of tempting goods. The shopkeepers' signs are probably commonplace, but they have a strange, romantic air to those who cannot read them.

dolent throngs. One is surprised to find how modern and substantial are the Government House, the Hong Kong and Shanghai Bank and the Supreme Court buildings. The British residents have polo, golf and cricket grounds and a race course and live a gay social life after the coolness of evening has swept in from the sea. Here we cannot fail to be impressed by the shipping, for we are at the gateway of the Far East, on the highway from Europe and India to the west, and China and Japan to the east. Ships from all over the world bring merchandise to Singapore, for it is the distributing center for the whole of the Malay Archipelago. At all seasons of the year the port is filled with strange craft: Malays with their fishing boats—the only home of many of them—Chinese junks and sampans, large and small steamers from Indochina and Japan, and great vessels loading cargoes of tin and rubber for the markets of Great Britain and the

United States of America. Besides the tin-smelting, rubber-refining and pineapple canning industries of Singapore, there is a great trade in rattan canes, which are there cleaned and prepared.

As we wander among the shops and markets of Singapore we meet all sorts and types of peoples. The majority of them are Chinese; Malays take second place. Although European and Japanese manufacturers have done away with much of the picturesque native dress, we can still see the stately Malay in his loose trousers, jacket and sarong, or tartan skirt, which is bundled around his waist and reaches down to his knees. On his head he wears a kerchief or a velvet cap, which he would never be without. The Malay considers his headdress even more a point of etiquette than his coat, though it may be only a thin wisp of palm frond tied around his forehead. After the Malays come the Hindus. The tourist will find Hindu jewelers, who sell precious

BLACK STAR

OPERATING TIN MINE IN THE KINTA VALLEY, NEAR IPOH, MALAYA

British Malaya is one of the world's important tin producers, and the output has increased in recent years. The limestone area on the west side of the central mountain range in and near the Kinta Valley is its richest source, and Ipoh is the most important city in the section. Only a few degrees from the equator, Kinta Valley is hot, with a heavy rainfall.

THE ORNATE TOWER of the Chinese temple looking down on the island city of Penang is by no means out of place. More than half of the people who live there are Chinese.

stones in the rough, and Chinese silk merchants. He can buy beautiful examples of Malay weaving—bright cloths inlaid with gold leaf from Selangor and striped shawls made in Kelantan. Odd pieces of pottery are sent down from Perak and Pahang, and from the former district, delicate silverware. He can buy embroidered mats and slippers made of fine silk and gold thread, and occasionally he will find pieces of wood-carving, the craft of the people of Negri Sembilan.

We may leave Singapore on a comfortable state railway which crosses a causeway over the shallow strait and winds through the mangrove swamps of the coast, past inland fresh-water swamps, over a way carved out of the jungle and past the jagged limestone cliffs from

which about 35 per cent of the world's tin is mined.

Malaya is too near the equator for seasonal changes, though the northeast monsoon blows off the Gulf of Siam from November to March, sometimes so violently as to demolish the bamboo huts of the natives and do serious damage to the rubber plantations. At Kuala Lumpur it is often 140 to 150 degrees in the blazing sunshine and humid with the sudden downpours that occur toward evening.

The rubber trees, which have largely replaced the sugar, coffee, spice, banana and tapioca plantations, are worked by coolies under white supervision. The trees are planted in regular rows, and European experts superintend the tapping. In Johore, a former Unfederated

AVA HAMILTON

A LAVISHLY DECORATED FLOAT leads the funeral procession for a rich Chinese woman of Penang. Hired mourners dressed in sackcloth coats and hoods trudge beside the hearse.

HUNDREDS OF SMALL BOATS CROWD A GREAT CROSSROADS HARBOR

Singapore Harbor is one of the busiest ports in the world, handling over 80 per cent of all the imports and exports of the whole Malay Peninsula. These small boats are used chiefly to carry goods produced in the interior to the port city for handling and shipment overseas. So over-crowded is Singapore that many of the people live all the time on their boats.

FLASHING SWORDS ACCOMPANY THE PERFORMANCE OF A DANCE

Dancing is a popular pastime among Malay villagers. To the music of drums and pipes, a group executes the dramatic postures of a traditional dance called the Ota Ota.

State lying in the south of the peninsula, nearly the whole of the country is planted with rubber. Rubber is not a native of the East, however. Although a very large part of the world's supply is now produced by Malaya, rubber was first brought to that country from Brazil in South America in 1876.

Pahang, on the eastern side of the central mountain range, is one of the richest tin-producing areas. The United States is one of the largest consumers of Malaya's rubber and tin. During World War II, however, the Japanese conquest of Malaya deprived Americans of this source of supply, and serious shortages of rubber and tin developed.

Rattan is one of the important vegetable products of Malaya. The rattan palm has hooked prickles which enable it to climb the tallest trees of the jungle. Rattan stems are cut into lengths of from five to thirty-five feet, dried in the sun on trestles, till the outer skin is peeled off, then split and exported in that state for furniture making.

If we follow the course of a river from its mouth, we find that it passes through crocodile-haunted swamps and over sandbars near the sea. Higher up it threads a winding course through miles of forest; nearer its source in the mountains we find it cascading over the cliffs.

Forests of green twilight, their high branches interlocking, deepen the silences of the interior. Certain of the trees grow

A YOUNG MOSLEM IN A STREET OF GEORGE TOWN, PENANG ISLAND

Although the majority of Penang's population is Chinese, many other types of Asians may be seen, among them Malays, Indians and Eurasians. The small island is just west of the Malay Peninsula; and George Town, its seaport, is on the eastern side, with large docks and a ferryboat to the mainland. The climate is hot and humid, and there is a high rainfall.

RUBBER TAPPING IN MALAYA: A PROCESS REQUIRING GREAT SKILL

Rubber trees are usually tapped for the first time in their fifth year. They must be tapped to just the right depth, for the latex—the gummy fluid from which rubber is made—lodges against a thin layer of cells between the bark and wood of the tree. It flows most readily in the cool morning temperature. The average yield of a tree is four or five pounds a year.

193

to 150 feet or more while beneath them trees half that height intermingle with their stems, and below these lesser trees grows a dense tangle of ferns and creepers, mosses, orchids and other flowering plants.

In the forests there is plenty of big game. Elephants do great damage to the plantations only a few miles north of Kuala Lumpur. The great beasts are captured in "drives" in which the blowing of trumpets and the beating of tomtoms frighten them into stockades, after which men with spears and torches prevent the captives from demolishing their imprisoning walls. There are two species of rhinoceros, and the Malay tapir is common. The Malay tiger is smaller than its Indian relative, and is not very greatly given to man-eating, because game, in the form of deer, is very plentiful.

In the hills north of Perak lives the rare Siamang ape, a powerful, long-armed creature. One old male seen by the writer had an arm span of nearly five feet. There are three other anthropoid apes known as gibbons, besides which the wizened faces of several kinds of monkeys peer at one or go crashing away, barking and jibbering. It is interesting to watch the country Malays with the coconut monkeys. They train them as pets, and send them up the coconut trees to pick whichever coconut they point out.

Squirrels are to be found everywhere, some bigger than a cat, other species nearly as small as a young rat. In mentioning rats we name one of the most constant troubles in Malaya, for they exist in enormous numbers, and do great damage to the crops. Bats haunt the vast limestone caves, snakes hunt through

MECHANIZED RICKSHAS transport passengers to the railway station, which looks like a wedding cake, at Kuala Lumpur. Kuala Lumpur, Federation capital, is on the west-coast railway.

BRITISH INFORMATION SERVICES

the tree tops and undergrowth, crocodiles and tortoises infest the swamps. But there are also hundreds of gorgeous butterflies, song birds, and birds of gay plumage.

The beautiful Argus pheasant is fairly plentiful, and so are several species of pigeon. There are few parrots, but brilliantly colored kingfishers dwell there in large numbers, and the clumsy hornbills are easy to find.

In the interior we come across a round-headed race of Negritos that hark back to the days before men learned to plant crops and pasture cattle. These hunt their meat with blowpipes or trap it, fish, and hunt wild roots and fruits. They make offerings to the spirits of the elements and to their ancestors. As shy as four-footed forest dwellers, these Semangs may be told from the Sakais because they are smaller, darker and frizzly-haired. They live in leafy shelters on high poles, and wear loin cloths, with belts of dried grass or ornaments of plaited rattan for the women.

The other aboriginal race of the peninsula, the Sakai people, is superior to the Semangs in culture. In the mountain districts of Perak and southward down to Selangor we find their pile houses grouped together in small villages. They are a sturdy race, with light brown skins and straight or wavy hair. Near the villages there are small cultivated patches of ground where the Sakais grow millet, sugar, tobacco and hill-rice. When they have garnered their crops they move on and make fresh clearings. They use bows and arrows, although they make these chiefly for sale to tourists, but their important weapon is the blowpipe.

BRITISH INFORMATION SERVICES

BASKETS OF PINEAPPLES, newly harvested, await canning in a busy food factory in the state of Johore.

The Sakais have many strange religious customs. If we could arrive at a rubber plantation at the time of one of their festivals, we would see them preparing a deep trench about thirty feet in length. In this they burn wood for two or three days, until the trough is filled with smoldering ashes. A number of the men of the tribe fast for some days before the event,

195

then, on the appointed day, walk barefoot down the trench. They do this with the idea that evil spirits will be driven out of them in the course of their uncomfortable promenade. The Sakais' feet are padded underneath with very thick skin, so they do not suffer as much as they would have us believe.

A number of small rivers crawl through the jungle to form the Pahang, which curves through Malaya to the China Sea, bearing innumerable sampans with palm-thatched cabins on its bosom. Were it not for the good roads that traverse the peninsula, it would matter more that the mouth of the great river is so choked by sand-bars as to be unnavigable to the many large vessels of the coast and trans-oceanic trade.

Near its junction with the sea the banks of this stream are dotted with the villages of the Malayans built on high piles, some of them far out over the water where it is possible on a hot day to fish directly from the kitchen porch. The front veranda is the reception room.

The peninsular Malay comes of a mixture of neighboring races and is really courteous and likable. He is olive-skinned and has straight lustrous black hair. His eyes are black or reddish-brown, sometimes slightly almond shaped, and his nose is generally flat and broad; but he has small, finely molded hands and feet, prominent cheek-bones, a square chin and even white teeth. It must be confessed that he is lazy, although when he likes he can work both hard and well. He is a Mohammedan, yet his womenfolk have considerable liberty; and he is more than usually kind to children. Anywhere in the peninsula where we come in contact with men of his race, we are sure to be treated with gentle courtesy, and to find a certain degree of loyalty. One departs favorably impressed with this Eastern land.

SINGAPORE, FEDERATION OF MALAYA: FACTS AND FIGURES

SINGAPORE

The island of Singapore (including Cocos and Christmas Islands), was formerly one of the Straits settlements, together with Penang, Malacca, and Labuan. Penang and Malacca are now part of the Malay Federation, and Labuan is under the Federation's jurisdiction. Singapore has the status of a Crown Colony. The island, 27 miles long and 14 miles wide, is separated from the Malay Peninsula by the Straits of Johore. Area, 220 square miles; population about 980,818. The chief industry is tin smelting, and for many years Singapore produced more than half of the world's supply.

The Cocos or Keeling Islands, a group of about 20 small coral islands, are attached to Singapore. Population is about 1,763. There are large coconut plantations; copra, oil and nuts are exported.

Christmas Island is also attached to Singapore. It has an area of about 62 square miles and a population of about 1,216. Inhabitants are employed by the company that works the enormous phosphate deposits.

FEDERATION OF MALAYA

A Federation of Malaya was established on February 1, 1948, in which the nine Malay States and the settlements of Penang and Malacca were granted the right of local self-government. Control of defense and foreign affairs still remains in British hands, as does ultimate legal jurisdiction.

The Malay States lie on the Malay Peninsula. Four of them were federated once before: Perak, area, 7,980 square miles, population, 962,400; Selangor, area, 3,167 square miles, population, 723,000; Negri Sembilan, area, 2,550 square miles, population, 272,900; Pahang, area, 13,873 square miles, population, 241,500. Total area: 27,570 square miles; total population: 2,199,800. The products are coconuts, rice, rubber, sugar, pepper, timber, gutta-percha, oils, resins and canes. Mining of tin, gold, tungsten and coal is carried on. The chief industries are the cultivation of rubber and the mining of tin.

The states formerly known as the Unfederated Malay States are: Johore, area, 7,321 square miles, population, 753,900; Kedah, area, 3,660 square miles, population, 561,400; Perlis, area, 310 square miles, population, 71,300; Kelantan, area, 5,746 square miles, population, 444,700; Trengganu, area, 5,050 square miles, population, 227,100. Their area totals 22,087 square miles, with a total population of 2,058,400. The principal town is Johore Bahru, with a population of about 21,776. Rubber, rice, coconuts, tapioca and tin are the chief products.

The settlement of Penang has an area of 110 square miles and its neighbor, Wellesley, two miles distant, has an area of 290 square miles. Their total population is 454,000. Malacca has an area of 633 square miles and a population of 244,600. Labuan is 35 square miles in area with a population of about 9,000. The total area of the Malay Federation is about 50,700 square miles and the total population is about 5,000,000. The capital is Kuala Lumpur.

LAND OF THE WHITE ELEPHANT

The Independent Siamese and Their Country

The Siamese call their land Muang Thai, the Land of the Free. The word
Siam (or Sayam) is probably the same as Shan, the Burmese name for the
Lao race, the Shan and the Siamese. Their country, however, is usually called
the Land of the White Elephant, for albino elephants are found in its vast
forests and are thought by the Siamese to be semisacred. This kingdom of
the Far East is one of the few tropical countries that remain in a state of
independence, and it shows the combination of an Oriental king with a certain
amount of Western civilization. With its mixed population, largely Buddhist,
Siam is a most surprising and interesting corner of the globe to visit.

SIAM (Thailand) is a country of southeast Asia. To the east lies French
Indochina, to the west, Burma, and
to the south, Malaya. Siam's greatest
length is about 1,000 miles, and its greatest
width, 500 miles. It has a long coast line,
about 1,700 miles, and many very fine
harbors. The most important river is the
Menam ("mother of waters") which has
its source in the mountains in the north

THAILAND, OR SIAM

and which flows 600 miles to empty into
the Gulf of Siam.

Some two thousand years ago Mongoloid tribes, the Mon-Annams, and a few
centuries later the Lao-Tais, overran the
territory we know as Siam, driving the
aboriginal Negritos into the mountains.
To their Chinese culture, colonists from
India added customs and beliefs. In the
sixteenth and seventeenth centuries Portuguese, English and Dutch traders successively appeared on the palm-fringed
shores of Siam, and the French tried,
without success, to secure the kingdom.
Destructive wars with Burma followed, in
the course of which period the Siamese
chose for king a warrior, Phaya Chakkri,
who established peace. Though both
Great Britain and the United States of
America made treaties with Siam early in
the nineteenth century, a Chinese monop-
oly largely prevented foreign commerce
until 1851. Then there came to the throne
a king who spoke English. The open door
followed. Though there was considerable
material progress in the years that followed, Siam remained an absolute monarchy until 1932. In that year a bloodless
revolution resulted in the formation of a
limited monarchy. Siam, which was one
of the Allies in World War I, became a
more or less unwilling partner of Japan in
the second World War.

The traveler in Siam will find many
huge walled enclosures called wats, which
contain the Buddhist temples, the dormi-
tories of the "bonzes," or student priests,
and their school buildings. To them at
sunrise come devout women bearing offerings of tea, rice and boiled bamboo

shoots. After them flows a stream of worshipers, also holiday-makers. Families will make journeys requiring several days' travel to pray at the wats. At the gates they will be stopped by dealers in gold leaf, for the images in the shrines are covered with gold foil, and the worshipers renew the gold on any spot that may have become tarnished.

The gardens of the wats are the refuges of aged cats and dogs, for it is against the teachings of Buddhism to take the life of any living creature. For the same reason the priests each possess a filter that their drinking water may not harbor any living organism.

The bazaars of Bangkok extend for two or three miles outside the city proper. They consist for the most part of rickety bamboo shops, booths and stands on which odorous dried fish, oil, brass bowls, little carved Buddhas—some no bigger than hazel nuts—primitive looms, sweetmeats, green and blue slippers and toys are displayed in colorful confusion. Itinerant candy sellers, with bell-shaped umbrellas over their wares, kite-makers and flag-makers mingle in the streets.

When a customer enters a Siamese hair-dresser's booth, the barber shaves his head with a razor and pulls out the hairs of his beard one by one with broad tweezers. There are also traveling barbers who carry with them their whole stock-in-trade, including a chair.

We see tailors in the bazaars, sitting cross-legged at their work. It is not through making clothes that they make the greater part of their profit, but by selling needles and threads.

White elephants are venerated. The Siamese do not look upon these animals as gods, but believe that the spirits of their wisest and noblest ancestors inhabit them. On that account the albino pachyderms used to be tended by the greatest mandarins of the country, and even today they are guarded with the utmost care.

PLOWING THE HARD WAY

The picture was taken after an epidemic of rinderpest had swept through the country, killing a large percentage of the cattle. The loss of draft animals forced upon farmers a battle for survival in its most primitive form. Science is doing a great deal to control such epidemics.

UNATIONS

AVA HAMILTON

A NET TO CATCH ENOUGH FISH FOR A WHOLE VILLAGE

The net is arranged on a sort of pulley so that it can be raised or lowered into the water with little effort. Many Thai villages are built along river banks and the people depend on the waterways not only for food but also as the chief means of getting from place to place. To prevent flooding in the rainy season, the little houses are erected on piles.

A GIANT BUDDHA BROODS AMID THE RUINS OF A TEMPLE IN AYUDHYA

Rich in the ruins of early Thai civilization, Ayudhya is one of the world's most historically interesting cities. It was the capital of Siam until it was destroyed by the Burmese in 1767.

SIGHTSEERS AND SHOPPERS MINGLE AROUND THE STREET MARKETS

The shopkeepers must hustle out at dawn to raise their brightly colored awnings and arrange their merchandise, for the street markets are crowded with customers from morning to night.

BANGKOK HAS SOMETIMES BEEN CALLED THE VENICE OF THE EAST

The canals of Bangkok were once the major means of transportation within the city. Although many wide modern streets have been built, the canals are still used by gondola-like boats.

BANGKOK, THE CAPITAL CITY, lies along both banks of the River Menam near its mouth, and its streets are largely waterways, though there are a few paved roads served by electric cars. The town is actually only about a mile wide but stretches for many miles along the sluggish river, connecting with canals which traverse the plains of Siam to distant towns, as roads would be too often flooded. Even the yellow-robed monks, with their shaven heads and unsandaled feet, go about in boats silently offering their begging bowls for enough rice to maintain life.

HOUSES MOUNTED ON PILES line the waterways, not only in Bangkok but throughout the country, and almost all goods are transported by water in Siam. This wooden, grass-thatched house is stoutly built and stands firm above the river. Some houses, however, in this strange country are built of light wood and bamboo and actually float upon the surface, and so are the more secure against floods. The floods may be very severe, for in many places the rivers disappear entirely in the dry season, but when the rain comes they are soon transformed into torrents wide and deep.

AVA HAMILTON

A DRAGON, BEARDED AND HORNED, GUARDS A TEMPLE ENTRANCE

The great eyes of this imaginative monster overlook the courtyard of a Buddhist temple in Chiangmai. Although the creature may appear grotesque to Western eyes, one cannot help admiring
the skill of its carver and the wealth of intricate detail he has shown. The predominant religion of
Thailand is Buddhism, and there are thousands of such ornamented shrines.

A voyage of about forty miles up the Menam River takes us to Ayuthia, the ancient capital of Siam. It is in the jungles to the north and east of Ayuthia that elephants are most common. Trained elephants play an important role in parts of the country. There are valuable teak forests in Siam, and many elephants are used in the lumber industry. One should see these huge animals lifting, pushing and carrying immense logs and trees.

Curiously, Siamese servants in foreign households, believing it wrong to take life, will sometimes leave a good situation rather than kill insects, and gardeners will abandon their work in preference to destroying a snake.

The Menam is a river of houseboats.

UNATIONS

TRANSPLANTING TENDER YOUNG SEEDLINGS IN A RICE PADDY

Rice is sown first on well-prepared, fertile seedbeds. After the seedlings are 25 to 50 days old, the farmer wades into the beds and gently pulls up the plants. These must be replanted in the paddies and carefully spaced, about 3 plants every 6 inches. The paddies are covered with about 4 inches of water banked in by levees which encircle the field.

205

CHARBOT

POMP AND CEREMONY accompanied the King of Siam wherever he went. Western influence has caused many old-time customs of the country to be discontinued. The inhabitants of the country have always been known as Thai, the Free People, and prefer to call their country Muang Thai. The government has been changed to a constitutional monarchy. Much pageantry still remains. Here outside the royal palace in Bangkok there are men of rank in silver lace, palanquin bearers and ceremonial umbrellas. A white pointed hat indicates that the wearer represents a god.

CHARBOT

SIAMESE DRAMA is blended subtly with music and dancing. The performers wear costumes of rich fabrics, decorated with embroidery and jewels, and they sometimes use masks. They interpret the story with delicate and graceful gestures, moving to the accompaniment of chorus and orchestra. The Siamese plays, as well as their music, are often centuries old.

AVA HAMILTON

A BAMBOO BRIDGE CONNECTS OLD AND MODERN CHIANGMAI

The Ping River flows through Chiangmai, largest city in northern Thailand. On one side is an eighteenth-century walled town; on the other, a town that has developed since the 1920's.

The ordinary floating homes are constructed of light wood and bamboo, the roofs being thatched with the leaves of the atap palm. There are rarely more than two rooms in each house, though there is usually an open front with a landing-stage. If they have two floors, the number of steps to the upper story must always be an odd number, for it is a Siamese superstition that an even number of stairs brings bad luck.

The river peddler is a feature of life on the Menam. He goes up and down the stream in a sampan, a boat of Chinese pattern, propelled by a single oar at the stern. No gondolier could be more skillful than a Siamese boatman, as he—or she—contends with the rapids.

The Menam abounds in fish, and the Siamese have many ways of fishing. One consists of erecting in the water, close to the bank, a large wooden wheel to which a wide net is attached and lowered to the bottom of the river. Having done this, men row out in boats and make a wide sweep over the water, yelling at the top of their voices, splashing the stream with long bamboo poles and beating gongs. The frightened fish are driven before them into the net, which the men on the bank draw up by means of the wheel. As the net rises, the boats flock around and take out the catch.

Children are well cared for in Siam. Mothers continue to carry, astride their hips, little ones old enough to walk. Siamese children are taught to be extremely courteous to old people.

It must be borne in mind that Siam is a country where the majority are very

AVA HAMILTON

FISHING AN EASY WAY IN RURAL THAILAND

Thai fishers do not bother with bait. They simply lower an empty net and wait a bit for fish to swim over it. Then they pull the net up and scoop their catch out of its center.

ELEPHANTS OF THAILAND are royal property and are looked after by a special government department. The regal collection of these immense beasts is large, but every now and then, to increase the numbers, a mammoth hunt is organized and wild ones are captured. The huge elephants we see here, with drivers astride their necks, are about to go on a big game hunt. For this reason the howdahs on their backs, beneath the shelter of which sit the hunters, are as light as possible—this is in marked contrast to the elaborate howdahs used on state occasions.

210

THE WAT PHRA KEO is one of the most magnificent of the many Buddhist temples in Bangkok. The brightly tiled roofs and gilded pinnacles so characteristic of Siam rise against a background of bamboos, banyans and tamarinds. Within the temple burn candles as thick as a man's body, and offerings of rich treasure are built within or under the figure of Buddha.

poor. Boys and girls have to start earning a living at an age when children in Western countries are still at school. The girls usually start as porters, and we may see quite tiny folk going to and fro carrying waterbowls, rice, fruit and sugar-cane.

The national game of Siam is *raga-raga,* or shuttle-ball, as many as ten youths playing this game together. A large ball of split rattan is deftly kicked from one to the other, the players using either heel, ankle or knee to return the ball. So expert are these "footballers" that they will often keep the ball going from foot to foot for an hour on end without allowing it to touch the ground.

In a Siamese bazaar we are sure to find a "guessing-shop." The proprietor of this gambling establishment stands behind a table upon which are a number of melons of various sizes. A pool is made up by a company of guessers, all of whom make bets with the shopkeeper as to the number of seeds inside a given melon. When all the wagers have been made the melon is opened, and he who has guessed nearest takes three-fourths of the money staked; the rest goes to the proprietor.

The old methods of trial have been forsaken. No longer is a prisoner tried by being ordered to eat poisoned rice or to walk barefoot across hot stones, so that if he could eat the rice with impunity, or cross the hot stones unscathed, he might prove his innocence.

In recent years, other changes have been taking place. The most notable has been that of making the government, for hundreds of years an absolute monarchy, into a limited monarchy with an elected assembly, and changing the name, Siam, to the ancient name, Thailand.

When France was defeated by Germany in 1940, the Siamese regained some of their former territories. After the Japanese invasion on December 8, 1941, Thailand was completely under Japanese influence, although in theory her independence was respected by Japan. The people, however, yearned for freedom. A strong underground movement persisted in Thailand and awaited the opportunity to collaborate with Allied forces. The restoration of a national sovereignty was established in early 1946, not many months after the end of the war.

THAILAND (SIAM): FACTS AND FIGURES

THE COUNTRY

Forms part of the extreme southeasterly projection of Asia which also includes Burma, French Indo-China and the Malay Peninsula. It is bounded on the northwest and west by Burma, on the northeast and east by French Indo-China, and on the south and east by the Gulf of Siam. Area, 200,148 sq. mi.; pop. (est.) 17,317,764. In 1945 Bangkok became the commercial capital as well as the administrative capital.

GOVERNMENT

Formerly an absolute monarchy, since 1932 a constitutional monarchy. The king exercises legislative power with the advice and consent of the Senate and House of Representatives, and executive power through a State Council of 14 to 24 members. There is universal suffrage for all persons over 20 years of age.

COMMERCE AND INDUSTRIES

The principal product is rice, which is the national food, but para-rubber, coconuts, tobacco, corn, pepper and cotton are grown. A large area is under forests and teak-cutting is an important industry. There are large numbers of livestock, including cattle, horses, buffaloes and domesticated elephants. Of the extensive mineral resources, only tin, wolfram, tungsten ore and sapphires are mined on a commercial scale. The chief industry is rice-milling. Exports are rice, tin, tin-ore, teak-wood, salt fish and rubber and the imports are silk and cotton goods, flour, sugar, vegetables, iron and steel goods, petroleum products, electrical equipment, machinery and automobiles.

COMMUNICATIONS

There are 2,032 miles of state railway and 792 post offices. Length of telegraph line amounts to 6,155 miles. An automatic telephone system was introduced in Bangkok in 1937. Three wireless stations have been built.

RELIGION AND EDUCATION

Most of the people are Buddhists, and there are 19,759 Buddhist temples and 113,644 priests. The Minister of Education is responsible for education. There are a number of American, French and British mission schools. Over 77% of the local schools and 23% of the government schools are situated in temples. There are two universities in Bangkok.

ANCIENT RIVALS OF THE FAR EAST

Jungles and Rice Fields of Indochina

In the former French Empire, Indochina consisted of the colony of Cochinchina and the protectorates of Tonkin, Annam, Laos and Cambodia. Following World War II, while the French were engaged in war with the Communist-dominated forces of Ho Chi Minh, Vietnam (combining Tonkin, Annam and Cochinchina), Laos and Cambodia became associated states in the French Union. Under this plan, the three Indochinese states obtained considerable self-rule in domestic affairs. The eight-year-old war between the French Union forces and the Vietminh ended in agreement to divide Vietnam. The larger portion to the north, taken by the Communists, included the industrial heart of Indochina, around the cities of Hanoi and Haiphong, and rich deposits of coal and metal ores. South Vietnam, the French Union section, has the capital and port city of Saigon in a large rice-producing region. Agricultural Laos and Cambodia remained as constitutional monarchies and associated states in the French Union.

INDOCHINA, with Thailand, forms a peninsula that extends from the borders with China and Burma down into the South China Sea. For a long distance, the Mekong River, flowing out of China, marks the curving boundary line between Thailand (Siam) and Indochina.

More than half of Indochina is quite mountainous. Three ranges cross the country from the southeast to the northwest and on the coast of Annam reach heights of more than ten thousand feet. The jungle-clothed highlands of the interior are comparatively cool; but the long seaboard has tropic heat and monsoon winds.

On the map the territory appears to be a thick letter **S**. At its upper end is Tonkin, in the valley and delta of the Song Koi (Red River). Laos, on the west, is high plateau country. Annam curves along the coast, its mountains sloping steeply to the sea.

Cambodia and Cochinchina form the tail of the **S** in the delta of the Mekong River, which flows down from the plateau. The heavy rains that come with the monsoons in summer swell the rivers to torrents. Although Indochina has more than 1,500 miles of coastline, much of it is rocky and dangerous for mariners. There are few good harbors.

Until the tenth century the greater part of Annam was occupied by the Chams, a people of Hindu culture. But a Chinese invasion of the third century B.C. had resulted in Chinese supremacy. In 968 Dinh-Bo-Lanh ousted the Chinese and founded an independent dynasty. Annam, however, again fell under the yoke of China for a generation early in the fifteenth century. When it was once more free, the real power from that time until the end of the eighteenth century was divided between the family of Trinh in Tong-

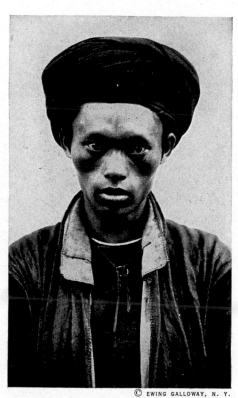

A NATIVE OF TONGKING (TONKIN)

213

SON OF HEAVEN is the title given by the Annamese, the chief race of Indo-China, to their king, who, on state occasions, sits richly arrayed upon a golden throne. His gorgeous robe and the great painted dragon, as well as his title, show Chinese influence.

CAMBODIA'S KING is a gorgeous figure, with his jeweled orders, pagoda-like crown and state robes. In the twelfth century his ancestors ruled a kingdom stretching from the Bay of Bengal to the China Sea, a kingdom of which but little remains to-day.

215

HEAVY LOADS FOR HUMAN SHOULDERS

Peasants in French Indochina, returning from their bargaining in the market, walk barefooted along the narrow roads fringed with dense tropical vegetation. Over their shoulders they carry long poles from which swing their large baskets filled with produce. The principal food crops of Indochina are rice, corn, yams, potatoes, coconuts, sugar-cane, tea and coffee.

216

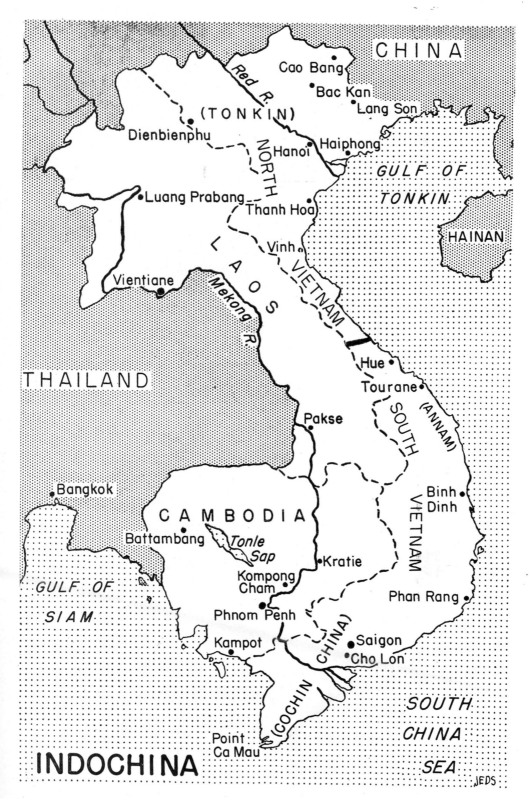

CHINA

Cao Bang
Bac Kan
Lang Son

(TONKIN)

Dienbienphu
Hanoi   Haiphong

GULF OF
TONKIN

NORTH

Red R.

HAINAN

Luang Prabang
Thanh Hoa

Vinh

VIETNAM

LAOS

Vientiane

Mekong R.

Hue

Tourane

(ANNAM)

THAILAND

Pakse

SOUTH

Binh
Dinh

Bangkok

CAMBODIA

Battambang   Tonle
Sap   Kratie

VIETNAM

Kompong
Cham

Phan Rang

GULF OF

Phnom Penh

CHINA)

Saigon
Cho Lon

SIAM

Kampot

COCHIN

Point
Ca Mau

SOUTH

CHINA

INDOCHINA

SEA

JEDS

217

IN ACTION off the coast of Vietnam—a power fishing boat. It is a modern vessel, equipped with a purse seine, and can make a much greater haul than old-fashioned fishing craft.

SAIGON, the capital of South Vietnam, is clustered on the right bank of the Saigon River. A transportation center, it is only fifty miles upstream from the South China Sea.

218

A CHARMING AND GRACEFUL WATER-CARRIER IN THAILAND

Thailand is, in the main, a rural country and the people's lives are governed by the planting and harvesting seasons. When times are normal, there is little poverty for the farmers are largely self-supporting. They raise their own food, and weave their own fabrics for clothing. The attractive young farm girl above is carrying water in containers made from bamboo logs.

king and that of Nguyen in Southern Annam, which about 1568 became a separate principality (under the name of Cochin China). Near the end of the eighteenth century rebellion overthrew the Nguyen, but in 1801 one of its surviving members, aided by the French, conquered the whole of Annam, Tongking and Cochin China. This proved an opening wedge for the establishment of French power in Indo-China.

Annamese the Dominant People

Annam, which now contains the dominant race, was a protectorate of France from 1884 until 1946. After that it became a part of the associated state of Vietnam within the French Union. As a result of the Indochina war, in 1954 a part of Annam was included in communist North Vietnam. Cambodia, Laos and Thailand bound it on the west. It has a narrow coastal plain from twelve to fifty miles wide, which is backed by the foothills of a range of lofty, forest-clad mountains the peaks of which mark its western boundary. The whole country has an average breadth of only ninety-three miles.

Annam's rivers are many, but are short and swift, and so are of no use for navigation. They are, however, important for irrigation purposes.

The Annamese, who dwell in the valleys and on the coastal plain, came originally from South China. They are small, wiry people, cunning and hard working, and have, since earliest times, been periodically at war with their one-time overlords the Chinese, with the Malay-like Chams who dwell in South Annam, and with the Khmers of Cambodia.

Lacquer Teeth to Preserve Them

Men and women dress alike, in indigo-blue tunics, wide cotton trousers and conical hats. Their feet are bare and their black hair is twisted up into a knot—the men's as well as the women's. Likewise, their teeth are usually lacquered black to preserve them, and their mouths are stained red from the chewing of betel nuts.

Most of them fish or are occupied in the rice fields that provide them with their principal food. They are fond of learning and the children all go to school. Boys too young for school are sent out to tend the big herds of water-buffaloes that are the chief beasts of burden.

There are also many Chinese people in Annam, most of whom are traders. The Annamese, though they do not like these traders, are painstakingly respectful to them and address them as "uncles."

In the jungles that cover the slopes of the inland mountains lives another race of people, the original inhabitants of the country. These are the Mois—a name that means simply "savage." There are many tribes of Mois, all speaking different languages, but little is known about the majority of them, for they live in inaccessible places, unharmed by the fevers that kill all invading races. The Mois are, for the most part, hunters, but they also grow rice in a primitive fashion. The women pierce their ears with thin pieces of bamboo and then replace them with larger and larger pieces until the lobes of their ears hang down over their chests. Then they wear heavy metal earrings.

Chams Once Dominant Along Coast

In olden days Southern Annam was a powerful empire called Champa, peopled by the Chams, the descendants of whom are now found only in the extreme south of the country. The Chams, Mohammedans and Hindus of Indo-Malayan descent, are an indolent people of small stature. The color of their skin varies between dark brown and red-brown, while their hair is black or auburn.

The usual costume of a man consists of a skirt and a long robe; that of a woman, a dark green bodice and a large piece of cloth wrapped around to form a skirt. White, or white striped with red and green are the favorite colors. Both sexes wear the hair long and twist it into a knot at the nape of the neck. Woman here proposes marriage; her children take her name and inheritance descends through her.

Chams never dream of applying soap and water to the little ones; but to appease

220

A DRAGON USHERS IN THE NEW YEAR, IN SAIGON

Saigon and its sister city of Cholon form a Greater Saigon of more than 1,000,000 inhabitants, mostly Annamese and Chinese. The Annamese profess the religion of Confucius; their language and culture in general resemble the Chinese, and so it is not strange to find New Year's celebrated in the Chinese manner, with dragons parading through the streets.

221

EWING GALLOWAY

A RELIEF DECORATING THE TEMPLE OF ANGKOR VAT IN INDOCHINA

Angkor Vat (or Wat) is a magnificent temple in Cambodia in Indochina. Dedicated to Vishnu, it was completed in the twelfth century. Later it was abandoned and its ruins were rediscovered in 1860 in the jungle. After 1908, it was cleared and a moated park now surrounds the ruins. They are the best-preserved examples of Khmer architecture that exist in the world today.

THE PURPLE GATE THAT GUARDS THE PALACE GROUNDS OF HUE

City walls enclose the ornate imperial palace at Hué, the port city that was formerly the capital of Annam, in central Viet Nam.   The palace was once known as a "forbidden city."

the spirits a mother will smear her baby's face with a mixture of flour and saffron, for she believes that the faces of the gods are yellow and they will be pleased at such imitativeness.   Should a mother have had a bad dream she will cover her baby's face with soot to hide it from evil spirits.

The Cham equivalent for a kiss is a kind of snort made at the back of a child's neck, just behind the ear, a caress that seems to fill the youngster with delight.   The young Chams are but poorly educated.   The priests teach them merely the rudiments of reading and writing.

Annamese towns all look very much the same; they consist for the most part of clusters of villages grouped together inside a girdle of walls and moats and defended by a huge citadel, which is often large enough to hold the whole population of the settlement.   In the villages the houses, thatched with palm leaves, are built with a wattling of bamboos and mud. The furniture consists of a number of low platforms used as tables in the daytime and as beds at night.

Each village possesses a communal hall which is kept for meetings that correspond to our municipal gatherings.   In the dwellings of the Annamese aristocracy there is usually a reception room fitted with a table in the middle, armchairs, a shrine at the back and sleeping stands on either side.   These houses are generally constructed of brick or wood, and are roofed with tiles.

Women do all the marketing—both the buying and selling.   The vendors squat down amid their merchandise and carry on a chattering that seems never to stop, all the time ceaselessly chewing betel, a custom universal throughout the country.

Hué, once the capital of Annam, held an important position at the mouth of the Hué River.   At the beginning of the nineteenth century it was strongly fortified by French engineers and ranked as one of the best-defended military posts in Asia.   The king of Annam, notwithstanding the fact that he lived in a large, strongly fortified palace in an inner enclosure of the citadel at Hué, had not really much power, for practically the whole administration of the country was in the hands of the French.

Cambodia, now an independent kingdom

223

ANGKOR VAT, CAMBODIA'S MAGNIFICENT RELIC

In Cambodia's jungle are ruins of a once beautiful city, Angkor Thom. It was the capital of the Khmer Empire, a Hindu-Buddhist civilization that flourished more than a thousand years ago. Near by is a resplendent Khmer temple, Angkor Vat. For centuries the Angkor ruins lay hidden and forgotten, but in recent years the jungle has been pushed back and restoration work begun.

of Indochina, is bounded on the north and northwest by Laos and Thailand, on the east by Annam, on the southeast by Cochin China, and on the southwest by the Gulf of Siam. It consists chiefly of the very fertile, alluvial plain of the Mekong, a mighty river that has its source in Tibet, and that forms, in its upper course, the boundary line between Thailand and Indochina. The Mekong flows through Cambodia from north to south, and periodically floods immense tracts of the country. At the junction of all the navigable waters of Cambodia, there stands Pnom Penh, the capital. The climate is tropical, and much of the land is covered with jungle, in which snakes, tigers and elephants are found. The land is fertile and produces vast quantities of rice, but some parts are so malarial that no one can inhabit them.

Fighting had been going on for centuries between Cambodia, Thailand and Annam. Cambodia had continually to pay tribute to the one or the other. During a part of the seventeenth and eighteenth centuries Cambodia was governed by two kings, one supported by Thailand and one by Annam; but by a treaty of 1846 the Annamese evacuated the country, and in 1863 Cambodia placed itself under French protection.

The Mystery of Angkor Thom

Where the first Cambodians originated is not certainly known. Centuries before the Christian era, immigrants from the east coast of India introduced into Cambodia both Brahmanism and the Sanskrit language, and the name itself is derived from the Hindu name of the mythical founder of the race, Kambu. But not until the fifth century A.D. did the Khmers as a nation rise into prominence. It is thought that the royal city of Angkor Thom (which means "capital city") was begun by Jayavarman III about 860 A.D. and completed some forty years later. It is pretty well established that the extraordinary temple of Angkor Vat was built early in the twelfth century for the worship of Brahma but later converted to the worship of Buddha.

The Thais (Siamese) were long subject to the Khmers, but about the middle of the fourteenth century they began repeatedly to attack, capture and pillage Angkor Thom until, after a century or so, the capital was abandoned. Indeed, when the Thais invaded Cambodia in about 1340 they carried off ninety thousand captives. Centuries passed. The creeping jungle of banyans and bamboo gradually buried the magnificence of the walled city. Then, in the late 1800's, a French naturalist, after a five-day boat trip through all but impenetrable jungle, discovered the stupendous stone temple near Great Lake (Tonlé Sap) and, north of it, the ruins of Angkor Thom.

The Four Faces of Siva

He found Angkor Vat an assemblage of vast, colored sandstone galleries rising to a central pyramid that towered above the palm trees; and Angkor Thom an assemblage of palaces and temples built within moated walls running practically two miles in either direction. There was the royal palace, rising in three quadrangular tiers beneath a central tower and four corner ones, and there was the temple of Bayon, likewise a square structure, with vast galleries and colonnades enclosing a huge tower and beset with half a hundred lesser towers each depicting the four faces of Siva, the Hindu destroyer and fosterer of crops. The walls were carved, beneath an overgrowth of olive and cerise lichens, with the figures of gods, men and beasts, and the inscriptions—obviously derived from the Sanskrit—told of what must have been (for that time) a great and wealthy people of Hindu extraction or at least pupils of Hindu teachers. But as to what had become of that people and that civilization, all was mystery. There have been a number of excavations at Angkor with a view to learning more of the ancient civilization of the Khmers.

Paved Roads to the Ruins

Today paved roads lead to the ruins and every tourist in this part of the world tries to visit them. Part of the way these

DOZENS OF "LITTLE MAIDS FROM SCHOOL" IN CHOLON, INDOCHINA

The demure little white-robed pupils, fans in hand, go to a French missionary school in Cholon. They appear to have rather mixed emotions at being photographed on their afternoon walk.

roads run through cleared land on which the jungle has been converted to fertile paddy fields. The Great Lake lies in a depression fifteen miles by sixty-eight and in flood time serves as a reservoir for the Mekong River. One finds purple banks of hyacinth and rose-hued rhododendrons, and swamplands brilliant with a rank growth of tiger lilies, which perfume the entire countryside.

The Pnom Penh of to-day presents a neat array of white buildings, parks and a museum of the antiquities of Indo-China which conducts manual training classes. Yet despite such modernity, seven-headed stone cobras guard the bridge, the open-faced shops offer the variable prices of the Orient and Buddhist priests in their long yellow robes mingle with crowds in which the native men and women are dressed precisely alike, in sarongs and pajamas. Peddlers roast bananas over charcoal or cook rice in portable stoves, and at night one hears the tom-tom beating out a rhythm for the drama-dancing girls, while pipers skirl and bamboo xylophones mingle melodiously.

The civilized Cambodians of the present day dwell on the banks of the Mekong River and around the Great Lake. They are a strong but gentle people, mostly tillers of the soil, but accomplished musicians and poets and lovers of literature, the dance and the drama. Most children are taught by the Buddhist priests in the many temples found in the land. The national costume of both men and women is a coat and a sampot—a straight piece of material, often of beautiful hand-woven silk, which is wound around the waist and loosely caught up between the legs. The average Cambodian prefers to live a lonely life among his rice fields. His house is built on tall piles as a protection against tigers and floods.

The wild tribes of Cambodia are also of the same race as the civilized Khmers. As is the case with the Mois, little is known of them, for they hide themselves from strangers in fever-ridden jungles.

THE ROAD FROM PEKING TO PARIS—VIA DONG-DANG, THAT IS!

Signs in an Indochinese town invite the traveler to stop at Dong-Dang, and point the way to
Paris, only 7,000 miles (12,672 kilometers) away, and to Peking, a mere 1,800 miles.

MAN POWER saws boards from a log in Hanoi, Tonkin Province. Most of Indochina's native industry is still carried on by methods as primitive as those used in this "sawmill."

The Khmer kingdom was at the peak of its power and glory from the ninth to the twelfth centuries, and during that period it embraced most of what is now Cochin China. For that reason much of Cochin China's early history parallels that of Cambodia. Its later history is linked with Annam's up until the time of the French occupation in the middle of the nineteenth century.

As far back as 1787 King Nguyen phua Anh of Cochin China signed a rather ineffectual treaty with King Louis XVI of France. This event marks the beginning of French influence in Indochina. However, the succeeding rulers of Cochin China were not friendly to the French and for many years they persecuted European missionaries and natives who had turned to Christianity. The situation became so serious that the French Government finally intervened and seized Cochin China (1862–67) and established colonies there. In 1887 the country was united with Cambodia, Annam and Ton-kin to form the Indochinese Union. In World War II the Japanese occupied sections of Cochin China. The country became part of Viet Nam, a state of the Federation of Indochina, in 1950.

Most of Cochin China's area consists of fertile alluvial plains—the delta of the Mekong and Don-Nai rivers—into which all of the country's rivers drain. From June to October floods of the Mekong inundate large sections of the land, and villages must communicate with one another through a widespread connecting system of natural and artificial waterways. This network of canals also aids in distributing the fertilizing flood waters so vital to the country's crops.

Saigon, capital of Cochin China, has fine public buildings, a tree-lined boulevard and an extensive port, together with radio communication with Europe. Its neighbor Cholon is the larger city by reason of its Chinese, who comprise half the population. These live in assemblages of native "villages." Cochin China has not only a good irrigation system but entirely modern rice granaries for its chief crop.

Laos, in the central interior, is a green and mountainous land, with deep river valleys. In its thick forests tigers, panthers, bears, monkeys, buffalo and snakes are plentiful. The rhinoceros, both the one- and two-horned variety, was once common, but today it is rarely found; native hunters have killed it off to obtain the horn, which they believe has medicinal qualities. Elephants are caught and trained as beasts of burden. Leopard, deer and wild boar abound in the mountains. Teak forests supply a timber for export. The wood is so durable that teakwood temples in southern India have survived two thousand years. The road from Savannakhet to Dongha is the principal route to Annam and is open throughout the whole year. Laos also has a number of public airports.

Tonkin, snug up to the borderline of southern China, was visited by French missionaries as early as the seventeenth century, though its modern development did not begin until about 1860. The state practically occupies the basin of the Red River, or Hong Kiang. When trade is normal, the busy port of Haiphong exports vast quantities of rice, grown on the river delta, to China. The city also has served at various times as an outlet to the sea for the southern Chinese province of Yunnan, connected with Tonkin by rail. Sampans and Chinese junks travel up and down the waterways, lined with wharves still redolent of tropic fruits, coffee and tobacco, pepper, cinnamon, corn, hides and rubber.

Though the long conflict in Indochina after World War II changed the picture, it once was not unusual to see ships flying the flags of many nations in the harbor of Haiphong. The freighters took on coal, limestone and bales of silk and tea, after unloading tools, machinery and cotton thread. Huge billets of Laos teak were hoisted aboard by cranes. Fish were sent to China by the thousands of tons.

It might be mentioned that for Indochina as a whole the exports so nearly equal the imports that a balance of trade usually exists in peacetime.

A great national road now runs from

EWING GALLOWAY

NATIVE DESIGN ELEMENTS lend themselves well to modern business architecture. The Bank of China in Hanoi, built by the French, is a blending of Eastern and Western styles.

PLYING CHOPSTICKS IN A HOME IN CAOBANG, TONKIN

For a dining table there are mats, and the family eats sitting on the floor. Rice is the main dish, and it is garnished with smaller portions of vegetables, pork or perhaps fish.

230

THE RUE GUYNEMER, STREET OF CHINESE RESIDENTS IN SAIGON

A tricycle jinrikisha stands against the curb, waiting perhaps for a Chinese merchant. Side-walk stalls are flimsy and cluttered, but the shuttered building behind looks well-kept.

231

the Chinese border across Tong-king and on the Siamese border of Cambodia, besides which there are motor roads, entirely passable during the dry season, traversing Tong-king and Cambodia on their way to Cochin China.

Tong-king is rich in minerals—coal, iron, salt, copper, zinc, phosphates—mined by natives working under French engineers, while the several towns hum with mill wheels. At Hanoi, the centre of the town is occupied by a lake spotted with islets on which stand colorful pagodas. The University of Indo-China, established in 1917, aims at turning out native lawyers, planters, traders, manufacturers and government assistants. Most of the attendants are, as it happens, Annamese. There is also a French School at Hanoi, which is making important researches into the native history, language and art, and which has made searching studies and excavations of the ruins of Angkor. There is a European College, a College of Interpreters attended by native students, a cathedral, a theatre and a race-course. But the tourist will be equally interested in the local color, such as that of the many native streets with their wares colorfully displayed in open booths. These local wares include the output of silk and cotton mills, tile and ceramic factories, as well as the lace made by native women in their homes.

INDOCHINA: FACTS AND FIGURES

THE COUNTRY

Indochina lies wholly within the tropics of southeast Asia, bounded on the north by China, on the west by Thailand and the Gulf of Siam, and on the east by the South China Sea. The country includes Laos, South Vietnam Republic (both in the French Union), Cambodia (independent since 1955) and communist North Vietnam. The area of Laos is 91,428 sq. mi., its population estimated at 1,200,000. The area of Cambodia, 53,668 sq. mi.; population, 3,750,000. The area of Vietnam is 127,259 sq. mi., divided approximately 77,000 and 50,000 between North Vietnam (made up of Tonkin and part of Annam) and South Vietnam (Cochinchina and southern Annam). A little more than half of the 25,000,000 Vietnamese live in North Vietnam. The total area of Indochina is 272,355 sq. mi., the population 30,000,000.

GOVERNMENT

Through a series of treaties, in 1950 Laos, Cambodia and Vietnam became the Associated States of Indochina within the French Union, with self-rule in internal affairs. Cambodia severed all formal ties with France in 1955. By a 1954 treaty, North Vietnam was established as a communist state, and South Vietnam remained within the French Union. Cambodia and Laos are kingdoms governed under constitutions which regulate the powers of the king, cabinet and national assembly in each country. Each of the three states has its own courts, civil service and national army. In Laos and South Vietnam, however, France—through a commissioner general in Saigon, a high commissioner in each of the two states and various French Union forces—controls such matters as foreign policy and military affairs.

COMMERCE AND INDUSTRY

Agriculture is the chief occupation of the people and the principal crop is rice. Other products are corn, tobacco, sugar, coffee, pepper, kapok and rubber. Livestock-raising is important and fishing is actively carried on. The chief mineral products are coal, phosphates, zinc, antimony, tin, wolfram, graphite and lead. There are forests of rare hardwoods, bamboo, rubber, coconuts, dyewoods and medicinal plants. The most important industry is rice-milling. In Cambodia, salting and smoking fish is the principal native industry. Raw silk is produced and is woven in Vietnam. The chief exports are rice (about 50% of the total), rubber, fish, coal, pepper, cattle and hides, copra, corn, zinc and tin ore, sticklac and teakwood; principal imports are cotton textiles, metal goods, machinery, kerosene and automobiles.

COMMUNICATIONS

There are nearly 2,000 miles of railroad, much of it government-owned, and an excellent highway system of about 17,000 miles. Telephone line mileage is almost 17,900, and telegraph line mileage is 3,030.

RELIGION AND EDUCATION

Buddhism is the principal religion. The educational system includes public and private elementary and secondary schools for both French and Indochinese. There are technical schools and colleges for higher education at Hanoi, Dalat and Saigon.

CHIEF TOWNS

Saigon, capital of the Associated States of Indochina, is joined politically with its twin city of Cholon; total population, 1,179,000. Hanoi, 237,000 (including suburbs) and Haiphong, 143,-000, are the chief cities of North Vietnam. Pnompenh, 111,000, is the capital of Cambodia; Vientiane, 28,000, is the capital of Laos.

FORMOSA, CHINA'S ISLAND PROVINCE

Its Jungle Tribes, Once Savage Head-hunters

Formosa was discovered by Portuguese navigators who sailed along its coast in the sixteenth century. It is a beautiful land, quite mountainous and heavily wooded. Its forests once harbored fierce tribes of head-hunters that preyed on shipwrecked seamen and camphor workers, but civilization has gradually tamed them. Most of the world's camphor trees grow on Formosa, and until artificial ways of making camphor were discovered the island was famous for this product. Japan, in her period of expansion and conquest in the Far East, forced China to cede her the island in 1895, but fifty years later, after World War II, Formosa was returned to China. When the Nationalists were pushed from the Chinese mainland in 1949, they established their headquarters on Formosa with their capital at Taipei.

WHEN the Portuguese adventurers sailed up the China Sea in the sixteenth century, they sighted an island about one hundred miles off the mainland of China. Its dense forests, rocky coast and the high range of mountains that runs down the centre of the island gave it such an enchanting appearance that the Portuguese navigators called in the Beautiful Island—Ilha Formosa.

As we sail along the east coast we cannot help being impressed by the beauty of the scene, the cascades gleaming in the sunlight as they tumble over the two thousand foot cliffs. Every now and then, as we round a headland, we get glimpses of valleys and ravines and perhaps of a tiny native village in a clearing.

Formosa lies in the volcanic chain that extends from Japan to the Philippines. It is one of a long line of islands which serve as a barrier to the Asiatic coast from the typhoon area in the warm Kurosiwo current. It is an oval island ending in a pointed tail at the south. Its area is just less than that of Hokkaido, and like some primeval monster of the deep, its back rises in a hump of mountain ranges. These reach farthest skyward in Mt. Sylvia, 12,480 feet above the level of the sea, and Mt. Morrison, named by the Japanese Niitaka or New High Mountain, 14,270 feet and higher than Fuji. While the mountains are not volcanic, there are steam and sulphur springs on the island. The higher slopes are shaded deep with pines, then a little lower, with gigantic Cryptomerias and Chamæcyparis. Below

six thousand feet the bush is composed of palms, banyans, cork and camphor trees, tree ferns and interlacing creepers, and is perfumed with lilies and gay with orchids. These forests are interspersed with all but impenetrable thickets of rattan or stretches of head-high jungle grass through which creep deadly reptiles and wild beasts. But the hill slopes are more dangerous, for there dwell aboriginal Malay tribes of savage, and often cannibalistic, head-hunters. Along the coast the climate is damp and altogether too hot for a white man, besides being malarial with fever-breeding mosquitoes. Off shore one sees coral and flying fish. The tourist who wishes to visit the tropic beauties of Formosa will find the climate in the north driest and best from October to December and that of the south in February and March.

The island, unlighted and unsurveyed, with its sheer cliffs on the one side and long shallows on the other, has been the scene of many a shipwreck, and until the missionaries came, about the middle of the nineteenth century, Formosa was known to white men chiefly by reason of the many wrecks that occurred along its coasts and the consequent treatment accorded the survivors by both the cannibalistic aborigines and the Chinese. Indeed, when the British brig Ann was lost off Formosa in 1842, forty-three of the fifty-seven persons on board were executed at Taichu. Over a generation later the crew of the shipwrecked Japanese junk Loo Choo was put to death by one of the tribes

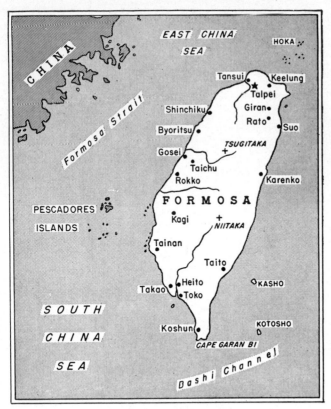

THE ISLAND OF FORMOSA

crossed to Formosa, where he drove out the Dutch and took possession of the island. But in 1682 after K'ang-hi came to the throne he turned it over to the Chinese imperial government and Formosa continued a Chinese possession until the war with Japan in 1894–95. The Japanese administered the island until the end of World War II.

The early Chinese settlers, it seems, ousted the aborigines in no gentle manner from their immemorial hunting and fishing grounds. Wherefore, when the Chinese went to the mountain forests for camphor or rattan, the savage hillmen laid ambuscades for them; and many a pig-tailed yellow head has been dried as a trophy. Little by little the head-hunters have become more civilized until they are no longer the great danger they once were. Many of the groups, however, have not become really friendly, and they continue to live as wild men. This is especially true in the eastern mountains of the island. Green savages, Chin-hwan, and wild savages, Sheng-fan, the hillmen are called. They keep ferocious dogs for hunting panthers, boars, bears and deer. Their thatched huts are usually made of bamboo and have but one small window and a door which it is possible to enter only by stooping. Some of the tribes build their houses half underground and line the interior with slate quarried from the hills.

The principal occupation of these savages is weaving. They cultivate millet, and the stores of grain are in charge of the women, who deal it out on a ration system. Among themselves, theft is almost unknown. They count on their fingers.

Such religion as they profess is confined chiefly to pleasing the God of Rain. They believe that when a man dies he must

of the southern coast, and as the Chinese government declined to punish the culprits, the Japanese invaded the island in 1874, and war was barely averted.

Added to other drawbacks to shipping, violent typhoons occur from four to five times a year during which the wind has been known to blow at a velocity of 125 miles an hour, while the rain falls in torrents. Keelung in the north has known years when there were 242 days of rain.

The island, with its wealth of camphor and other natural resources, has belonged to three other nations in turn. In 1624 the Dutch built a fort on the east coast, near where Anping now stands, and there maintained a settlement for roughly forty years. When the Ming Dynasty ended in China, Chêng Chi-lung, a defeated adherent of the Mings, harried the coast as a pirate, but was finally cast into prison and died. His son Coxinga thereupon determined to leave the mainland and cross a bridge over a chasm, and that those who have been successful in war will pass easily, as will those who have been industrious and of use to the tribe. Others, who have not been good weavers, will fall in and so will never enter paradise. In troublous times it is the custom for a selected party to go up into a cave in the mountains and there to sing and perform a weird dance. The echoes of their chants are interpreted as the sayings of the gods—indications of what the people are to do.

Among these head-hunters a human skull is regarded as a valuable kind of cup. A man may not marry until he has

WIDE WORLD

A RIVER OF FORMOSA, HEAVY WITH SILT FROM THE UPLANDS

In a dry season, a sluggish Formosan river carries an abundance of mud and gravel from the mountains and narrow plains of its upper course down to the coastal lowlands and the sea.

235

A REMNANT OF JAPANESE OCCUPATION, NEAR TAIPEI, FORMOSA

This torii, or gateway, leads to a former Japanese shrine not far from the island's capital. The island, which is separated from the China coast by the Formosa Strait, was under Japanese rule for fifty years. Its climate is tropical, with ample rainfall. More than half the people depend on farming, with rice the most important crop and sugar the chief export.

A TEMPLE OF MANY FAITHS IN TAIPEI, CAPITAL OF FORMOSA

The architecture of this Japanese-built temple reflects characteristics of three Oriental religions: Confucianism, Shintoism and Buddhism. It suggests that the Japanese, during their fifty-year rule of the island of Formosa, tried to adjust differences among their subjects. Taipei is a modern city, with several industries, and has an estimated population of half a million.

MAIN STREET IN FORMOSA'S MODERN CAPITAL

In his island of safety above the rush of automobiles, bicycles and rickshaws, this helmeted policeman looks down on all the world. He directs the traffic along the smoothly paved streets of Taipei
(formerly Taihoku) by means of modern electric signals. Although Formosa is still very primitive
in many ways, Taipei is a surprisingly modern city in appearance.

AN EARLY STEP IN THE PAPER-MAKING INDUSTRY

Workers are stripping bark from trees at a pulp and paper factory at Lotung. The peeled wood will be washed, cut up and ground to pulp as the next step in the production of paper.

CUTTING MACHINE AT A PAPER MILL NEAR TAIPEI

The machine cuts huge rolls of paper into sheets of precise size. Other machines in this factory will fold and glue the sheets into bags, for use at home and for export.

FOOTPOWER, AN IMPORTANT SOURCE OF ENERGY ON FORMOSA

The nimble footwork of the Formosan girls furnishes the power for the primitive paddle wheel
that pumps water from an irrigation ditch into their father's rice paddies.

OX-DRAWN, RUBBER-TIRED WAGONS MOVING INTO THE CAPITAL

From the mountain forests, where oak, cypress, Japanese cedar and other valuable timber trees grow in profusion, comes one of many convoys with sawn lumber for the busy builders of Taipei.

OLD CARS, SHAFTS AND CONVEYERS IN THE SUISHAN COAL MINE

The Suishan mine is inland from the northern port of Keelung and the capital, Taipei, in the valley of the Keelung River. The mine has been improved with the help of foreign loans.

EWING GALLOWAY

WINNOWING RICE BY LETTING IT FALL FROM BASKET TO BASKET

The wind will carry the lighter chaff away, letting the precious kernels fall to the basket below.
This is tedious labor which yields only a few pounds of rice for a day's work.

ONE IN THE BALCONY, PLEASE. A young man buys his ticket at the vividly decorated box office of a Formosan motion-picture "palace." Movie-going is a popular recreation the world over.

presented his intended bride with a number of skulls, for only after a certain number of heads have been placed beneath the foundations of their new house can they take up their residence. The finest form of decoration is not a picture, but the skull of an enemy. The customs in connection with courtship and marriage are curious. The young man takes a bundle of wood to the girl's home and leaves it in front of the door. When there are twenty bundles, he returns. If the wood has been taken in, it is a sign that his suit is accepted. In the marriage ceremony, bride and bridegroom sit back to back on the floor of the hut, dances and various rites are performed, then a slight cut is made in a leg of each and the blood is mingled. They are now supposed to have acquired mutually satisfactory temperaments.

Before setting out on a head-hunting expedition, the hunters consult the omens and follow the movements of a certain jungle bird, supposed to tell them whether they will be successful or not. When the party has left the village, a sacred fire is kept burning day and night, all weaving is stopped, and the hemp is not even prepared for the loom during the absence of the warriors. If the expedition be successful, the heads are placed in the center of a circle, food is put into their mouths, and wild dancing goes on all night. The successful warriors have a special mark tattooed on their faces; and boys whose fathers have been famous as head-hunters are also allowed this badge of honor.

Boys and young men must live in a large hut apart from the rest of their fellows until they are warriors or are married. The Formosans argue that this tends to make the men of the tribe hardy and accustomed to shifting for themselves.

Formosa has for long been the greatest camphor-producing area in the world. It has vast numbers of camphor trees, the product of which is valuable in medicine,

PATIENT OXEN haul heavy machinery and oil drums over the dirt-surfaced street of a Formosan town. A great deal of Formosa's transportation is still done by plodding ox-cart.

BLACK STAR

RYUZAN-JI: AN ELABORATE BUDDHIST TEMPLE IN TAIPEI

Dragons and foliage twist and turn around the pillars and flare from the corners of the up-curved eaves. The structure is a classic example of Buddhist architecture in Formosa.

in the making of celluloid and smokeless gunpowder, in protecting furs from moths and in many other ways. The best forests are situated along the northern hills, where the trees are exceptionally large and productive. Before the coming of the Japanese the method of extracting the camphor was wasteful. Vast quantities of trees were cut down, and only a little camphor was obtained by the crude system of refining. The Chinese had placed Formosa in charge of a viceroy appointed by the emperor, and he had control of all the camphor in the island; but he simply regarded it as a means of amassing a fortune. As a result, the savages in whose territory the camphor trees were found were so ill-treated that they often massacred the Chinese workers, whose

friends then murdered any of the tribesmen they could capture.

The Japanese then introduced scientific methods of dealing with the camphor trade. The trees were felled and the chips taken from them were refined by modern processes, so that there was very little waste. It is estimated that there are still eight thousand square miles of unexplored territory in Formosa, most of it forests of camphor trees. The early Chinese settlers knew the value of the camphor, and they constructed an embankment along the borderline of the native territory as a protection against the raids of the head-hunters.

The Japanese in their turn built a guard line through the forest. This included much of the country that had scarcely, if

WHAT THE WELL-DRESSED RICKSHA BOY will wear. Smiling proudly, a Formosan coolie models his short raincoat. The pointed straw hat serves as protection against the rain and the sun.

SORTING AND FOLDING NEWSPAPERS AT A KEELUNG NEWS STAND

Extra! Extra! Read all about it! Squatting beside his baskets in the open market at Keelung, a news dealer glances at a headline as he folds his papers and waits for his first customer.

CHIPPING WOOD OF CAMPHOR LAUREL AT A FORMOSAN DISTILLERY

Camphor is obtained by steaming the leaves, wood and bark until drops of the gum are driven out to the surface. Formosa is the world's outstanding producer of camphor gum and oil.

ever, been explored; for they had found that it was worse than useless to send military expeditions into the territory of the head-hunters. The tribesmen knew every inch of the ground and could prepare successful ambushes, whereas in this guerrilla warfare the Japanese soldier, hampered by his heavy equipment, made poor headway in climbing through the dense jungle.

Every effort was made by means of the guard line to get in touch with the natives and to pacify each tribe by peaceable means. The Japanese even strove to induce the head-hunters to adopt farming as a means of livelihood.

During World War II, the Japanese made Formosa a strong military base; and for this reason it was bombed frequently by Allied planes during the last years of the war. When Japan was defeated, Formosa, without much ado, was returned to China, which was then under the Nationalist Government of Chiang Kai-shek. Consequently, since 1945 Formosa has been involved in the changing fortunes of China.

As everyone knows, civil strife continued in China after World War II ended. Antagonists for more than two score years, the Nationalists and Communists took up their quarrel with even greater vigor than before. The Western world watched with growing dismay as the Communists by degrees gained the upper hand and then, at the end of 1949, succeeded in pushing the Nationalist forces from the Chinese mainland altogether. It was then that the Nationalist Government established itself on Formosa and made the island a focal point in the whole explosive Far Eastern situation.

However, the Nationalist Government never became directly involved in the Korean conflict of 1950–53, partly at least because it had so recently suffered defeat on the mainland.

Since then the bitter strife between Nationalists and Communists has flared up elsewhere, particularly in regard to the islands of Quemoy and Matsu. Both of these little groups lie in Formosa Strait, much closer to the Chinese mainland than to Formosa. The United States had pledged itself to defend Formosa but whether or not it would help the Nationalists to hold the Quemoys and Matsus was a matter of controversy.

Nationalist leaders still cling to the hope that they can return to the mainland. Meanwhile, Formosa is largely dependent on American aid and good will.

FORMOSA: FACTS AND FIGURES

THE COUNTRY

An island which lies between the Philippines on the south and Japan on the north with the China Sea on the west and the Pacific Ocean on the east. The area is 13,890 square miles and the population is about 8,750,000. Taipei, the capital, has a population of 504,000. In 1895 Taiwan was ceded by China to Japan. As a result of World War II, Japan surrendered control of the island to Nationalist China.

COMMERCE AND INDUSTRIES

The agricultural products are rice, of which two crops a year are grown, tea, sugar, sweet potatoes, ramie, jute and tumeric. Camphor, the most important product, is worked in the forests. There are active fisheries. Industries include flour milling, sugar, tobacco, iron-works, glass, bricks and soap. Minerals include gold, silver, copper and coal. Most of the commerce is with Japan. The exports are tea, sugar, rice, camphor and coal and the imports are cotton and silk goods, wood and planks, oil cake, petroleum and opium.

COMMUNICATIONS

Roads are being constructed, and there are 2,500 miles of railway. Length of telegraph line is 734 miles and length of telephone line is 2,946 miles. There are about 193 post offices.

EDUCATION

Since the end of World War II, the Japanese educational curriculum has been abolished and one similar to that of the Chinese mainland has been introduced. There are 1,191 elementary schools; 206 middle, normal and vocational schools and 6 universities. Enrollments in all classes have increased sharply since 1945.

DEPENDENCY

Pescadores, or Hokoto Islands, a group of 12 islands lying west of Formosa, is under the Formosan government. Their area is about 50 square miles.

THE LAND OF THE DRAGON
Some Glimpses of China

Far in advance of the Western world, China developed a complex civilization, in which the arts, literature and invention flourished. However, as time went by, it froze into a rigid pattern. The best and only accepted way to do anything was to do it as one's ancestors had. Through these centuries, China was governed along feudal lines down to the smallest village. The great tide bringing about more democratic forms of government elsewhere did not reach China until early in the twentieth century. Though a republic was established in 1912, it failed to unite China. For long years after, internal strife and foreign invasion kept the nation impoverished. Following the war with Japan, from 1937 to 1945, civil war flared up more violently still between the Nationalists and the Chinese Communists. The Reds, grown strong during the conflict with Japan, at last swept the Nationalists from the mainland in 1949. Today the Chinese people are governed by a ruthless dictatorship.

CHINA was for many centuries a far-off wonderland, a place of mystery. To Europeans, during the Middle Ages, it was known as "far Cathay," and many tales of its marvels and magnificence were told by the few travelers who managed to get a glimpse of it. To the Chinese themselves it has been "The Flowery Kingdom." They do not forget that their race was civilized long, long ago, while the people of all northern European nations were savages, so they have always regarded themselves as heavenly people—"Celestials"—and the rest of the world as barbarians.

As far as possible for many years they kept foreigners out of their country. However, as early as 1557, in return for aid given against pirates, permission was granted to some Portuguese to put up warehouses on the end of a peninsula at the mouth of the Canton River. The Chinese, thereupon, built a wall across it to keep the barbarians from mixing with the Celestials. This place, Macao, became a Portuguese colony, and has remained one ever since, but it was not really recognized by treaty as Portuguese territory before 1887.

Traders from England followed those from Portugal, after about a century; but it was not until after war with Britain that, in 1842, Hong Kong, an island off the Canton River, became a British Crown Colony. At that time, five other coastal towns, including two famous ones, Shanghai and Canton, were opened to foreign traders. These were known as the Treaty Ports. For a time Japan held Manchuria and the island of Formosa, as well as Korea. As a result of World War II, Manchuria became part of China and Korea achieved independence. Formosa has become the last stronghold of the Chinese Nationalist Government.

Who are the Chinese, these people who have seemed so exclusive, and what is the land so many millions of them have guarded so dearly? In ages of strength China has included lands on all sides of it, and in times of weakness it has been the domain of foreign rulers. The China under consideration in this article is China proper—the almost circular cluster of eighteen provinces between Tibet and the Pacific Ocean and between Mongolia and the southeastern peninsula of Asia. A section on Manchuria appears at the end of this chapter.

The Chinese belong to the great yellow race of mankind. They are small in stature, their eyes are almond-shaped and frequently slanting, their skin is yellowish and their hair black and straight. Coming into China about 4,000 years ago, though nobody knows whence they came, they drove the people already living there to the mountains of the western provinces, especially Yunnan, where millions of them still exist.

Early Chinese history, like that of other ancient nations, has a long period (over a thousand years) where tradition and fact cannot be disentangled. After this came nearly a thousand years more when development went on in a number

THE GREAT WALL OF CHINA was begun in the third century B. C., but long stretches of it were added hundreds of years later. It is about 1,500 miles long, with a general average height of 22 feet. At intervals were placed towers, 40 to 60 feet high. The wall, built as a protection against savage invaders, was not altogether a success as a means of defence. The section at Nankow Pass, shown in this picture, seems to be in good condition; this is due probably to the fact that at points of special danger the structure was most strongly built and most often repaired.

CHINESE MONKS find quiet in this tree-sheltered holy place, with its pagoda and graceful marble bridges. It is situated on the island of Pu Tu, on which only monks may dwell. The island is especially dedicated to Kwan-yin, the goddess of mercy, who is said to keep a close watch over sailors. As a very great many of the Chinese earn a living on the sea and the rivers, the goddess is most popular, and many thousands of pilgrims visit the island. Some of them even travel long distances in the hope of securing their own safety and that of their relatives.

251

of separate feudal states more or less under an emperor. Finally a strong ruler of the third century B.C. drew these states together under his firm hand. Soon Shi-Hwang-ti, "the first universal emperor," brought an end to feudal conditions, made canals and roads, and (about 220 B.C.) started the building of the Great Wall, to keep out barbarians. During the feudal period, silk had become an important product, some of the finest bronzes had been made, Confucius (Kung-fu-tze) and other great teachers had lived, and masterpieces of literature had been written.

A Glorious Age in China

Looking over centuries of advancing civilization, during which paper was invented, the first printed book was produced and navigators were beginning to use the compass, we come to the thirteenth century A.D., when Jenghiz Khan and his Mongols overran northern China. His grandson, Kublai Khan, after overthrowing the Chinese rulers, made himself emperor, reigning with great splendor at Peking. But in 1368 the Mongol rule was ended, and the Ming dynasty, last of the Chinese imperial line, held control until 1644. This was a time of notable expansion in porcelain-making. But China now began to lag behind Europe. Shutting her doors to the outside world, the nation lost creative force.

Again came an invading force from the north, Manchu Tatars, some of whom had been living in northern China for centuries. Their leader ascended the throne at Peking in 1644, and at this time the Chinese began to wear the pigtail—a queue, with the front of the head shaven— as a badge of Tatar sovereignty. Nearly three centuries later, during the revolution, queues were cut off in token of release from imperial rule.

An Old Empire Comes to an End

The current of foreign trade thrust into China's ports (as we have already noted) swept the government and the people into the stream of world relations. During the nineteenth and early twentieth centuries, wars, treaties, "concessions" (lands set apart for foreign residents), railways built with foreign capital, reaction to neighboring Japan on one side and Soviet Russia on the other, strong pressure of outside thought and customs—a crowd of disturbing and arousing experiences brought about revolution. In 1911 the Manchu dynasty fell; in the following year a republic was set up. For the sake of harmony the great leader of revolt, Dr. Sun Yat-sen, consented to let Yuan Shih-kai become the first president.

Yuan proved to be highhanded; soon the Kuomintang or Nationalist Party, that had been organized by Dr. Sun, was in revolt. Yuan succeeded in crushing this rebellion, only to face another crisis. In 1915 Japan made her notorious Twenty-one Demands on China—demands that would have reduced that unfortunate country to the status of a satellite state. Thanks to the vigorous protests of Great Britain and the United States, the original demands were greatly modified. Yet in yielding to them, as she now did, China enabled the Japanese to win a foothold in the land.

Yuan Shih-kai died in 1916 and was succeeded by the well-meaning but weak Li Yuan-hung. In the following year China entered World War I on the side of the Allies. She could not contribute much to the Allied victory and did not benefit particularly as a result of the negotiations that followed.

Chaos in the New Republic

In the meantime conditions had become chaotic. The Kuomintang had set up a separate government in the South, with the capital at Canton; the government of the North had become constantly weaker. The governors of certain provinces raised their own armies and became *tuchuns* or war lords. They fought constantly against one another as well as against the governments of the North and South. The devastation caused by civil war made millions homeless; banditry flourished in the ravaged areas of China.

Sun Yat-sen died in 1925. His disciple, Chiang Kai-shek, commander of the Kuomintang army, took steps to unite

WALKING HIS PET BIRDS brings a smile of contentment to the face of an elderly Chinese. Governments may come and go but, when he can, he still follows the customs of his youth.

253

CHINESE FUNERAL PROCESSION

The dead are held in the greatest reverence in China, where funerals are as elaborate and expensive as weddings. Unlike Western custom, white is the color of mourning. Although a man may die, he is still considered part of the family and no one takes his place. For instance, the youngest son is still the youngest son even if his older brothers are dead.

all China under his rule. He conducted a fierce campaign against the Communists, who had become influential in the South; then he marched on Peiping (Peking). By 1928 the country was ostensibly united; the capital was set up in Nanking. However, internal strife continued. Chiang engaged in ceaseless fighting against the Communists, who were strong in certain districts; moreover, he had but slight control over certain war lords.

To internal difficulties was added the threat of foreign domination. In the year 1931 the Japanese began to occupy rich Manchuria. By 1932 they had overrun the entire area and had organized it as the puppet state of Manchukuo. Japan continued to extend her influence in northern China. The Chinese did not dare to resist by force of arms, but they seriously hampered the Japanese by organizing passive resistance, while they prepared for future attack.

The Japanese Attack China

At last the Japanese, exasperated, determined to crush China; in July 1937 they launched a terrible attack. China lost her seaports one by one; her capital, Nanking, was captured; and large areas of the coastal provinces were occupied. Yet instead of crushing China, the invasion united the country as never before. The Chinese resisted fiercely. Chungking, in the western province of Szechwan, became the wartime capital. Eventually, the struggle with Japan became a part of World War II; and when Japan finally was defeated, the seized territories were returned to China.

War in China did not end with the defeat of Japan. Hostility between the Communists and Nationalists flared up again. War raged throughout the scarred land until 1949 when the Reds drove the Nationalists from the mainland. What could be salvaged of Chiang's army was moved to the island of Formosa. There the Nationalists prepared for a Red invasion.

At the start of the war in Korea the United States sent a fleet of war ships to protect Formosa. The blockade lasted until February 1953. In July 1953, after thirty-seven months of fighting, a truce agreement was reached in Korea. The entry of Communist China in the Korean war in November 1950 complicated peace talks. The Reds were unwilling for any peace treaty to be signed that would win them neither Formosa nor a UN seat.

China's Religions

There are three main religions in China—Confucianism, Taoism and Buddhism. Confucius was a wise man who was born in 551 B.C. and taught a beautiful rule of conduct, similar in some respects to that of Christ. Temples to Confucius are common in China, and his teachings are known throughout the country.

Lao-tse, the founder of Taoism, who lived at the same time as Confucius, taught the way by which mortals should in time become immortal. This teaching has degenerated into a belief in omens and charms, in lucky days, soothsayers and magicians. It includes the worship of idols and of various spirits, such as the god of the city—for every city has its own god—the spirit of the household, the spirit of the mountains, and so on.

Memorial buildings called pagodas, of which there are nearly two thousand in China, are believed to bring good luck to places near by. They are usually constructed of brick. The most famous of them all, the green and white Porcelain Tower of Nanking, had at its summit a gilt ball from which were hung on chains five large pearls, each of which was supposed to protect the city from one of five disasters—floods, fires, dust-storms, tempests and disturbances among the citizens. From the eaves of the nine stories of the building were suspended many bells and lanterns. This beautiful tower, built by the son of the first Ming emperor, in honor of his wife, was entirely demolished in 1853 during the Taiping rebellion.

Buddhism, the third great religion, has its temples, wayside shrines, monasteries, nunneries, and sacred mountains. Shansi, in the north of China, has the sacred Wu-tai Mountains, where there are numerous temples to which pilgrims throng from all parts of China and Tibet in the hope

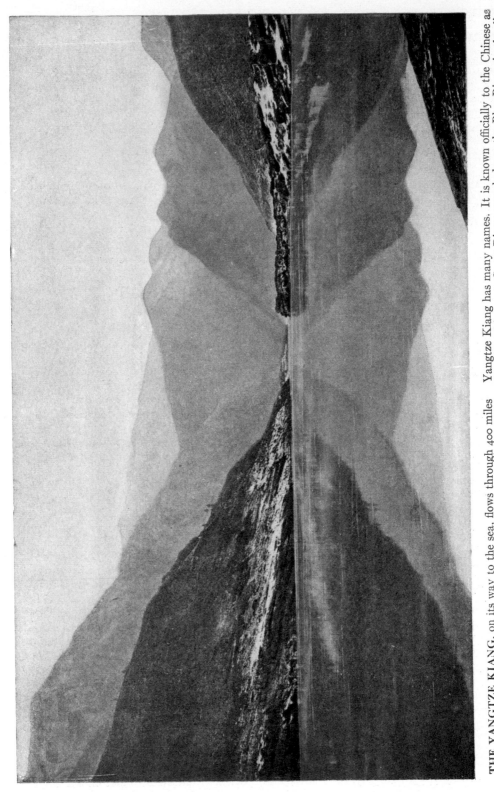

THE YANGTZE KIANG, on its way to the sea, flows through 400 miles of such magnificent mountain scenery as we see here, immediately above the town of Ichang. The river is not always so placid, however, for in places there are gorges with rapids that are very dangerous to shipping. The Yangtze Kiang has many names. It is known officially to the Chinese as the Changkiang, or Great River, popularly as the Blue River; in the districts near Tibet it is the River of Golden Sand; elsewhere it is the White Waters and the Long River. It is over 3,000 miles long.

UNPAVED, ROCK-STUDDED and crossed by streams, this ancient highway runs from Peking, the capital of Communist China, to Kalgan, the "gate" to Mongolia. Long years ago the road was the main route of caravans that carried tea from China to Russia. The road runs through a wild, mountainous region and crosses a bend of the Great Wall. Today there is a railroad between Peking and Kalgan; and Kalgan has become the leading commercial and communications center of Inner Mongolia. Other highways link Kalgan with Ulan Bator and Tolun, farther west.

MISSIONARIES FOUNDED ST. JOHN'S UNIVERSITY IN SHANGHAI

Many schools of all levels were set up by missionaries in China. Young Chinese flocked to them, anxious to add to their classic Chinese education by learning the ways of the West. Since the Communists took over the Government, most of these schools have either been closed or their studies changed to suit the purposes of the Communists.

NOISES OF A MODERN CITY VIE WITH TEMPLE BELLS IN SHANGHAI

Here we see both new and old methods of transportation in a busy street which runs through what was called the International Settlement before World War II. Long the banking and trade center of China, Shanghai lost its modern, international flavor in 1949 when the Red Army succeeded in driving Nationalist forces from the city.

261

CARTER

OLD WAYS AND NEW meet in the person of an elderly Chinese of Shanghai. Such richness and color in dress as he displays are frowned on by China's communist overlords. His newspaper represents the "new." Once reading was the mark of the scholar alone; but today so many Chinese can read that daily newspapers are turned out on a mass scale.

PRIDEAUX

A CHINESE ACTOR, in dress that is rich and historically correct, plays the part of the heroine. In modern China, as in the England of Shakespeare's day, women do not appear on the stage, so that men and boys have to take the female parts. Some Chinese plays, usually the most popular, are long, and several days may be needed for their performance.

JUNKS SCUDDING BEFORE THE BREEZE

Chinese rivers and coastal waters are busy highways, with junks and sampans scudding in and out between larger craft. These small craft are fishing boats, water taxis, freight carriers and even homes to countless thousands of Chinese. The junks are flat-bottom affairs, with two or three sails and a small cabin amidships, usually a crude shelter roofed over with mats.

of witnessing the reputed miraculous opening of a golden lotus flower. Buddhist priests are called upon chiefly for the rites attending birth, death and burial.

Religion under the Communists

According to some reports, the Communists have not abolished these old religions outright but are controlling them. Buddhist temples and property, for instance, have been taken over by the Government although some funds may be left to take care of the priests.

On the other hand, there can be little doubt that ancestor worship, which was a kind of national religion in the old China, has been profoundly affected. In the determined effort to change the character of the Chinese people, reverence for ancestors and tradition is an obstacle to the Communists.

Ancient Rituals

The ritual of ancestor worship in the case of a death was elaborate. When a parent or grandparent died, the person's name and particulars of his life were written on a piece of wood—an ancestral tablet. It was given a place of honor in the home of the eldest son, who burned incense before it and conducted family worship for the departed spirit. The coffin containing the body was covered with a pall—red for men, blue for women—and taken to the family grave. The family followed, led by the eldest son and accompanied by neighbors and friends, the younger relatives in white—one of the colors of mourning. At the grave, firecrackers were exploded and sometimes a theatrical performance was given.

The mourners carried along food, paper money and either models or paper cutouts representing the chief articles used in life. These, it was believed, the spirit would need in another world. It was also held that every dead person has three souls, each of which was worshiped, at regular intervals, with offerings in the home, at the grave and in the temple of the village or city god. If these rites were not carried out, the spirit would be unhappy in the other world and therefore

his descendants would be miserable on earth. Mourning lasted three years.

As the worship of an ancestor had to be conducted by a son, couples without sons adopted boys lest they should die with none to worship them. Every rich family had an ancestral hall in which the tablets and family records were kept. Here, in winter, the Feast of Ancestors was held. Wine, fruit and other delicacies were offered at the shrine and were afterward consumed by the family.

Joy at the Birth of a Son

There was great rejoicing at the birth of a son. Ginger was hung at the street door to ward off evil spirits or strangers who might bring the child ill luck. To protect the newborn baby from such hazards, it was disguised in the cast-off clothing of a grownup. Often the baby was made ill by being fed on sweet cakes.

When the boy was nearly a month old, his head was shaved. This was a very important day in his life. For then he was given a name, dressed in fine new clothes and carried by his father's mother to the temple, where offerings were made and the gods were thanked for the gift of a son. A feast called the "ginger dinner" was given for relatives and friends, who were invited to it by receiving an egg colored red. According to custom, men and women did not dine together. The men feasted in a restaurant and the women at home. Pickled ginger and tinted eggs were always served on these occasions, and every guest brought a present.

How Age Is Reckoned

The real birthdays of Chinese children are never celebrated. A baby is counted as one year old at birth. Another year is added on the Chinese New Year's Day, which, like Easter, is a movable date. It is, of course, everybody's birthday and, at least in the past, was an important general holiday. Then all the people donned new clothes, fresh red paper mottoes were pasted on the doors, fruits and sweetmeats were set out and at night there were fireworks. In order to be free of worry and enjoy the day to the full, everyone was

IN NINGPO is the great Tien-how-Kung, or "Queen of Heaven" temple. The roof is the main architectural feature of a Chinese building, and to it, accordingly, the architect gives the greatest part of his attention. The double roof, such as we see in this photograph, with its carved and lac- quered eaves and its ornamentation of dragons and other figures, is held to be a most satisfying artistic device. The town of Ningpo was visited by the Portuguese early in the sixteenth century, but they were soon driven out, and it did not really become open to European trade until 1842

MERRIMAN

VIVID SIGNS line a narrow street in Kiukiang, which is a river port city on the south bank
of the Yangtze Kiang in central China. Four miles to the south of the city, in a wooded
mountain region, is White Deer Cave, where Chu Hsi lived and taught. He was a revered
Confucianist philosopher of the thirteenth century.

HAND-PAINTED WHILE YOU WAIT

These girls, who look so pleased with the silk handkerchiefs they are examining, have just had them painted by this Kunming artist. Kunming, the capital of Yunnan Province, is the chief city of southwest China. It was of considerable strategic importance during World War II, when it was a U. S. Army air base and the headquarters of the Chinese military command.

supposed to pay all his debts before the holiday arrived.

The old China had some other charming customs. On the first full moon of the New Year came the Feast of Lanterns. Then all sorts and sizes of lanterns, some in the shapes of dragons and fishes, were hung up everywhere in the streets and over the doors. Another feast day was celebrated by a family picnic. In the summer came a gala day on the water— the Dragon Boat Festival.

The old and the new China have one terrible thing in common and that is the abysmal poverty of the great mass of people. Flood and famine still play havoc, taking an even greater toll of life than they otherwise would because the people have few bulwarks against disaster. When one has only a minimum of food at the best of times, there is little resistance to disease or the effects of starvation.

This wretched poverty is the biggest single problem with which the Communist Government must contend. Early in their climb to power, the Reds won the allegiance of many of the peasants by their promises of a reform in agriculture. They took land from farmers with ten acres and gave it to those with only a half acre or none. But in the mid-1950's they seemed to be following the Russian pattern—collectivization—which has never worked any too well in the Soviet Union itself. According to a plan scheduled to be completed by 1965, the Reds are attempting to collectivize all of China's 100,000,000 farmers. This means a tremendous upheaval in village life and a struggle between the Government and the peasants, whose last remnants of pride and dignity are based on ownership of their little plots. The issue may prove to be a decisive one for the Red regime and for the world.

At the same time the Communists are making an all-out effort to industrialize China. In this they are being helped by the Soviet Union, which supplies technical aid and quantities of machinery. In fact, about three-quarters of Communist China's trade is with the Soviet bloc of countries. Manufacturing and transportation do seem to be making rapid progress. A number of industrial towns, such as Anshan (in Manchuria), are said to be jammed with tens of thousands of work-

EASTFOTO

CHINA'S RIVERS near the towns and cities teem with sampans. These small boats with mat roofs are usually propelled by sculling with a long oar. Some of them have sails.

BRIDE AND BRIDEGROOM alike dress in gorgeous costume for the wedding. The young man and his parents arrange the marriage with the parents of the future bride, and husband and wife do not usually meet until the wedding ceremony. The Chinese wife exchanges the life of a servant in her father's house for a similar life of drudgery for her husband's family.

GRANDMOTHER AND GRANDSON enjoy the air together. The birth of a boy is always welcome in a Chinese family, and from his earliest days he has infinitely better treatment than a girl. It was once not uncommon for parents to kill a girl baby, or to sell her as a slave after a few years. Some very little girls work long hours in the silk factories.

HONG KONG: FRAGRANT HARBOR

Victoria, city of Hong Kong, is viewed here from Kowloon on the narrow Kowloon Peninsula across the harbor. The city streets sprawl up the mountains which surround the harbor.

ers fresh from the farms. They labor under harsh discipline and have a standard of living little higher than the peasants.

The most frightening aspect of present-day China is the way the people's minds have been enslaved. Terror and "brainwashing" are commonplaces. By psychological techniques the people are conditioned to accept and follow whatever they are told, no matter how false or absurd. In *China under Communism,* by Richard L. Walker, one of the most thorough studies of the subject, the author gives his opinion that "psychological mass coercion . . . is bringing about the dehumanization of Chinese civilization."

Schools are a natural channel for propaganda, and it is the children and young people who are most completely captured.

Before the coming of the missionaries in the nineteenth century, China had by no means ignored education. A complicated, exacting system of schooling had been built up over the centuries since before the time of Christ. Bright boys were selected and trained to read and memorize the classics, such as the works of Confucius. After arduous periods of schooling and

testing, the best of the best emerged as "model scholars of the Empire." To them was opened the path to the highest political positions in the land. All China revered the scholar.

The educational zeal of the missionaries found fertile ground. Millions of Chinese sought to better themselves by learning to read and write. Many went abroad for an education, and many stayed in China to attend missionary or newly founded government schools. Even before the Republic was set up in 1912, the Government began to meet the demand. The old examination system was abandoned in 1905; Chinese schools became more and more like models in the United States and Britain. The multitude of the illiterate decreased as modern scholars simplified the long list of characters that must be learned in order to have a reading knowledge of the Chinese language.

After the defeat of Japan, education, like everything else in China, was disrupted by the war between the Kuomintang and the Communists. What has happened since the civil war is hard to determine, but most signs indicate that the

272

Communist regime encourages education, at least to the extent of instructing the people in the theories of communism. Also, schools are necessary if the Reds are to have the technicians who can build up and man their industries. Missionary schools have been suppressed because, according to the Communists, Christians substitute alien ideas for the interests of the state.

Mineral resources in China are poor when we consider the great size of the country. There is coal in large amounts in Shansi, Shensi and other northern provinces. Iron-ore reserves are low and are of poor grade. Tungsten and antimony are in abundance.

The long rivers, the people and the fields of rice and wheat are the principal ingredients of China's wealth. The country has especially fertile soil, particularly the yellow-brown earth, or loess, of the Hwang Ho basin. Unfortunately, the loess region does not receive as much rain as less fertile areas. The Hwang Ho, which means "yellow river," and is also called "China's sorrow," is often swollen by monsoon rains. It then overflows, wrecking the towns in its path, and rushes on, laden with the "gold" of the loess. Before the river disgorges its rich cargo into the Yellow Sea, it lays down great quantities of loess soil in the densely peopled and heavily farmed North China plain. Fertile earth is thus brought to a region where it is needed most.

The other great river of China is the Yangtze Kiang, which rises in the western mountains, not far from the source of the Hwang. The first third of its course, called the Kinsha Kiang, or "golden sand river," runs southward. After turning east in Yunnan Province, the Yangtze falls through splendid gorges into the central China plain and flows on into the East China Sea above Shanghai. Six hundred miles of the lower Yangtze are navigable.

Silk is one of the things we owe to China, although the Chinese were so anxious to keep the industry to themselves that there was a time when anyone who tried to take silkworm eggs or mulberry-tree saplings out of the country was doomed to die. But about 550 A.D. two pil-

BLACK STAR

HOUSES ARE SCARCE IN HONG KONG, TOO

The buildings that dominate the heights overlooking the harbor are new flats. There is a great demand for housing in the colony. The British race course is shown in the foreground.

YOUTHFUL, DEFT, BUSY—A BASKET-WEAVER OF HONG KONG

One of the most useful objects in China and throughout the Far East is the cane basket, which the barefoot boy here weaves with considerable skill and speed. Mainland China, ordinarily the biggest customer for the goods of Hong Kong, was shut off from trade with the British outpost after the Communist Government of China entered the Korean conflict.

A PUBLIC SCRIBE, OR LETTER WRITER, IN SHANGHAI

In parts of the East, where many people can neither read nor write, necessary letters are dictated to a public scribe, who pens the epistles for a fee. His job is really quite similar to that of a Western public stenographer, although his "office" is likely to be only a table set up on the sidewalk, which he can easily shift in search of clients or even as the whim may seize him.

grims succeeded in carrying to Europe some silkworm eggs concealed in their bamboo walking staves. Thus the world came to share the precious product.

In the valley of the Yangtze Kiang and some of the provinces south of it, the rearing of silkworms and the unwinding of the cocoons have usually been carried on as household industries. For, at least until the Communists came, China was a land where the home was the center of most activities. Even today it is likely that most households weave the cotton for their clothes and that in farming sections each family tries to live on the food grown on its own little plot. However, many cotton, woolen and silk mills have been built,

and there are also flour mills, glass factories and iron works.

Side by side with the silk is another great industry, the cultivation of the tea plant. Tea also we owe to China. It is strange to think of a tealess England, yet tea leaves never reached there until 1645. In China, tea-growing is also apt to be a family concern. The plant is cultivated in small patches.

It is claimed that porcelain has been made in China for more than two thousand years. "China ware," as it came to be called in Europe, is of all descriptions, from fine cups of eggshell thinness to heavy bowls of a rich green made to imitate jade. There were many factories

THE BARRIER GATE BETWEEN MACAO AND RED CHINA

Macao, west of Hong Kong, is the oldest foreign settlement in the Far East, founded in 1557. With two smaller islands it forms a Portuguese colony. Through the gate, over which flies the Portuguese flag, many thousands of Chinese pass each day on their way to and from China. They are allowed free entry and exit by Macao, which is noted as a pleasure resort.

in China, the most famous being that of King-te-Chen in Kiangsi, which supplied the royal household from about 1370. It was destroyed in the Taiping rebellion of 1850, but has been rebuilt. The secret of the manufacture of the most celebrated variety of this Chinese porcelain is completely lost.

In the south we find that rice takes an important place. It is grown in small patches, flooded artificially with water from the nearest river. After the soil has been churned up into a porridgelike state, seed is sown thickly in a sort of nursery corner. When the seedlings are about twelve inches high, they are pulled up in bunches, separated into groups of four or five plants each, and replanted in the flooded fields. Some of these fields yield three crops a year.

Sugar-cane and cotton are cultivated, and fruit-growing is carried on to a considerable extent. Oranges, which Arabs are said to have brought to Europe, are grown all over south China. Bananas are to be had nearly all the year round; pineapples, cape gooseberries, peaches and apricots are abundant, while palm trees supply several millions of palm-leaf fans annually. But the most useful plant of south China is the bamboo. It supplies the material for the framework for the huts of matting which the poorer peasants call "home," and is also employed in the making of furniture of all kinds, umbrella frames, clothes-lines, tools, etc., and when it has been soaked and pulped it is made into paper. Its dried leaves are made into sunhats and raincoats, and its young shoots are pickled for food.

With such a vast population everything that can be eaten is eaten. Birds'-nest soup, for instance, is a Chinese delicacy. The nests, which are small, and like thin cases of gelatine, are found in great numbers in caves by the sea. They are boiled until they make a thick, white substance which is the first course at every grand dinner. A seaweed called agar-agar, a sea-slug known in Europe as beche-de-mer, sharks' fins and eggs that have been preserved for a long time, are all eaten and enjoyed, while among the poorer people, in times of scarcity, cats and dogs, rats and mice form part of the diet.

BLACK STAR

A BASKET-MAKER'S DREAM COME TRUE

Although basket-weaving is considered one of the simplest of the arts, it has reached a high degree of perfection in some of the Oriental countries. The Chinese, for instance, use bamboo and rattan to fashion baskets that are unusually fine in quality and beautifully finished. In addition to baskets, this shopkeeper seems to have every possible variety of wood container.

HOMEMADE WINDMILL OF A YANGTZE RIVER RICE FARMER

Water from the Yangtze is channeled to farmlands by a series of ever narrowing ditches. Farmers
draw the water for their fields from these irrigation ditches by primitive windmills.

THE TERRITORY OF MANCHURIA

At various times Manchuria has been considered a part of China. Manchuria is, however, a distinct region separated by mountains from China proper. The people of Manchuria, the Manchus, once were also distinct from the Chinese, but there has been considerable intermarriage between the two stocks.

The Chinese used to call Manchuria *Tung-san-sheng* (the three eastern provinces)—Liaoning, Kirin and Heilungkiang. Later, when the Japanese wrested Manchuria from China in 1931, they included the neighboring province of Jehol.

In 1945 Manchuria again became a part of China, and this time it was divided into nine provinces—Liaoning, Kirin, Heilungkiang, Liaopeh, Nunkiang, Hsingan, Sungkiang, Hokiang and Antung. Chinese now refer to Manchuria as *Tung-pei* (the northeast). When World War II ended, the Chinese Communists were already in possession of most of Manchuria; and as the Chinese civil war continued, the Communists gradually gained the whole territory.

Many Kinds of Animal Life

Hot in summer and intensely cold during a winter of four months, it has products and animals of both hot and cold climates. The country abounds in bird life, including such edible birds as pheasants, partridges and quails, and in the mountains and on the steppes are found bears, antelopes, deer of many kinds, hares, squirrels and foxes.

The Manchus have small farms where dogs are bred for their thick winter coats and a Manchu girl will often have six or more dogs for her dowry. These dogs are Chows, like those that we keep for pets, just as we do the Pekingese. The latter is in China a very tiny animal, called the "sleeve dog," because it is carried in the wide sleeves of its owner's robe.

The land is rich in minerals, with valuable deposits of gold, silver, asbestos and lead, as well as great coal and iron mines that have been well developed. Much of the coal is carried out of the open mines in large wheelbarrows.

The rivers of Manchuria supply many kinds of fish, including sturgeon and trout and a variety of salmon called the tamara. The skin of this salmon is made into clothing and is worn by the people of a certain district, who are called, in consequence, the Fish Skin Tartars.

Millet the Chief Food

The Manchus are naturally a race of hunters, but when their country was united with China, Chinese settlers introduced agriculture. Corn, rice, wheat and barley are grown, but the principal grain cultivated is millet, which forms the staple food of the working people. The grain is boiled, put into bowls and eaten with chopsticks together with vegetables fresh, cooked or pickled that are added for flavor. From millet is distilled an alcoholic liquor called "samshu," which is sold all over the country. The refuse becomes food for herds of pigs. Millet stalks are used for fencing and firewood, and the poorer people weave them together and plaster them with mud to make houses.

What Is Made from the Bean

By far the most important article cultivated for export is the bean, of which many varieties are grown. Several of these yield an oil which is used all over China for lighting and heating, and the part left after the oil is pressed out, known as "bean cake," is sent south to fertilize the sugar-cane fields. Piled up along railroad tracks or wharves, the "cakes" look like cart wheels or grindstones. Some varieties are ground into bean-flour or used for vermicelli, others are made into a strange sort of cheese called "bean curd." From the soya bean, which is cultivated on about twenty million acres, is made the famous "soy" sauce. The products derived from this plant seem almost numberless and are of astonishing variety. The income from it is enormous.

Besides being linked by the Trans-Siberian railway to Europe, Manchuria has a railway line to Port Arthur (Lu-

PARK IN DAIREN IN THE WINTERTIME

Dairen, much-disputed ice-free port in Manchuria, was declared a free port in 1907. Although it is still technically free, Russia has the right to lease half its port facilities without charge.

PHOTOS, EASTFOTO

HUNDREDS OF SPINDLES OF LINEN THREAD

The girls above are working in the spinning department of a flax mill at Harbin. Plans for the mill area are said to include housing, educational and recreational facilities.

shun) on the Yellow Sea. This port and
Dairen, also on the Yellow Sea, give Manchuria access to the Pacific. Much of the
interior shipping, which used to be done
by means of the rivers or in springless
carts that had to go bumping over incredibly bad roads, is now handled by new
or improved railroads. In normal times,
Manchuria exports considerable farm
products, especially those made from soybeans, one of the country's chief crops.

Instead of living on their farms, the
Manchus build their little mud and stone
habitations in huddled groups or villages.
Pigs and chickens share the enclosures
with them, and heat is secured by burning bunches of straw or stubble in a
"kang," a brick ledge about two feet high
in one end of a room. Inside it are flues
to spread the heat through the bricks, and
on top of it the members of the household
sit by day and lie down by night.

In the warmest districts of Manchuria,
as well as in certain provinces of China
proper, wild silk is obtained from a cater-
pillar which feeds on oak leaves. From
its silk are made the fabrics called pongee
and tussah. About four million dollars'
worth of this wild silk is produced here
every year. Camel's hair and sheep's wool
are woven into rugs, but, curiously
enough, neither here nor in China is wool
used for clothing; padded garments of
silk or cotton, costly furs or common
skins, according to the rank of the wearer,
are used to keep out the cold. For out-
door use in winter the working people
wear shoes of tough oxhide stuffed with
coarse grass to make them warmer.

The women never bound their feet even
though the people accepted some other
customs of the Chinese. The Manchuri-
ans are no longer mostly wandering herds-
men as they once were, but have become
farmers and have intermarried with the
Chinese until few pure Manchus remain.

Mukden was formerly the capital; later
the Japanese made Hsinking (Chang-
chun) the capital. The People's Government for the Northwest have set up their
headquarters at Mukden, however. The
fortified city of Port Arthur is a joint
Chinese-Soviet naval base.

© Gleason

BANDIT CHIEF'S LIEUTENANT

Formerly hordes of bandits made trade and
traveling dangerous. Merchants and insurance
companies paid them large sums to get safe
conduct for both goods and persons.

There is much beautiful mountain
scenery in Manchuria. A peak in the
province of Kirin is known as the "Ever-
White Mountain" on account of the white
pumice stone at the summit. It is the
crater of an old volcano. This is said to
be the birthplace of Nurhachu, the father
of the first Manchu emperor of China,
and as such was maintained as a sacred
place by the imperial family.

When the Japanese established Manchuria (calling it Manchukuo) as a separate state, they worked to develop the
country economically and also to change

the attitude of the people. The Japanese knew that a sizable part of the population was made up of recent immigrants from China. In fact, in some years this immigration had been as high as a million individuals—persons who had found no chance for success in overcrowded China and so had chosen to become pioneers in the undeveloped north. The Japanese reasoned that these millions could have no love for the old home, since it had been unkind. Here, the conquerors thought, they could develop both land and people along new lines—Japanese lines, of course.

They sought to make Manchuria a modern industrial state that would in time provide opportunities for emigrants from the Japanese islands, for these, too, were overcrowded. They also saw that a prosperous and well-populated Manchuria (or Manchukuo) would be a fine market for the products of Japanese factories. It would also be a source of raw materials for their factories.

There was much to encourage their dreams. Manchuria is rich in timber, for building, and in minerals of various kinds. For example, it has the most extensive coal deposits known. There is iron ore, also, and great quantities of oil shale from which petroleum may be extracted. Many industrial products can be made from Manchuria's abundant crops of soy beans.

The Japanese, largely with their own capital and under their own management, made an extraordinary start in developing the mines and industries during the few years they were in occupation of the territory. Their defeat in World War II drove them out of the mainland of Asia; but the factories and other installations they had built remain.

The Japanese Policy Is Continued

The Communist Government that was set up soon after the war in Manchuria continued the industrial policies of the Japanese; only, of course, now everything belonged to the state.

In February 1950 Manchuria, by treaty, joined the Communist Government of China, becoming again a part of China.

As you can see by the map, Manchuria

CHINA, WHERE A FIFTH

and Korea have a common border more than five hundred miles long, half of it defined by the Yalu River. Across this border poured great numbers of so-called Chinese Red "volunteers" to fight against the United Nations forces in the Korean War.

OF THE WORLD'S POPULATION DWELLS

CHINA: FACTS AND FIGURES

THE COUNTRY

Bounded west, north and northeast by the Soviet Union, north by the Mongolian Republic, east by Korea, the Yellow, East China and South China seas and south by Indochina, Burma, India, Bhutan, Nepal, Kashmir and Afghanistan, Chinese territory includes the 18 provinces of China Proper (area, 1,373,370 square miles; population, 397,522,237); Formosa (13,890 square miles; population, 7,647,703); Tibet (469,294 square miles; population, 3,700,-000); Sinkiang (660,976 square miles; popula-

287

tion, 4,012,330) ; Sikang and Chinghai (431,987 square miles ; population, 3,102,000) ; 3 provinces of Inner Mongolia (326,792 square miles ; population, 5,054,126) ; Jehol (69,491 square miles ; population, 6,109,866) ; and 9 provinces of Manchuria (413,306 square miles ; population, 38,584,268). Total area, 3,759,115 square miles ; population, 483,870,000.

GOVERNMENT

A republic after 1912 and controlled by the Nationalist (Kuomintang) party after 1926-27, China became a Communist People's Republic in October 1949, the Nationalist Government thereafter being confined to Formosa. The People's Republic is based on an Organic Law that sets forth the general aims of communism and the eventual election of an All-China People's Congress. Powers of government—executive, legislative and judicial—are in the meantime vested in a 56-member Central People's Government Council. The council, headed by a chairman and 6 vice-chairmen, has set up a State Administration Council (Cabinet) that manages the ministries and commissions of government.

COMMERCE AND INDUSTRIES

About three-fourths of China's population is agricultural. The average farm is about 3.3 acres and is intensively cultivated. Unaided human farm labor predominates ; there are relatively few draft animals and fewer farm machines. The principal farm products are cotton, silk cocoons, hemp, flax, tea, fats and oils, peas, beans, potatoes, tobacco and sugar. Production of staples, wheat in the north and rice in the south, is insufficient ; both must be imported to meet domestic needs. Of about 150,000,000 head of livestock, 55,605,000 are hogs. Chief forest regions are northern Manchuria and southwest China proper ; teak and tung are the principal trees. Leading mineral products are coal, pig iron, steel, copper, lead and cement ; there is also an output of wolfram (tungsten), antimony, tin, bauxite, magnesite, pyrite, gypsum and phosphate. Chief manufactures are textiles, paper, power machinery and chemicals. Exports : soybeans, hog bristles, tung oil, peanuts, tea and mineral ores. Imports : machinery, gasoline, kerosene, lubricating oil and chemicals.

COMMUNICATIONS

Railways, 14,405 miles opened to traffic ; highways, 126,320 miles ; state airlines, 55,269 route miles. There are about 7,000 miles of inland waterways. Telegraph lines, 97,360 miles ; 673 radio transmitting stations.

RELIGION AND EDUCATION

Ancestor worship, though not a formal religion, is widespread. Confucianism, Buddhism and Taoism are the chief religions. There are also native Moslems and Christians. Missionaries have been murdered, expelled, imprisoned or closely watched as subversives. Communist regime has conducted a vigorous literacy campaign and a program of technical instruction for workers. There are over 43,000,000 pupils in primary schools, 2,050,000 in secondary schools and 175,000 in colleges and universities.

IMPORTANT CITIES

Shanghai, 3,853,511 ; Tientsin, 1,679,210 ; the capital, Peking (formerly Peiping), 1,602,234 ; Canton, 1,276,429 ; Mukden, 1,175,620 ; Nanking, 1,037,656 ; Chungking, 1,000,000 ; Pinkiang (Harbin), 760,000 ; Tsingtao, 752,800 ; Hankow, 749,952 ; Talien (Dairen), 543,690.

MANCHURIA

Forms the major part of the North East Regional Government of the People's Republic ; area, 413,306 square miles, and population, 38,584,268. Recognized as part of the People's Republic in Sino-Soviet treaty of 1950. Former Japanese commercial holdings, a railroad and the Kwantung ports of Dairen and Port Arthur remained under Soviet control.

KWANTUNG

Formerly Japanese, ceded to China in 1945 while ports of Dairen and Port Arthur were leased to Soviet Russia. According to Sino-Soviet pact of 1950, the cities were to return to China not later than the end of 1952.

TANNU TUVA

Now called the Tuva Autonomous Region as a part of the Soviet Union, it is located in northwestern Mongolia. Area, 64,000 square miles ; population, 65,000. Kysyl Khoto is the capital.

FOREIGN POSSESSIONS IN CHINA: FACTS AND FIGURES

HONG KONG

A British Crown Colony, it consists of a number of islands and a portion of the south China mainland at the mouth of the Pearl (Canton) River ; total area, 391 square miles (Hong Kong Island, 32 square miles), and population (1952), 2,250,000. A governor is assisted by executive and legislative councils. Fishing is the primary industry ; there is also shipbuilding and repairs, textile spinning and weaving and manufactures of rubber goods, paint, cement and other goods. United States and colonial-government bans on shipments of war goods—including rubber and oil—to Communist China have caused a drastic decrease in Hong Kong trade. Railways, 22 miles ; road, 425 miles ; 11 airlines have flights to all parts of the world. About 160,000 pupils in primary and secondary schools ; also 3 teachers' colleges and University of Hong Kong.

MACAO

Portuguese province opposite Hong Kong ; area, 6 square miles, and population, 187,772. It is under the administration of a governor and has been important for commerce with mainland China. There has been a trade recession due to the embargo of shipments to China. Macao is also famous as a pleasure resort.

IN UNKNOWN SINKIANG

Life in China's Westernmost Province

We have read of Russian Turkestan in Volume III. Sinkiang includes Eastern Chinese Turkestan, Kulja and Kashgaria. This territory embraces all
of the Chinese dependencies between Mongolia on the north and Tibet on the
south; but though it extends for six hundred miles from north to south and
twelve hundred from east to west, its population numbers less than two million. Turks, Mongols and Chinese, each in turn have overrun this land
of the nomad, which forms a strategic wedge into Central Asia. No doubt
the Russians are interested in Sinkiang. Its three large cities are in the west
near the Russian frontier and Pakistan and India can be reached by journeying
over the high passes of the Himalayas. The archaeologist is interested because in the Taklamakan Desert in south Sinkiang are towns buried in the
sand from which ancient manuscripts, wall paintings and even many articles
of clothing have been recovered.

SINKIANG, or Chinese Turkestan
(also spelled Turkistan), is the most
westerly province of the Chinese
Republic, of which it forms an important
part, for it has great mineral and other
resources. It is still a land of which little is known. No railway connects Sinkiang with the outside world. It can be
reached from Peking only by horseback,
camelback or in carts along the trade caravan route through Inner Mongolia.

Sinkiang is divided into two unequal
parts by the Tien Shan (mountains).
Dzungaria, to the north, is tableland.
The larger portion to the south is occupied mainly by the great Taklamakan
Desert. So dry is this region that the
snow line on the mountains is above 11,-
000 feet. Streams and rivers formed by
the melting snow either disappear in the desert or flow
into salt lakes. The Tarim
River, the longest stream,
ends in Lob Nor basin.

Generally speaking, then,
Sinkiang is a land of deserts
and sand dunes, though the
rivers and streams make a certain amount of cultivation possible by supplying water for irrigation canals. It is bounded
on the north by Siberia, on the
east by the province of Kansu
in China proper and by the
Desert of Gobi in Mongolia,
on the south by Tibet and the

northern frontiers of India, and on the
west by Russian Turkestan and Afghanistan. Urumchi (Tihwafu) is the capital,
but the most important towns for trade
and commerce are Kashgar, Yarkand and
Khotan. The climate is the same as that
of other regions far from the sea—in summer it is hot and in winter very cold. In
the spring high winds are frequent, and
raise clouds of dust, enveloping the country in a haze that often takes days to disperse.

On all sides save the east, Sinkiang is
hemmed about by mountains which wall
it in like a horseshoe. Some of the ice-
clad peaks rise to over fifteen thousand
feet and it is a difficult and dangerous
thing to cross them at any time of year.
Just beneath the snow fields are grassy,
flower-enameled meadows which are used

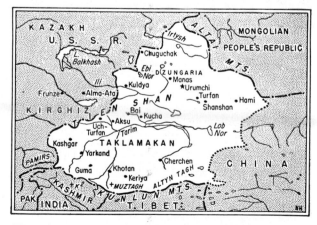

SINKIANG, WHERE WEST CHINA MEETS RUSSIA

A TURKI MOTHER AND HER CHILD BY AN OASIS WALL

At Kara Shahr, a town and oasis near Bagrach Kol, a salt lake of central Sinkiang, a Turki woman prepares to set out on a journey over the bleak foothills of the Tien Shan range.

A GOOD-HUMORED KALMUCK, HIS FAMILY AND STRONG FELT TENT

The Kalmucks, whose tribesmen long ago settled the lower Volga basin in Europe, now roam the rugged uplands of Sinkiang, raising and breeding horses and tending large flocks of sheep.

ON THE WAY TO KASHGAR: TRADERS AND BURDENED CAMELS

Kashgar is the first town that eastward-bound caravans reach after they cross the ranges of central Asia. Even in medieval times there was trade between East and West along this route.

PHOTOS, AMERICAN MUSEUM OF NATURAL HISTORY

A GATE WITH PEAKED EAVES WELCOMES TRAVELERS TO KARA SHAHR

Kara Shahr is chiefly a horse-raising center, known for the manufacture of saddles. It is on the south side of the Tien Shan in central Sinkiang near a salt-water lake, Bagrach Kol.

SWEEPING GRAIN, WHICH HAS BEEN WINNOWED, INTO A MOUND

Wheat is tossed in the pan at the left so that the light chaff is driven off by the wind, leaving the kernels. After each panful is winnowed, it is dumped and carefully swept up.

REPAIRING GRAIN CARTS ON THE PLAIN NEAR URUMCHI

The body of the cart is made of woven straw and it is placed on wooden wheels, which are heavy and cumbersome. It is easy to imagine that the first wheel invented looked like these.

YOUNG RECRUITS ON THE STREETS OF KULDJA, NORTHWEST CHINA

Called up for compulsory military training, these sixteen-year-olds regard their future responsibilities with serious faces. Kuldja is in Sinkiang Province near the Russian border.

293

VEILED MOSLEM WOMEN IN A NARROW STREET OF YARKAND

The veiling of women was not part of the original Islamic code, but of later Semitic origin. The rule requiring Moslem women to wear veils and men to wear fezzes is gradually being relaxed.

for summer feeding-grounds by the no-mad shepherds. The northern slopes are the best watered. Beneath this upper grass belt comes a sweep of rock-ribbed country cleft by canyons and practically uninhabited. Farther down on the edge of the plain comes a second grassy belt watered by the Tarim and its tributaries and other mountain streams before they evaporate or sink into the sands. They are full-fed in spring and summer by the melting of the snows above and there is therefore no such dearth of water as might be expected on the fringes of the desert. Here the flocks return in winter when the higher meadows are quite exhausted.

The plain itself is unfit for agriculture or human habitation save on the oases, whether natural or formed by irrigation ditches from the rivers. On these oases the cities and trading centers have been built, and to them the camel caravans from India and Russian Turkestan wind over the wind-bitten passes, their banners hoisted on spears, with grain and other things in exchange for the native wool, felts and rugs, jade, silk and cotton. As these oases are from one to two hundred miles of desert or mountain travel apart, there is naturally no strong central government.

There is one other kind of habitable

country in Sin-Kiang—the lakes and reed swamps of the Lop-nor. These are the home of a fisher-folk, the Lopliks. Barring their small numbers, it is probable that all but ten per cent of the population live in the oases. The remaining ten per cent represent the nomadic stockmen.

It is an interesting sight to see the animals being taken on their semi-annual migration. The fine herds of ponies are guided by the younger, more active men, the long-legged camels by the men, the placid oxen by the women and the sheep by children mounted on ponies or oxen. The baby camels are often so unequal to hard travel their first spring that they have to be strapped to their mothers' backs on top of the packs; while the weaker lambs will be thrown across the saddle or tucked into the saddle-bags. Lambs bleat, ponies neigh, cattle low and camels utter their raucous note, while the dust rises in a yellow cloud that can be seen for miles; and at night the cook-fires gleam red beneath a starry sky as chunks of lamb are strung on wire spits and broiled, or other food is prepared before the round felt tents.

The higher meadows have as background peaks of red porphyry and glistening ice hung in white mists, which at times stream in the wind like banners and at times disperse, leaving the great domes and pinnacles to reflect the sunlight. Ice Pass (the Muzart) is itself eleven thousand feet high and down it flows a glacier raked by fissures impossible to cross. The most used pass is that between Aksu, on

AMERICAN MUSEUM OF NATURAL HISTORY

A KIRGHIS WITH A GOLDEN EAGLE TRAINED FOR FALCONRY

Falconry is a sport of ancient Oriental origin in which a bird is trained to capture its prey on the wing. The Oriental falconer carries the bird on his right wrist, the European on his left.

A SHELTER FOR CATTLE GETS A WEATHERPROOF ROOF

Flat boards are laid first, then a layer of straw and finally a covering of gravel. This will protect the shed against the torrents of rain that frequently fall in western Sinkiang.

PHOTOS, TRIANGLE

A BAD-TEMPERED HORSE IS TRUSSED FOR SHOEING

The animal is used on the rocky trails and icy passes of the Tekes Valley in the west. In such rugged terrain, a lost shoe could well mean death for both horse and its rider.

the south, and Kuldzha. Such is the Sin-Kiang that greets the traveler's eye.

For twenty centuries its history has been one of control first by China, then by the Turks, then by Mongols and now again by the Chinese. Jenghiz conquered it in the thirteenth century and Tamerlane made conquest of it over a century later. The Chinese acquired it by force in 1758, but in 1862 when the Mohammedan rebellion reached this remote province, the natives slaughtered thousands of Chinese and were free of them until 1876. Now the Chinese call it the New Dominion. This wedge into Central Asia is of great importance to China, but the influence of Soviet Russia is much stronger in the region than that of the Chinese Government.

Its sparse population, collectively termed Turkis, though the tribes include Kashgari, Kirghiz, Taranchi and others, chiefly Mohammedan, shows a greater resemblance to the Iranian stock of Western Asia than to the Chinese. They are light-hearted and cheerful, easy to govern, and without any desire for advancement either educationally or in any other sense. Both men and women are good riders, and if a horse or donkey is not available they

TRIANGLE

CARRYING WATER IN A LAMA MONASTERY IN THE KASH VALLEY

These young novices, members of the Kalmuck tribe in Sinkiang, are preparing to be Buddhist priests. In addition to studying, they must also take care of the manual labor for the order.

are equally at home astride the lumbering ox.

Their houses, low and made of mud, are generally without windows and devoid of architectural beauty. Outside the towns most of the houses have a courtyard and veranda and are surrounded by trees, under which in the summer the women sit and weave the rough but durable white cloth from which they make their wardrobes.

Boots Are Removed Indoors

The people can best be seen on a market day. All roads lead to the bazaar, and they are crowded from early morning by a mixed crowd of men, women and children mounted on ponies or donkeys, all going to the places allotted to the venders of particular articles. A winter market day shows the national costume in its many colors. That worn by the men is a long coat of bright colored cloth reaching to the knees and fastened at the waist by a sash. Men also wear trousers like pajamas. Their coats have long sleeves which may be pulled down over the hands, thus taking the place of gloves. Leather knee-boots, with detachable slippers that are kicked off on entering a house, and a cloth or velvet cap edged with fur—the headgear common to both men and women—complete the costume.

Ladies of fashion wear embroidered silk waistcoats over short coats, which are covered by long coats, and over all are white muslin cloaks reaching to the heels. The women wear lattice-work veils, usually edged with embroidery, which hang down over the face and hide it as required by Mohammedan law. But in midsummer, when heat-waves rise dizzyingly, everyone wears loose white robes.

Camels Sleep Beside Their Drivers

Tea-shops, with floors of mud on which the customers squat on their heels, provide refreshment. The tea-urn sings merrily and there is a tiny china teapot with a bowl for each person. The seller of meat dumplings and small cakes is there to supplement the tea. He takes coins in payment, using his mouth as a purse as he deals out change to veiled ladies or solemn-eyed priests. Hotels are unknown, but accommodation can be had in the inns, or serais, where camels, carts, horses and men are lodged side by side. These inns are merely roofs with mud walls and floors. Nothing is provided for the comfort of travelers, save a cook-fire. When a mounted tribesman with a sword is met, he is known to be on government business and is entitled to free food, lodging and transportation.

The meat market supplies beef and mutton, but horse-flesh is a dainty and commands a high price. The principal articles of food are mutton and rice, with onions, potatoes, turnips and spinach. There are many forms of roast and boiled joints, soups and pilau, or pilav—a mixture of meat and rice flavored with fried onions and other vegetables. Tea is the chief drink and is served with sugar but without milk. However, mare's milk is highly esteemed, the more so when it has been fermented and lightly churned in a colt-skin. It is then called "kumiss." Bread is made in the shape of little circular rolls with a hole through the centre of each. Only two meals are taken by the Turkis.

Good Food Is Plentiful

On market days the restaurants are well patronized. The customer may have tiny meat dumplings known as "mantu," pastry cooked by steam, soups of vermicelli, macaroni and mutton, stews made in curds and whey, doughnuts of fat and flour, salads of carrot, radish and onion chopped fine, mustard and cress.

Fruits of all kinds—melons, apples, pears, apricots, peaches, nectarines, pomegranates, plums, cherries and mulberries —grow in profusion in some parts of the country and appear on the table at the feasts which are popular during the summer months.

The inhabitants of Sin-Kiang are a pleasure-loving race and they have various forms of sport and games, but none is more popular than "baigu," a game, played also in Russian Turkestan, in which the carcass of a sheep or goat serves

BOSSHARD FROM BLACK STAR

A POTAI, an ancient milestone, marks a centuries-old caravan route. It seems likely that sentries were once posted at the top, to give warning of approaching friends or foes.

KALMUCK LAMAS offer the hospitality of their temple to passing travelers. The Kalmucks are Buddhist Mongols. Some tribes live on the Dzungaria plateau in northern Sinkiang.

as a ball. The players, who are all mounted on fast ponies, form in line. There are often as many as 120 players, one of whom is selected from the center of the line to start the game. He takes the carcass and dashes forward with it,

THE TURKI use their sturdy livestock for mounts when they are hunting for small game.

well in front of the eager crowd, swings around in a wide circle and hurls it to the ground. This is the signal for the rest, who set off in full cry. The rider who gains possession of the carcass will have a dozen men hanging on to him: all is fair in this game. A man may beat his opponent's mount, or he may seize a player and unhorse him or compel him to give up the trophy. The din is terrific, for the yells of the players mingle with the thunder of hoofs and the jingling of stirrups and ornamental trappings; dust rises, leather creaks, horses snort, as the contestants strive to get hold of the carcass and place it at the feet of the principal guest.

At the end of a game players and spectators adjourn for the Turki equivalent of tea and cakes. Dancing then goes on to the music of an orchestra, consisting of a dulcimer, a native banjo and a tom-tom, or small drum. The Turki has, however, his own idea of music.

The system of revenue and taxation shows the methods of Chinese officials in remote parts of the republic. There are official regulations fixing the amount of taxes to be levied, but they depend mostly upon the amban, or magistrate, of the

BAREFOOT AND PANTALOONED, a small boy totes a bundle of dry sticks and twigs almost as big as himself. The children of Sinkiang learn to toil hard while still very young.

TRIANGLE

HAIR STYLES FOR YOUNG MEN

Tunghans of Sinkiang, descended from Chinese and Arab ancestors, preserve many of the customs of both people. The young mother proudly displays her two small sons whose hair is cut to protect them from "the evil eye."

cause suffering, he would accept the remainder in cash—at the then prevailing rate.

Theatricals play a prominent part in the lighter side of life in Sin-Kiang, for they are the national pastime of the Chinese and are much patronized by the Turkis. The scenery is of a rough and ready kind and much is left to the imagination. There are no dressing-rooms for the actors. All changes of costume, the arranging and plaiting of the hair, painting and powdering are done in the open, in full view of the crowd, who treat everything as a matter of course. For the site of the theatre it is usual to take the courtyard of an inn or a point in the street where it is fairly wide, and there the company set up their stage and prepare for the play.

Meanwhile, the street is littered with beams and posts, and pedestrians trip over coils of wire. Gaudy screens, trees and foliage are placed in position, and soon the theatre assumes a size that stops all traffic, which has to be diverted down side alleys. Foot passengers who wish to gain the other end of the street must follow suit or climb under the stage.

particular district, for bribery and corruption are common. An example of this is given in the following true story. A large amount of firewood was demanded. The amban summoned the chiefs and subordinate officials, who were sent out to collect the wood, with the result that the price of wood rose to nearly three times as much, and still not more than half the requisite quantity had been supplied. The people then came forward to say that the commandeering of further stocks of fuel must inevitably cause hardship in the district, upon which the amban showed a fatherly benevolence and stated that, as it was not his intention to

In the Taklamakan Desert between the Tarim (Yakand-darya) and the Khotan-darya rivers is a sea of sand dunes rising from sixty to three hundred feet in height. Here, where frequent dust-storms make animal life impossible save for a few camels, the explorer Dr. Sven Hedin has discovered ruins of the ancient city of Lôu-lan (Shanshan) buried in the wind-blown sand. Dr. M. Aurel Stein has found, near Lop-nor, part of an ancient Chinese wall. Nor are these all of the discoveries that have been made of an ancient civilization long since overwhelmed by the wind-blown sands.

WHERE A LIVING BUDDHA REIGNED

Mongolia, Home of a Once All-powerful Race

When we hear the name "Mongolia" we picture to ourselves a huge desert out of which came, many centuries ago, a vast army of horsemen who overran Eurasia from the China Sea to Moscow and from Siberia to Delhi. But the tables have been turned, and now this interior section of Asia has come under the domination of two of the lands that were overrun—Russia and China. The country is divided into the Tuvinian Autonomous Region of Soviet Russia, the Inner Mongolian Autonomous Region of the Chinese People's Republic (Inner Mongolia) and the Mongolian People's Republic (Outer Mongolia). "Mongolia" now usually means the Mongolian People's Republic, which is, in theory at least, an independent republic. However, it is linked closely, by treaty and economically, to Russia. Soviet troops are stationed there.

SUNSHINE and yellow sands, with the azure of distant mountains piled like clouds on the horizon, that is the scene typical of Mongolia in fair weather. The temperature often rises to 140 degrees at midday but may fall to 70 by night. There are gravel plains and sagebrush but also gentle hills and hollows, sheer red mesas and canyons. The scourge of the traveler is the suffocating sandstorms in which, with a shriek of wind, a solid yellow mass will advance across the unpeopled wastes.

Spring is the rainy season when forage grass grows upon certain areas, though Western Mongolia lies in the broad belt of salt and sand which extends across Asia. This Desert of Gobi or Shamo, once an inland sea, is a plateau of an average height of four thousand feet, though it is broken here and there by slight depressions which give the land an undulating appearance. The grasslands of Mongolia make it possible to breed sheep and cattle. The roads that cross Mongolia are the same great routes that were used by the Mongol conquerors. The Inner Asian trade route to Eastern Turkestan is still the main communication between East and West. It stretches across Asia for 3,500 miles; and much of the way, which lies often through deep and muddy gullies and at times over ten-thousand-foot passes, is too narrow for passing. Caravan leaders must watch the way ahead for miles to see if there is an approaching procession of dust spirals to indicate the approach of another camel train. If there is, the caravan must manage to arrive, or wait at some wider place where it will be possible for the two to pass. On the desert itself trees are almost unknown. For a thousand miles from east to west and 450 to 600 from north to south, there are but a few dwarf specimens. Water is found only in wells or occasional small lakes.

The Altai (Gold) Mountains, however, are one of the most fertile regions of Asia, besides being possessed of valuable mineral resources. Timber is abundant in their forests of pine, larch, birch and spruce; and in summer this part of Mongolia is, surprisingly, a paradise of green grass and bright flowers.

The area of Mongolia is probably nearly 2,000,000 square miles, partly under Chinese control. The sparsely peopled land is hemmed in by forbidding mountain walls, those of Siberia on the north and Sin-Kiang on the south, while Western Mongolia is intersected by the Altai Mountains. The mountain walls rob the interior of the moisture of the winds, precipitating it upon their own white summits.

Naturally the Mongols and the Kalmucks and Chinese immigrants who share the grassy uplands are nomads and shepherds, for no part of the desert has ever been placed under irrigation, and practically nothing is raised in the entire million and a quarter square miles save herds of asses, sheep, camels, reindeer and horses. There is gold in Outer Mongolia but it has not been mined. Urga, the capital and only city, is a frontier

ELABORATELY ADORNED GUESTS ATTEND A WEDDING

The Mongols are highly skilled silversmiths. Headdresses similar to the ones above, made of silver and gem stones, with fringe and tassels, are the badges of married women in Inner Mongolia.

emporium for the caravan trade with China across the Gobi Desert, and long trains of camels, plod beneath bulging packs of wool, skins and hides, furs and horns. Since 1917 there has been motor freight service across the desert requiring but four to six days between Urga and Kalgan, China, a matter of five or six weeks' travel by camel.

To-day, it is estimated, a hundred thousand camels are employed, while the entire caravan trade employs over a million camels and three hundred thousand ox-carts. This mode of freighting is enormously more expensive than water or even rail transportation and railroads are a need that will be in part supplied by a new line started in 1930.

Explorations in Mongolia

Roy Chapman Andrews, leader of various Central Asiatic Expeditions of the American Museum of Natural History, has spent much of his time since 1920 in Mongolia. His party used camels for heavy transport only, at least after the first expedition. For reconnaissance work they had a train of automobiles. Their explorations and those of Henry Fairfield Osborn, who was there in 1922, have found this region to be a treasure-house of the life story of the earth. Their belief is that the earliest ancestors of man possibly originated in "Gobia"; indeed, that man existed on earth between two and three million years ago, and that Mongolia was at some time an earthly paradise, possessed of enough rainfall to permit great forests to flourish and with enough winter cold to stimulate man to use his wits to devise means of shelter at that season. Mr. Andrews found a fossil forest where logs, stumps and chips lay preserved as they had fallen, many thousands of years ago. It may have been on the leaves of these trees that some of the largest dinosaurs had browsed.

Skeleton of Pre-Mongol Man

The expedition traced the bed of an ancient stream in which thousands of animals had perished in the Eocene or Dawn Period of the Age of Mammals. They found deposits of fresh-water clam shells, and high dunes on the one-time fresh-water lake shores. They excavated the skeleton of a pre-Mongol man over six feet tall who must have lived in Mongolia long before the time of Tutankh-Amen. He must have been a huntsman, to judge from his implements, and in view of the winter cold and the relics of his activities, he must have dwelt on the sunny side of these dunes in skin shelter huts.

One may say Mongolia suffered four periods of mountain uplift, that which (by erosion) formed the floor of the present Gobi Desert, that which raised the mountains of Northern China, that which raised the Himalayas on the south and that which raised the Altai Mountains in the Central Asiatic plateau.

Colossal Prehistoric Beasts

The succession of life in what is now Mongolia, according to the discoveries of the Museum expeditions, began with a stupendous creature now called the Asiatosaurus, a beast with an incredibly long neck, a small head and fleshy, tapering tail. The next outstanding form was the Deinodont, whose forelegs were shortened to mere feeble appendages, as he had taken to walking on his powerful hind legs in a semi-upright position. There was a Velociraptor, a similar but far smaller form that developed speed in running and so was able to find food and in particular to escape the enemies that he was too small to fight. There was a succession of rhinoceros-like creatures that began as comparatively tiny forms but which became larger and larger till they reached their maximum in the Baluchitherium. Last to develop were the small horse-like Hipparian, the somewhat larger Camelus and the ostrich-like Struthiolithus.

The more colossal of these beasts were, according to Mr. Andrews' theory, unable to find enough food or else, when the climate changed till it became impossible for them to remain in Asia, they were unable to carry their great weight on the long migration to Europe and North America that then became necessary, and

A LONELY OUTPOST IN INNER MONGOLIA where horsemen and camel drivers find rest and refreshment before resuming their travels across the sparsely settled country. The Mongols, skilled and daring riders, breed large herds of ponies for their own use and for sale in China.

THE SOLDIERLY STEEPLES OF THE GREAT LAMASERY IN JEHOL

The Great Lamasery, residence of a high lama, the religious leader of many Mongol Buddhists, is one of several in the vicinity of Jehol. It is modeled after the monasteries of Tibet.

so they perished by the way. The bones of these prehistoric creatures are preserved in the sandstone, limestone, clay and slate deposits beneath the desert sands. And among them has been found a mammal that must have been as long as a skyscraper is tall. They have called it the Mongolian Colossus. They also excavated in Asia specimens of the forerunners of incredibly large Titanotheres such as dwelt in some past age on the continent of North America. This beast must have browsed on the tops of forest trees. It is, up to date, the world's biggest mammal and a new species, at that.

While it was the inhabitants of millions of years ago who most interested Mr. Andrews, he found some interesting present-day dwellers in Mongolia with which the remainder of this article will treat. He found, for instance, Mongol temple priests who forbade the killing, on certain spots they hold sacred, of the deadly reptiles that sometimes crawled for warmth into the beds of the explorers during the chill of night. But one should not leave the subject of exploration without a reference to the geologists Berkey, Granger and Morris who have discovered that Gobi is to-day very like the deserts of Utah, Wyoming and other portions of the American desert northward to or beyond the Canadian border.

As to the human dwellers on the Gobi Desert, the nomad Mongols, averse alike to agriculture and organized government, had always raided the more fertile provinces of China, and at the height of their power possessed the best weapons of the world in their day. Their rise forms one of the most romantic chapters of history. They were first consolidated in the twelfth century by the establishment of the so-called Empire of the Great Moguls, and

SPINNING YARN IN A WOOLEN MILL AT ULAN BATOR

The city is both the capital and the center of industry in the Mongolian People's Republic.
One of its most important manufactures is the production of wool cloth. Ulan Bator means
"red hero" and refers to a Mongolian revolutionary leader who helped to establish the communist-
led government in the 1920's. The country retains close ties with Russia.

GUARDING SHEEP ON THE PLAINS OF KAZAKHSTAN, EASTERN RUSSIA

Kazakhstan is one of the sixteen republics that make up the Soviet Union. It has a climate that is bitter cold in winter, hot and dry in summer. Nomadic tribes once wandered on this vast pasture land with their sheep and cattle, keeping a sharp lookout for hostile tribesmen. The snow-covered Altai Mountains are shown in the background.

STURDY PEASANT OF THE ALTAI MOUNTAIN COUNTRY

The Altai Mountain Range in the middle of Asia stretches over western Mongolia and Kazakhstan in eastern Russia. The inhabitants of the area, Kazakhs and Kalmucks, are Mongolians, and until recent years some of them were still nomads, living in tents through winter snow and summer heat. They are skilled at weaving wool into felt and rugs.

A STRANGE STRUCTURE with elaborately carved and colored decorations of shields, animals and Buddhist symbols. It is the tomb of an Inner Mongolian prince of the East Tsunnit Khan.

ULAN BATOR, the modern capital and cultural center of Outer Mongolia, was once the old city' of Urga. When the Living Buddha died in 1924, the present government was set up here.

ON THE OPEN RANGE of Mongolia are found small, wandering herds of the only truly wild horses in the world. Elsewhere, wild equines are descended from horses once tame.

A MONGOLIAN CATTLE-BREEDER ASTRIDE HIS SHAGGY PONY

The ponies that rove the Mongolian plains are sturdy animals that can race with surprising speed. It was such steeds that carried the dread hordes of Genghis Khan. The raising of live-stock is the chief activity of the nomadic tribes—mainly Khalkhas—of the Mongolian People's Republic. In addition to horses, cattle, sheep, goats and camels are bred.

312

AN EARLY MORNING SCENE IN A VILLAGE OF INNER MONGOLIA

The covering on these hovels is coarse wool felt. Much of the land in this part of northern China is more suitable for grazing than for farming, and that is one reason why these people have been nomads, tending sheep and cattle since bygone times. Many of them raise camels and horses. Inner Mongolia shares with the Mongolian People's Republic the vast desert area called the Gobi.

SOVFOTO

THE MONGOLIAN MINER is expected to produce his annual quota of ore, which is fixed by his government.

fourteenth century Tamerlane (Timur), who was the most amazing conqueror the world had ever seen, for one summer he sacked Moscow and the next he stood at the gates of Delhi.

When at the height of their fame the Mongols were Mohammedans. Had they so remained, they might even now retain a prominent place among the nations of the East. Their downfall, which followed soon after the rule of Tamerlane, was due largely to the introduction of Lamaism, a form of the Buddhist faith which forces all sons save one of every family to enter a monastery. Lamaism was introduced from Tibet toward the end of the thirteenth century and rapidly gained adherents.

When the Mongol Empire fell apart, a portion of it came under Russian, and a part under British domination, while Mongolia itself—as we know it today—became a Chinese province.

Treaties were established between China and Russia as early as 1689 and goods entered European Russia by way of the Siberian steppes. By a later treaty (1725) the frontier city of Miamchen in Mongolia became one of two gateways for the Chinese trade, while Siberian Kiakta became the other.

The Chinese revolution of 1911 led to the natural division between Outer and Inner Mongolia. Separated by the wasteland of the central Gobi, Outer Mongolia on the north became an independent nation protected by Russia. The southern portion, Inner Mongolia, was eventually absorbed into China as the provinces of Jehol, Chahar, Ningsia and Suiyuan.

In expelling the Chinese officials from Urga in 1911, the princes of Outer Mongolia set up the rule of the Living Buddha (Urga Hutukhtu). Disorder following

soon thereafter, their empire stretched from the Sea of Japan to the Adriatic Sea. It was then that the Mongols came near to dominating the Old World. Under Jenghiz Khan in the thirteenth century an army was organized which penetrated the Great Wall, ravaging and plundering the Chinese provinces; and Jenghiz Khan later conquered most of Inner Asia, sweeping westward as far as where Odessa now stands, capturing what later came to be known as Moscow, invading Poland and Hungary and capturing Budapest.

Later in that same century Kublai Khan dominated the scene of action, and in the

the Russian revolution gave the Chinese another opportunity, in 1919, to broaden their power in Mongolia, but they were driven out of Urga once more in 1921. This time the Soviet troops organized a government. Then when the Living Buddha died in 1924 and revolution ensued, the Mongolian People's Republic was proclaimed. The capital city of Urga was renamed Ulan Bator. The new nation is, of course, strongly influenced by the Soviet Union. Russian is widely spoken in addition to the native Mongol language, and most of the country's trade is conducted with its huge neighbors, Soviet Russia and Red China.

In the course of their war with China, the Japanese set up a puppet government for Inner Mongolia in 1937. Prince Teh Wang, a direct descendent of Genghis Khan, was named president of this Mongolian Federated Autonomous Government which collapsed in 1945 when Japan was defeated to end World War II. Following the liberation of China, the struggle for power between the Nationalist Government and the Communists extended into Mongolia, which became the Inner Mongolian Autonomous Region when the People's Republic of China was proclaimed in 1949. The boundaries of the region are uncertain. Parts of what was formerly Inner Mongolia are now included in North China.

The Mongol dress, a study for an artist, is like a long and ample dressing-gown of varied color, fastened at the waist by a sash. Beneath are shirts and coverings according to the period of the year. For headgear the rider of the plains has a rounded, turned-up hat, the centre rising to a cone-shaped crown of red, yellow or ochre. For the feet he has leather boots reaching to the knees, al-

ways two or three sizes too large, for as the winter advances successive layers of felt socks are added. Stuck in the girdle is the long pipe without which a Mongol never moves, flint and metal to supply the want of matches, and a riding-whip.

With the women the dress is somewhat similar, with their very long sleeves well padded at the shoulders. The hair and its careful dressing is the feminine strong point. It is plaited and threaded through a flat framework curved outward like the horns of a sheep, these terminating in a silver tip covered with beads and other ornaments. They wear earrings of turquoise and other precious stones easily

EASTFOTO

A MONUMENT to the wild horses of Mongolia and the men who break them stands in a park of Ulan Bator.

procurable in this land of minerals while strings of beadwork and necklaces adorn the neck and shoulders. The boots are, of course, far too large for their tiny feet, but then provision must be made for extremes of temperature, and, moreover, they are receptacles for the pipe and tobacco, riding-whip and the brick tea and even the drinking-cups.

Goats' Hair Felt Tents

The home of the Mongol is a large felt tent, a semi-circular construction on a lattice framework with an opening at the top for light and the escape of smoke. The felt covering the framework is made from goats' and camels' hair. The difficulties of house-moving are reduced to a minimum, for the family range themselves around the inside of the tent and, lifting the structure bodily, walk away.

The contents of a Mongol larder are easily supplied, for they consist of milk, mutton, cream and a form of cheese made from goats' milk. The Mongols drink copiously and often of fermented mare's milk, which they keep in leathern bottles in exactly the same way as the Jewish patriarchs or their nomadic forbears did centuries before them.

The conservative Mongols treasure the romantic theory of the bride being carried off from her father's tent. A wedding is a great event, especially when the belle of the encampment is the prize. Arrayed like a princess, the slant-eyed young woman with her flat yellow face and stiff black hair, mounted on a fiery charger, gives the lead in a breakneck race to the young men who aspire to her hand. To ward off undesirable lovers she uses her heavy whip with force and accuracy, and a well-directed slash across the eyes puts the unwelcome suitor out of action.

A Savage Custom

The customs of the Mongols are often remarkable. Instead of burying the dead in the usual way, the body is put out on a knoll in the vicinity of the camp, and there left to the tender mercies of dogs and birds of prey. Should the remains not be disposed of within a few days the deceased is considered to have led a wicked life, since even the dogs are shocked and refuse to touch the body. The sequel to this discovery is the chastisement of all the members of the deceased's family with the idea of saving them from a similar fate.

Among the Mongol lamas, or priests, who comprise forty per cent of the male population, the medical profession is favored, since it affords an opportunity of acquiring wealth and position. Their medical practice is, unfortunately, founded on superstition and witchcraft. There are quaint observances respecting doctor and patient. One is that the medico lives in the patient's tent until the sick person is either cured or dies. Payment of the fee incurred is a question of results.

The Mongols have strange ideas concerning the origin of complaints from which they may be suffering. They will declare with all sincerity that the deity is angry with them and has visited them with a fever, a cold or whatever it may be, because they have inadvertently cut a stick from the stunted trees surrounding a monastery, or because in digging a hole in the ground they have destroyed life in the shape of worms and insects.

Hard Lot of a Mongol Prisoner

The prison system and mode of punishment in Mongolia are similar in their cruelty to those of the Middle Ages in Europe. Here offenders are placed in an oblong box measuring about five feet by two and two feet in depth—very like a coffin. There, chained and manacled, they are left to pass weeks, sometimes months and not infrequently years, according to the seriousness of the crime. They can neither stand up nor lie down, but must perforce assume a semi-crouching posture, so that their limbs become shrunken and useless. They are taken out for a few minutes daily and food is passed to them through a small hole in the side of the box. For covering at night a totally inadequate sheepskin coat is provided when the thermometer drops to 20 degrees below zero.

A Peep at Peking (Peiping)

Once the Paris of the Orient

Under various names and dynasties, Peking served as the capital of China for a thousand years. After an interval of twenty-one years, from 1928 to 1949, when the city was called Peiping, it again became a capital, this time of the Chinese Communists. On its battlemented walls, its palaces and in its streets, invader and conqueror have left their mark. Much of its old-time splendor and romance disappeared after the revolution of 1911, though Peking remained the cultural center of China, with a number of universities. It was often called the Paris of the Orient. The city's most characteristic color is gray, from the dust that settles on streets and roofs when the frequent dust storms of winter bring yellow-gray loess from Inner Mongolia. In this chapter we tell you about some of the ancient glories of Peking.

OF all the cities in the world Peking is, perhaps, the most remarkable, with its huge walls, its historic past and its curious mixture of things old and new. It has a history that few cities can equal. It dates centuries before the Christian era, for a city existed here or near here about 1100 B.C. In the course of time this spot came to serve as a provincial capital; then, after other centuries of change, the city was named Chung Tu and was made the royal residence of the Tatars. From them it was taken by the Mongol leader, Jenghiz Khan, and rebuilt by his grandson, Kublai Khan.

The name Peking, which means Northern Capital, dates from the third Ming emperor, who moved the seat of government there from Nanking, the "Southern Capital," where the court of his two predecessors had been established. In the year 1928, some five hundred years later, the Nationalist Government shifted the seat of power back to Nanking, changing the name of Peking to Peiping. At the end of 1949, the Chinese Communists made it their capital, as Peking once more.

It may be said with truth that the history of China is contained within Peking, for here reigned the emperor, known as the Son of Heaven. His word was law, and he was believed by his subjects to rule over everything beneath the sun and to have no earthly rival. Therefore, as all states and countries throughout the universe were regarded merely as his vassals, their emissaries could be received at the Chinese court only as inferiors.

The present city is very much the same as the one created by the Ming emperor Yung Lo, who reigned from 1403 to 1425, but he built on the foundations laid by the great Kublai Khan. The Manchu emperor Ch'ien Lung did much to improve Peking during the latter half of the eighteenth century. The city is situated in a plain that extends southward for about seven houndred miles and eastward to the Gulf of Chihli, ninety-one miles distant. Forty miles to the northwest is the Great Wall. The soil of the plain is so light and so loose that we are vividly reminded, when the wind raises the dust, of the story that the city was carefully located on the driest spot in the province.

It is from the walls that we can get the best impression of the city. They are about twenty-four miles in circumference, approximately forty feet in height and enclose four cities. Since the fall of the monarchy in 1911 and the substitution of a republic, parts of these cities have fallen into dilapidation. Of the four, three form a nest: first comes the Tatar City, in the heart of which lies the Imperial City, enclosing in its turn the Forbidden City. Each of these is surrounded by its own walls. In the central enclosure—"forbidden" ground to all foreigners until the Boxer rebellion in 1900—are the palaces and exquisite pleasure gardens of the former emperors and their households. Here for a thousand years lived the royal masters of China, unseen of common mortals.

In the Imperial City were the residences of princes and high officials. The whole

THE OLD SPLENDOR of China is seen in the moated Imperial Palace, now the Historic Museum of Peking. Any foreigner, or "barbarian," was once unwelcome in this Forbidden City.

THE LOWLY FRANKFURTER SPEAKS EVERYBODY'S LANGUAGE

In far-off Peking, one of China's most ancient cities, a street merchant happily watches a tray of simmering frankfurters as he waits for passing customers. Peking was once the capital city of the mighty Kublai Khan's empire. The emperors of the Ming Dynasty finally made it their capital, too, and they gave it its present name, meaning "northern capital."

A WINDOWED GATE OF BRICK IN THE CITY OF MANY GATES

Walls surround both the Inner, or Manchu, City and the Outer, or Chinese, City on the south.
Those around the Inner City are fifty feet high, broken by huge gates and defense towers.

area surrounded by the mighty walls of the Tatar City is much older than the Chinese City, which joins it on the southern edge and in which are the shops and the homes of most of the population of Peking.

For a long time no one was allowed to walk on the walls, because it would have been an act of great disrespect on the part of the observer to look down upon the emperor and the palaces in which he lived. It was only after the war between the Chinese and the British and French, in 1860, that an order was given permitting foreigners to enjoy the privilege of walking along the top of these ramparts. This was a great advantage, since the roads are often ten inches deep in dust during the summer, and in winter are masses of mud and slush so deep that carts are often bogged up to the axles.

There are many wonderful buildings in the old city; but one of the most interesting is the Observatory standing on a site first used by Persian astronomers at the court of Kublai Khan. It is probably the oldest astronomical observatory in the world. We know that hundreds of years before astronomy came to be studied with care by Western men of science, the Chinese had evolved a system of their own, which led them to believe that the earth was the centre of the universe, and that the sun, moon and stars moved round it and gave it warmth.

In the seventeenth century Jesuit priests came to the city from Europe, and made known the wonders of Western astronomical science, which the Chinese endeavored to apply to their own system. They worked out eclipses and forecast them with great accuracy, but the results of science were hard to reconcile with the

EWING GALLOWAY

ONE OF THE WATCH TOWERS OF TATAR CITY

Outside the walls of the Imperial City is the imposing Drum Tower. It and the companion Bell Tower, in imperial days, sounded the two-hourly change of the watch. A water clock and sticks of incense kept the official time.

traditions of the race. For centuries the people had been taught that the only efficient method of counteracting the dreadful consequences of an eclipse was to assemble all the priests, nobles, and astrologers and to beat drums and other instruments to frighten the dragon that was trying to devour the sun.

Near the Observatory we shall find the ruins of the famous Examination Halls, where examinations for official posts were held for centuries. The higher positions in the civil and military service were filled only from among those who had passed the examinations held here, and this system was the leading feature of Chinese administration. The possession of a literary degree was not only a distinction but also a passport to an official appointment. The final examinations, which occurred every third year, were presided over by the emperor in person, and the candidates were all those who had successfully come through eliminating trials previously held at the various examining centers in the provinces.

The Examination Halls contained about 10,000 cells, each nine feet long by four feet wide, into which light and food were admitted through a narrow grating in the wall. Every candidate was thoroughly searched before entering to make sure that he had with him nothing that might assist him in the coming ordeal. He was then given a cell, locked in and left there during the time (perhaps a week or more) required for the examination.

The questions were so hard that many of the more highly strung candidates went mad under the strain. No one could hope to sit for this final examination until he had spent years in intense study, and if he should make the slightest mistake in composition or the fault of misplacing a character, he knew he would not pass and would not be allowed to present himself for examination again. Many of the questions set at the examinations were taken from the works of Confucius, who lived more than 2,400 years ago and whose teachings have greatly influenced the Chinese race during all these centuries.

The center of foreign life and activity

SURROUNDED BY THE TOOLS of his craft, a public letter-writer sits in the market place. His dress is traditional Chinese. His client wears a combination of Western and Chinese clothing.

HENLF—MONKMEYER

CLOUD TOWER AND GUARDIAN LIONS. It is told that once a year, in the time of the emperors, the spirits of past rulers climbed down the marble tower to give advice to the sovereign.

LIFELIKE LAUGHING BUDDHA

In the neglected Buddhist temples about Peking there are many works of art depicting Buddha as partaking of human emotions. Buddhism is now decaying in China.

in Peking was the Legation Quarter, an international colony where the foreign representatives lived. This quarter was below the Tatar Wall in the southern part of the Tatar city, on land allotted for the purpose after the Boxer troubles. Here are all forms of architecture, because each nation endeavored to set up a portion of its country, with its own particular style of architecture, within the walls of Peking. Each nation had a separate compound for its own buildings, and no foreigners, with the exception of missionaries, were supposed to live in any other part of the city. At one time the quarter's walls and gates were guarded.

The imperial splendors of the Forbidden City, with its artificial lakes and beautiful trees, though they have lost some of their luster, still suggest in their very names the mystic wonders of a fairy world. There are, for instance, the Jade Rainbow Bridge, the Palace of Earth's Repose, the Throne Hall of Purple Effulgence and the glorious Dragon Throne of the Son of Heaven. Foreign ministers were first given audience within these royal precincts after the uprising of 1900;

but to the public the gates remained closed until 1924, when the former emperor was at last sent forth from within the walls that had so long guarded an imperial residence. After that a permit would gain admittance for the humble as well as the notable visitor.

Since the Communists have made Peking the capital of mainland China once more, the city has undergone many changes. Partly because of all the government workers who have flocked there, the population has increased enormously, perhaps to as much as three million.

The new rulers are ensconced in the old Forbidden City, long ago so secret and mysterious. The Imperial Palace itself is now an art museum. Within the ancient Imperial City, which surrounds the Forbidden City, are the Hall of Po-

GUARDIAN OF A TAOIST TEMPLE

Such fierce-looking images as this are to be seen at the entrances of Taoist temples to frighten away evil spirits. Many observances have been borrowed from Buddhism.

SUMMER PALACE OF THE MANCHUS, SIX MILES WEST OF PEKING

A broad lake mirrors the sylvan Western Hills and the ruins of the magnificent palace sanctuary of Tz'u-hsi, Dowager Empress and one of the last of the Manchu rulers. Tz'u-hsi was the power behind the imperial throne for almost fifty years, acting as regent first for her son and then for her nephew. She died in 1908; the Empire fell after the revolution of 1911.

APARTMENT OF THE DOWAGER EMPRESS IN THE SUMMER PALACE

The exquisite woodwork of the entrance to the Empress's apartment in the Summer Palace, though losing the bright sheen of its lacquer to the wearing effects of time and weather, still suggests the splendor of the court in the old days. In the court the statues of two cranes and an elk remain, inanimate witnesses to the last days of a wily and strong-willed woman.

325

EASTFOTO

THE BALUSTRADES surrounding an imperial shrine in the Forbidden City were carved from
white marble.   An interesting column of animal figures marches across one of the tiers.

litical Diligence, now a warren of government offices, and the Hall of Magnanimity, which houses the National People's Congress.

Kublai Khan had broad avenues constructed, which cross the city in a checkerboard pattern. But off these main streets there still remains a maze of *hutungs*—narrow bypaths, hardly more than alleyways, deep in dust or mud depending on the season. For Peking is a dusty city; clouds of powdery yellow particles blow in from the plain to the west when the wind is in the right direction.

The *hutungs,* lined with the blind walls of inward-facing houses, have names that indicate something of their past: Ditch of a Thousand People, Dog's Neck Lane, Human Hair Lane, Chase the Thief Lane. Through these crowded streets push ped-

EASTFOTO

BLOSSOMING TREES herald the arrival of spring at the beautiful Summer Palace lake. The famous centuries-old pleasure garden of Chinese rulers has become a public park.

A GAS STATION STRIKES A MODERN NOTE ON ANCIENT STREETS

The tank was left over from the days before the Communists came to power and is still put to use. There are cars for officials and some trucks for the rapid transportation of goods.

dlers hawking their wares: caged crickets, herbs to promote long life, fried greaseballs, darting goldfish in bowls. Each street vendor makes a distinctive sound. Rattles, flutes, clashing metal, bells, drums, tuning forks and human vocal cords make an uproarious din. At his side, a tradesman is sure to have an abacus, with which to count. Street selling such as this is an ancient custom, which the Communists either cannot or have not tried very hard to stop.

"Squeeze," an Old Custom

Another old custom, however, does seem to have been eradicated pretty completely, and that is "squeeze." In the old days, servants would keep a small sum as a kind of commission on purchases made for their employers. The Chinese did not consider this dishonorable; their wages were wretchedly low in any case. Eventually there was hardly any transaction from which "squeeze" was not extracted all along the line. What we would call graft and bribery became commonplace, and "squeeze" always plagued the Nationalist Government. When the Reds came to power, the custom became a crime against *their* Government—the unforgivable sin in the communist calendar. So there can be little doubt that "squeeze" has been attacked ruthlessly.

Modern Cars and Pedicabs

Peking is one place in China where high-powered modern cars and trucks are not rarities. The passenger cars, of course, belong to important officials, and the trucks are the Government's. Side by side with them are primitive horse- or donkey-drawn carts. The old ricksha, which was pulled by a runner, has been replaced for some years by the pedicar, or pedicab, which is a tricycle, the cyclist sitting behind his passenger. Usually a pedicar is owned by its driver. As the vehicles are thus a hated remnant of private enterprise, the Government would like to abolish them. To ban them outright, however, would cause considerable unemployment. Instead, the supply of spare parts for the pedicars is gradually

being cut down. The most common means of transportation in the city is the bicycle.

Traffic in Peking is wild. To avoid pedestrians and the jumble of bicycles and other small vehicles on the sides, big cars race down the middle of the avenues, each driver trying to force the others to give way. Horns must be blown fifty yards before and after leaving a traffic-control policeman and when meeting another vehicle. The result is practically continuous hooting.

For a time after the Red regime came to power, colorful dress for adults was frowned on. Gay clothing was considered too frivolous and smacked of the old ways. Dark blue or gray dungarees became an almost universal uniform for both men and women. However, perhaps in an effort to counteract the dreary effect, parents dressed their children in the most gaudy hues they could find. Then, in 1955, a new order came down from on high. For women, the drab, baggy trousers and tunics could be replaced by dresses, and in bright colors, too. This meant a return of the *chi pao*, or *chang san* (long gown), but it must not be too close-fitting. Men were now permitted to wear Western-style suits.

Pekingese, Chief Dialect

More fundamental are the changes affecting language. China has long had a number of spoken dialects—Cantonese in the south, for example. Since the Communists have established their capital in the north, however, Pekingese is becoming the universal tongue. Long ago, it was the accepted form of Mandarin, the language used by the official classes of the Chinese Empire.

Reform of Written Chinese

At the same time, the Communists are reforming written Chinese, attempting to make it more simple. As you may know, it has no alphabet; every word has a character of its own. So, to write or read Chinese easily, thousands of characters must be memorized. These same characters are also used in written Japanese— in fact, Japan borrowed them. Though

PEKING'S HALL OF CLASSICS is an old imperial university, and the emperor used to sit in the main hall to preside over examinations or explain the old literature. In the grounds are tablets upon which have been carved extracts from the thirteen Chinese classics. They were set up by the famous Chinese Emperor Ch'ien in the eighteenth century.

TWO FEARSOME DRAGONS guard the entrance to one of the buildings within the Forbidden City. When China became a republic, some of the halls and palaces were used as government offices and barracks. Many of them, however, have remained empty since the day in the year 1924 when the young emperor received orders to leave the Imperial Palace.

331

the meanings may be somewhat different, educated Japanese could still read Chinese. The similar written language was one of the strongest cultural ties between China and Japan. Today, the Red program for simplification is changing written Chinese to such an extent that soon it will become completely unintelligible to the Japanese. In their zeal, the Communists do not seem to have considered how this will affect such matters as trade with Japan—which the Communists would like to increase.

Years ago Peking was a glamorous cosmopolitan city, but no more. Street cars stop running after 10 P.M. Night life has been abolished. Apparently with the idea of providing some form of relaxation, the Communists have introduced what are called Physical Interludes. There are three such interludes a day, broadcast over loudspeakers, which are almost everywhere. At such times, everyone is earnestly advised to do squats and knee bends then and there, to the count of the broadcaster. The Chinese once had a delicious sense of humor, so one can only wonder what their secret feelings must be about such an absurd spectacle.

Besides the old structures that the Government has taken over for its uses, new edifices have been built for administrative purposes. Hotels, hospitals, a theater and suburban houses have been erected as well. Going in the face of the old tradition in Chinese architecture that buildings should lie close in harmony with nature, skyscrapers are altering the skyline of the ancient city of Peking.

EASTFOTO

VIEW OF PEKING showing the grounds and buildings of the Imperial Palace. The spacious, rectangular plan of the city was adopted by Kublai Khan and kept by later rulers.

THE CHRYSANTHEMUM ISLANDS

Japan—from Kyushu to Hokkaido

The Japanese love gardens and flowers, and their national symbol is the shaggy bloom of autumn, the chrysanthemum. Its petals resemble the rays of the sun; and to the people their land is Nippon, or Nihon—"home of the sun." Of all the modern nations, none has had a longer and more continuous history than Japan. Like the pine tree, sentinel of its landscape, Japan has bent but not broken to ill winds—even the problems that followed defeat in 1945 and the loss of considerable territory. Endlessly adaptable, the people have been able to meet change without losing their identity or their traditions.

ONE should see Japan from the air, perhaps, for a broad first impression. There were ten of us and a jeep aboard the overloaded old Army transport, all equally battered and sun-dried from the arid brown hills of northern Luzon, in the Philippines, at the end of August. Okinawa's beaches were behind us. As we flew up the long miles of Japanese coastline from the tip of Honshu to Tokyo Bay, one thought came to mind at each look through the porthole in the fuselage: "How green this country is."

It is an impression that has endured. Japan is not the show window Tokyo, with its rather pitiful pretense of modern Westernism, or the steel mills of Yawata or the great trading cities of Osaka, Nagoya and Kobe. Western techniques, steel and trade gave Japan her power before World War II, of course. Yet they were only a quick graft made in less than ninety years, from 1853 to 1941, onto an older trunk, a graft that produced the Japan of twentieth-century history. The real country—the trunk—that lives on in the traditions of the Japanese and nourishes the newer shoots is the green land.

The essential Japan is still its lush rice paddies and its waving plantations of bamboo. It is the fishing ports scattered along sixteen thousand miles of rocky coastline where the Pacific sometimes recalls the Mediterranean of the Italian Riviera. It is the farm villages, which have scarcely changed since the artist Hiroshige sketched them around 1850 for his wood blocks of the Tokkaido post road. It is the snowcapped volcanoes—Fuji, Asama and the rest—and the forests of pine and birch that climb them to the timber line.

This is the land Jimmu Tenno saw with his companions when, according to traditional belief, he became the first emperor of Japan in 660 B.C. It matters little whether he was the grandson of the Sun Goddess, as the myth has it, or, as is more likely, was the leader of a band of Malay or Chinese adventurers from the south, who found an almost empty country and settled down to stay.

"The flowering land of the reed plains," he called it. Today, overpopulated and undersupplied with the necessities of life, it is still a nation deeply rooted in its own soil. Almost half the population work the flowering plains or fish the surrounding seas, and the proportion of farmers and fishermen has been increasing, not decreasing, since World War II.

The ancestry of the modern Japanese people is complex. Faces that look almost Malay and those that appear almost Mongol throng the cities of Japan. If the music of the samisen is reminiscent of the Tartars of the lower Volga, the sharp lines of Japanese fishing boats are those of the South Sea proa. Too, the houses are often built on stilts, another feature of the South Sea islands.

Nevertheless, the melting-pot period, in which all the various strains must have been blended, is long past. In recorded history, Japan has never known a successful foreign invasion and never admitted a broad stream of immigration. These factors and long periods of isolation from the

WRIGHT

MIYAJIMA THE SACRED on which no one is allowed to die, is a mountain-island that rises from the still waters of the Inland Sea. Forests of pine and maple and grassy glades cover the mountain slopes, and down the ravines fall cascades, with never-ceasing music. The island is dedicated to the three daughters of Susa-no-o, the Sea-King. There are three temples. One temple stands on the shore, another on the hill above and a third on the highest peak, eighteen hundred feet above the sea. The island is well worth the tourist's time.

FUJI THE PEERLESS (as Fuji-san-Fuji-yama, to give it its authentic title, is called) whether we see it from north, south, east or west, is never anything but lovely, at all seasons and at any hour of the day or night. It stands in the centre of a plain surrounded by less lofty mountains. To the south of it stretches the sea. To the north five lakes lie at its foot, from all of which wonderful aspects of the sacred mountain can be obtained. Thousands of pilgrims climb up to its crater in the summer when it is bare of snow world have made of the Japanese a completely distinct group of people. A Japanese could scarcely understand such phrases, for instance, as "of Anglo-Norman descent" or "French Canadian."

As the record shows, Japan is an adaptable nation, though this is far from meaning that the old is set aside. Perhaps nowhere else do the present and the past walk so closely together as in Japan. In the formative years of the late 1800's and early 1900's, Japan, as has been said else-

where, took the form of her army from Germany, her navy from Britain, her constitution from Prussia, and her economic system from the United States. But the *spirit* under which all this was done remained that of old Japan. Equally so today, past and present move side by side— the village with its ox carts also has its municipal motor truck.

Japanese politics and Japanese moving pictures alike have set forth the same theme in the years since the Allied occu-

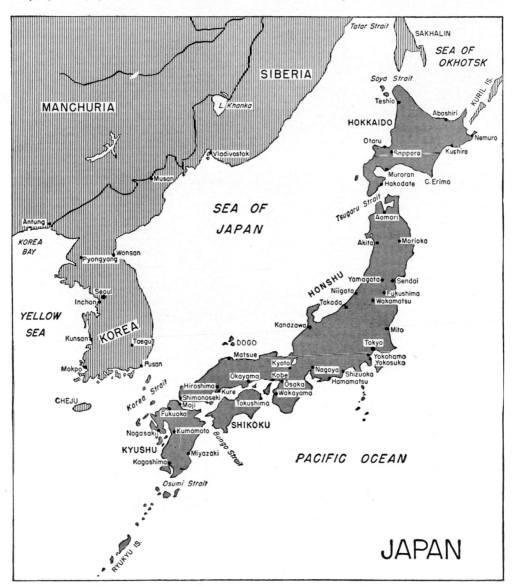

FISHERMEN REPAIRING TEARS in a purse seine. After a school of fish is encircled by the net, a rope at the bottom is drawn like a purse string, making a bag to hold the fish.

pation ended. Popular leaders press for "the reverse course." To them, the road to national salvation and happiness is the road back to the old days. Dramas about the samurai, the old warrior class, are what Tokyo audiences flock to see on the screen.

It would be fruitless to attempt here more than the barest outline of the long history of Japan before the "opening" by Commodore Perry in 1853. Generally, it is a story of clan feuds, full of battles, sieges, treachery and adventure. Probably the flavor of medieval Japan is best conveyed through the Kabuki drama, which became enormously popular again after the occupation ended. The stories it tells are of Benkei, the Japanese Robin Hood, of the forty-seven ronin (outlaw samurai) who avenged their master. In fact, the whole repertory of Kabuki consists of half-factual, half-legendary tales.

Some sketch of the country's history, however, is necessary for an understanding of modern Japan. The settlement of the sons of the Sun Goddess was no peaceful one. For more than a thousand years

the Japanese thrust northward against the Ainu, the white-skinned, hairy, probably Mongoloid people who apparently had taken the islands from its earlier, neolithic (New Stone Age) inhabitants.

Wars and Clan Rivalry

These were wars of extermination. Today only some fifteen thousand Ainu remain on the northernmost island of Hokkaido, wards of the Government on government reservations, like the Indians of North America. In this long conflict, the military tradition was firmly established in Japan. Power slipped from the hands of the imperial court in Kyoto (the capital from 794 to 1868). Clan leaders vied for the title of shogun—the Generalissimo for the Subjugation of the Eastern Barbarians —who exercised the real authority. In the Kamakura period of the twelfth century, Japan came under its first truly national administration, the Bakufu of the shogunate—literally the "camp office" of the general. It was what we would call a bureaucracy today. The frequently poor, always weak emperors remained the spir-

337

A DAIRY BARN on Hokkaido, the only island that has any room for grazing. Japan produces only a little milk, butter and beef. The hip-roofed building looks decidedly Western.

itual heads, the national symbols, of the country—the link with the divine descent of Nippon. At the same time, the clans, as one wrested control from another, wielded power in the imperial name—a situation that a much later military regime revived before it launched Japan on a disastrous course of conquest in the 1930's.

Physically, little remains to mark the ebb and flow of the Ainu campaigns and the rivalries of the Tairo, the Minamoto, the Fujiwara and the other great feudal families. However, the clansmen were the castle builders of Japan, the more so after Europe and China sent the secret of gunpowder and artillery to Japan.

The castles in Himeji, Osaka, Matsu-

yama and elsewhere still stand as examples of Eastern, medieval fortification against gunfire. Generally the clan castle was perched on a hilltop, all but impossible to approach. Huge walls of solid, handlaid, unmortared masonry topped with guard towers surrounded a central keep. The walls of the imperial palace in central Tokyo are the fortifications of old Yedo castle. Farther north on Honshu, at Sendai, are the ruins of the castle of the Date clan. The massive stonework stands as a reminder to the Japanese, if any reminder is needed, of the deeply imbedded system of clan and family loyalties, even to the death, that is an inheritance from their past.

Doubtless the feudal system worked

IN THE NORTHERN ISLANDS, winters can be severe, with heavy falls of snow. These bundled-up youngsters, like children everywhere, relish a frolic among the feathery drifts.

A TIME-WORN TORII of camphor wood, most beautifully designed, is the entrance gate to the ancient Shinto temple on Miyajima, the sacred island. There is a day in every year when a long procession of boats crosses the Inland Sea and passes through this gateway, bringing thousands of pilgrims to the water-lapped steps of the temple. This, built on piles, seems at high tide to be floating upon the water. When the tide is out we may stand on dry ground beneath the torii, and feed the graceful little deer that haunt the island.

342

STEPPING-STONES are a feature rarely omitted in the lovely temple gardens of Kyoto. The beauty-loving Japanese invariably have a stream or a lake in their gardens, for they realize that the picturesqueness of the drooping clusters of wistaria and upright spikes of purple or yellow iris, and of the gay kimonos of their wives and children, is doubled when seen mirrored in the quiet waters. They often build bridges most inconveniently arched simply for the sake of their reflection. In the water swim great red-gold carp and ancient tortoises.

343

SORTING SILK COCOONS. Each one is examined for quality and condition of the thread.

hardship on the village that grew in the shadow of the lord's tower. Up until the Industrial Revolution, which hit Japan in the late 1800's, the basis of the country's economy was rice. "A man of five koku" was an adequate description of a retainer entitled, for his service, to twenty-five bushels (five koku) of rice a year. The castle was the granary. The farmer in the paddy, then as now the backbone of the nation, had title to his rice only through his overlord. The warrior samurai, the lord's hired fighter, quite legally might whip off the peasant's head with a sword for disobedience.

The history of the clan era of Japan is also the story of hundreds of scattered peasant revolts, not only against the feudal lords but also against the wealthy priesthood. In general, the revolts were attempts somehow to ease one burdensome system after another of landholding and taxation. The idea of land reform, hailed as new under the occupation—as the Communists also hailed it in China—is centuries old in Japan.

The upshot today is the tiny family farm of one or two acres, cut into separate strips of paddy, woodlot and upland field. Only about one-third of Japan is arable. But where the land can be farmed this is the picture—divided and subdivided handkerchief-sized plots of green with few cattle and fewer machines. The paddies climb the hills in terraces where the slopes are steep. Water buckets go up, and reaped produce comes down on the backs of boys and girls as well as men and women. Habits of work begin early.

Feudal Policy—Isolation

The feudal system of the castle builders boasts two major achievements that altered the course of history in Japan, and perhaps in all Asia. The keen, tempered swords of the shogun's "house men" and of the clan leaders in the thirteenth century beat off the first and only serious attempt at an invasion of the islands. Except for that, the country might have become part of the Chinese Empire. Three centuries later, a shogun of the Tokugawa family cut Japan out of the world and, in the era of the discovery of the New World by Europeans, turned the islands into a kind of hermit kingdom. Contact with the balance of the human race was forbidden. Thus the final flowering of the feudalists of Japan was a command to time to stand still.

As for the first of these events, by the middle of the 1200's, the Mongol wave had swept the East. Kublai, the great khan of the Mongols, sat on the throne of China. The wave lapped at the shores of Japan. There were negotiations and threats. Some heads of Mongol envoys appeared on pikes in Kamakura, headquarters of the shogunate. In November 1274, a fleet of 450 ships sailed from Korea, the part of Kublai's empire nearest to Japan, to subdue the "King" of Japan, as diplomatic correspondence of the day called him.

It appears that the Mongol expedition-

A DISPLAY OF DOLLS, in a Kobe shop, entrances a toddler. Those on the lower shelf look like the traditional wrestlers. One of Japan's customs is a yearly Festival of Dolls.

WESTON

THIS SERVANT OF BUDDHA will sit thus, in his brocaded robes, for hours seeking self-mastery through introspection. He is one of the Zen sect, which comes nearer to the Buddhism of India than to any of the other sects in Japan. Its priests have always been learned men. The faith was introduced from China about the twelfth century.

CEREMONIOUS POLITENESS is one of the attributes of the Japanese of all classes. Reverence to parents and to the aged is, indeed, taught them by their religion. Here we see a hostess in her house of paper and wood and cool matting greeting her guest. It is considered correct for both to kneel on the floor and bow several times to the ground.

THE HARBOR OF OSAKA, on the southwestern coast of Honshu. The busy port at the mouth of the Yodo River and the head of Osaka Bay has miles of modern piers and breakwaters.

ary force was well equipped. Some Japanese authorities list 15,000 Mongolian spearmen and bowmen, 15,000 Korean seamen and auxiliaries, and "secret weapons," unknown to the Japanese, which flung heavy missiles at a distance. The force landed near Hakata, or Fukuoka, in northern Kyushu, today a quiet little country town, best known for its manufacture of graceful, delicately painted earthenware dolls and figurines.

The planning of the invasion was less thorough, for it evidently failed to take into account the fact that November is a month of typhoons in the Japan Sea. The Mongols pushed ashore, with their short,

powerful bows behind a wall of shields. Only local levies—Kyushu tribesmen—faced them, for the Mongol attempt had been well concealed. Not until Tsushima Island, which is in Korea Strait, had fallen, apparently, did the Shogun know that the force was on its way. In one day's fighting the tribesmen took heavy losses and fell back at dusk behind their earthworks to await the next assault.

It never came. At night a typhoon blew up from the south, as typhoons do today, in gusts at times of more than one hundred miles an hour. The Mongol fleet was scattered and the landed stores abandoned. When the survivors straggled back to Pusan in Korea, Kublai reckoned his casualties at 13,500, almost half the force. For the first time the Japanese talked of the "divine wind"—the *kamikaze* that fought for the descendants of the sun and seven centuries later gave its name to the suicide squadrons of Japanese pilots in the Pacific war.

The Mongols tried again in 1281. But this time the shogunate was better prepared and the Khan's wave was ebbing. Under the orders of the Shogun Takimune, the Kyushu landlords built a "great wall"—possibly a stone-faced earthwork —across the landing place at Hakozaki Bay. Fast Japanese ships, easy to maneuver, harassed the clumsier Korean transports. Once landed, the Mongols made little progress against the Japanese troops. Then for a second time a storm scattered the fleet. Again, historians believe, the invasion losses reached 50 per cent. Never since has Japan been invaded. (The Empire was not invaded but surrendered in August 1945.) On the shore of Hakozaki Bay were planted the seeds of a belief in the divinely fostered invincibility of Japan—a legend that may not yet be dead.

If military prowess was the first theme of feudalism in Japan, the second, as we have said, was isolationism. The military aspect froze society into rigid classes; and withdrawal from the world brought about a conservatism, a clinging to the past, unparalleled in history. When the Tokugawa clan emerged as rulers after the battle of Sekigahara, which put an end to the tribal wars in 1600, it harbored one abiding policy: a determination to retain unchanged, forever if possible, the social conditions, the economic and political system over which it then presided.

Living Habits Are Regulated

The scope of the policy's application can scarcely be exaggerated. Japanese navigators who, in earlier days, had cruised from Ceylon to Acapulco (Mexico), were prohibited from foreign voyaging. No ship could be constructed of more than coastwise capacity. Laws laid down what might be worn, drunk and

eaten by each of the social classes, regulating even personal habits.

The peasant, said the code, should rise early, refrain from the consumption of rice

JUDO, OR JUJITSU, makes use of the opponent's strength and weight to disable him.

A NEW HIROSHIMA has arisen from the rubble of destruction left by the atomic bomb. After the war, rebuilding went on rapidly; and today Hiroshima is again a thriving community.

in favor of inferior grains. If his giddy wife should show a tendency to waste her time visiting temples or roaming in the hills, he was to divorce her promptly.

Foreign commerce, in both goods and ideas, dwindled to a trickle, filtered through the Dutch trading station at Nagasaki—in effect a quarantine. This post, on an island, was the only foreign one permitted and it was closely restricted. Only one Dutch ship could anchor there in a year. Christians were persecuted, less because of a hatred for Christianity than because the religion was a "foreign import." It might bring other foreignisms in its train to overset the established regime.

The regime did endure for 250 years.

While the Western world passed through the last stages of the Renaissance, the social revolutions of the American colonies and of France and the Industrial Revolution, Japan remained a state frozen by law and custom into its feudal forms. It was remote and aloof from the streams of all civilizations except its particular inbred culture.

There are few visible reminders of the Tokugawa era. The Dutch island off Nagasaki is part of the mainland now, connected with the city by a streetcar line. However, at Nikko, in central Honshu, the tombs of the early Tokugawa shoguns are still a national landmark. Elaborately decorated, tricked out in red and gold, they are planned to impress more than to

THE WORLD CHURCH OF PEACE in Hiroshima was built on the site of another church,
destroyed by the A-bomb. Contributions for the new structure came from all over the world

appeal. Besides, they are more representative of the Chinese taste of the powerful, new-rich Tokugawa dynasty than of native Japanese architecture, which is simple and austere. The tombs illustrate neatly the nature of the shogun's claim to something close to divinity for the supreme lord and the paramount order.

Probably a more lasting and more significant inheritance is the remarkable sameness of places and things in Japan. Travelers notice few local differences. Barring some minor variations in food delicacies (the best tea is found in Shizuoka, central Honshu, and the best raw fish on the island of Shikoku), a few quirks of dialect and an occasional special tradition, the village in Kyushu and the village in north Honshu are identical. Uniformity of custom, uniformity of behavior, even uniformity of thought was the rule.

If the clan wars and the feudal system are the sources of Japanese thought in military, social and economic fields, Buddhism is the spiritual parent of Japanese art and culture. For hundreds of years the Buddhist priesthood was the repository of learning and the closest link with China, the fountainhead of everything de-

BLACK STAR

A BUSY DOCK in Yokohama Harbor. An ocean-going freighter, anchored in deeper water, looks down on a jumble of fishing craft. Many families make their homes on these boats.

A HANDSOME LENGTH OF BROCADE emerges from a loom in a silk-weaving factory near Kawacouchi. Though there is an electric-light bulb, the loom is powered by a water wheel.

HILL

KYOTO is a city of a thousand temples. One of the best known is the Yasaka Pagoda. If we climb the ladderlike stairs and reach the balcony around the top, the entire city will lie maplike at our feet. In midsummer the sun-drenched streets will be roofed over with matting and in the all but dried river bed temporary houses will be erected.

HILL

THERE IS A GARDEN to every Japanese house. It may be but a few feet square, or it may cover an acre or two, but it is always artistic and well cared for. Where people have means, there is almost sure to be a stream with lotus flowers and a bridge or steppingstones, stone lanterns and fir trees and a miniature Fuji-yama with a shrine upon it.

sirable. The written Japanese language itself was borrowed from China as well as the foibles and luxuries of the court.

On occasion early Japanese emperors emptied their treasuries to build great Buddhist temples, such as those at Nara and Kyoto. The Japanese found no conflict between Buddhist beliefs and the old cult of ancestor worship, or Shinto. The Grand Shrines of Ise, in southern Honshu, were really family places of worship of the imperial ancestors. Yet these shrines sometimes borrowed for their upkeep, when the emperor's treasury was empty, from the richer Buddhist establishments.

Buddhism arrived in Japan some time about A.D. 550 when a king of Korea, it is related, sent an image of Buddha and some of the sutras (Buddhist scriptures) with the recommendation "that this religion be adopted." It blossomed in Nara, laid out as the new capital of Japan in 710. Today the remnants of past grandeur overshadow the little town, an hour's ride from Osaka. The Emperor Shomu's Great Buddha Hall, often burned down and often reconstructed along the ancient lines, though on a smaller scale, still is the largest wooden building in the world.

The Great Buddha itself stands 53 feet high and contains more than 550 tons of metal—copper, tin and lead—plus the remnants of the original gilding from gold mined in Japan for the first time as the figure was being cast. The first pagodas in Japan were built on the grounds of the temples that surround the Great Buddha Hall. As Nara was being built, the Emperor Shomu ordered the construction of a Buddhist temple in each of the old provinces. Today such local shrines are the most familiar of all buildings in Japan. Some 45,000,000 Japanese are registered members of more than 150 Buddhist sects.

"Japanized" Buddhism

The extent of the impact of Buddhism on the medieval Japanese mind still is a matter of debate. Japanese writers themselves have contended that Buddhism, over the centuries, was increasingly "Japanized." Earlier teachings were reinterpreted and purely Japanese sects were established. In Zen Buddhism, for instance, with its self-centered ideas of discipline and personal insight, the samurai found a creed for the warrior and a justification of code and caste that are a long way from the gentle teachings of the Gautama (Buddha) himself.

Nevertheless, for centuries, Japanese art, sculpture, architecture and literature were in effect a Buddhist outgrowth. Buddhism must take a place with the feudal system, isolationism and a deep-seated belief in the divinity or semidivinity of the race as one of the keystones of Japanese thinking, even today.

The whole system of ancient Japan collapsed at last, of course, under the guns of Commodore Matthew Calbraith Perry's Black Ships in 1853. Indeed, by then, the system already carried within itself the germs of its own destruction. These were the rise of the mercantile classes, the change in unit of value from rice to money, and the increasing inability of the sho-

JAPAN TRAVEL BUREAU

DAIBUTSU (Great Image of Buddha) in Kamakura, a forty-two-foot bronze.

A GION FESTIVAL held in Tokyo brings out wide hats, pleated skirts and fans—the last said to symbolize prosperity. The Gion religion is an offshoot of the Shinto cult.

HELPER AND PET, a cormorant catches fish for its master by diving under water. A string keeps it from flying away, and a ring around its neck prevents it from swallowing the catch.

362

ARMY BARRACKS at Sukiran on Okinawa, one of the Ryukyu Islands held by the United States. The island has a native government but has also become an American military base.

gunate to find new answers to the old problems of taxation, land tenancy and national poverty.

The story of Japan's transformation from an isolated feudal community to a great power is well known. It speaks well for the vigor of the nation that the process was accomplished in less than a hundred years. What is more, the country bred itself a generation of statesmen, under the young, progressive Emperor Meiji (reigned 1867–1912), that, for ability, has been matched neither before nor since.

The coming to the throne of Meiji is called the Restoration. The shogunate was abolished, and Meiji became the supreme civil ruler. In 1889, he handed down a constitution as a gift to his subjects. It established the Diet, or Parliament, of two houses. Feudalism, or at least its outward forms, was done away with. Now was launched the tremendous drive to catch up with the Western world in the industrial and military fields.

When Meiji died, authority passed into the hands of the Genro, or Elder Statesmen. After World War I, however, real control was taken over by the military class and their allies, the big industrialists. It was this group who embarked on a campaign of conquest, beginning with the seizure of Manchuria in 1931.

After 1945, the Japanese Empire was reduced to about half its prewar size—to practically the same area it had in 1853. It acquired a new constitution, which included such Western ideas as freedom of speech, press, assembly and person, and also placed most of the power in the lower house of the Diet. At first the use of armed force was renounced completely. However, by the peace treaty of 1951, Japan was expected to contribute to the defense of the Pacific. Also, by an agreement signed at the same time as the treaty, the United States received authority to keep troops in the islands for an indefinite period.

Today the cities of Japan have a half-Western look, and there are many other evidences of Western influence. The democratic philosophy imported by the occupation also appears to have been accepted. Yet how deep the Westernization goes no Westerner can say.

Grave handicaps burdened Japan after the occupation and the war in Korea ended. Until then, the country's economy had received a large measure of support from first United States aid and then from the expenditures for war supplies. These sources of income were much reduced after 1953, and the bamboo curtain also shut out Japan's greatest prewar market, China. Yet Japan must trade to live.

It is the natural supplier of manufactures to Asia. At the same time the islands command the western Pacific and must be held for the West against the communist threat on the mainland of Asia. Thus the Japanese problem is a world problem. Late in 1954 there was no doubt that Japan would have to receive more help from the noncommunist world. Such help could take the form of direct financial aid or trade treaties giving Japan a chance to sell more goods to the West.

The Japanese people would do their share. They are practical, capable and hard-working. With even moderate prosperity and some hope for the future, there is little doubt that Japan will remain on the side of the West.

By LINDESAY PARROTT

JAPAN: FACTS AND FIGURES

THE COUNTRY

Japan, as constituted after defeat in World War II, consists of four islands, Honshu (mainland), Hokkaido, Kyushu and Shikoku and some 500 islets, with a total area of 142,427 square miles and a population of 87,000,000. The islands lie in the Pacific Ocean off the coast of east Asia, commanding the approaches by water to Vladivostok (Soviet Union), the Yellow Sea, Korea and north and central China.

GOVERNMENT

Under the constitution of 1946 the emperor has no executive power. This is exercised by a prime minister and a cabinet, chosen from the Diet, or Parliament. The Diet makes the laws. It consists of a House of Representatives and a House of Councillors. Members of both bodies are elected. On April 28, 1952, the peace treaty, signed at San Francisco, California, in September 1951, became effective. The treaty brought Allied occupation to an end and made Japan once more a sovereign nation.

COMMERCE AND INDUSTRIES

After World War II, the large estates were split up into small farms that today cover most of the arable land of Japan. The average farm is barely two acres. In 1949, the Government bought more than five million acres from landlords and resold it to more than four million tenant farmers. Rice, Japan's major crop, occupies more than half of the cultivated land of the country. Wheat, barley, rye, tobacco, tea, beans, peaches, pears, apples, grapes, persimmons and mandarins are also produced. Mulberry trees are widely grown, and the annual output of silk is about three-fourths of the world's total. The country possesses small quantities of minerals including gold, silver,

copper, lead, zinc, iron, chromite, coal, sulfur, salt and petroleum.

After agriculture and the manufacture of textiles, the principal industries include the making of paper, pottery, vegetable oil, leather and matting.

RELIGION AND EDUCATION

Japan has no state religion, and all faiths are tolerated. The principal forms of religion are Buddhism and Shinto. There are about 45,000,-000 Buddhists, 11,000,000 Shintoists and 350,-000 Christians, the majority Protestants. The Roman Catholics have an archbishop and three suffragan bishops.

Elementary education is compulsory up to the age of 15, and free. Six years are spent in primary school and three in the middle school. Attendance for three additional years in high school is optional. Japan has 6 universities: Tokyo, Kyoto, Tohoky at Sendai, Osaka, Nagoya, Kyushu in Fukuoka, and Hokkaido in Sapporo. It also has 38 other schools of university rank, of which 36 are co-educational. English is the language of commerce and a required study in the high schools. Military training in the schools was abolished in 1945 after Japan surrendered to the Allies.

CHIEF TOWNS

In normal times there is considerable foreign trade. Most important ports are Yokohama, Kobe and Osaka on the Pacific coast of the main island, and Nigata on the coast of the Japan Sea.

Populations: Tokyo, 6,277,500; Osaka, 1,956,-100; Kyoto, 1,101,900; Nagoya, 1,030,600; Yokohama, 951,200; Kobe, 765,400; Fukuoka, 392,-600; Sendai, 341,700; Kawasaki, 319,200; Sapporo, 318,900.

TOKYO, THE PHOENIX CITY

Capital of a Beauty-loving People

Like that fabulous bird, the phoenix, which, every five hundred years, burned itself on a pyre of aromatic gums, and arose from the ashes in new vigor and beauty, Tokyo has more than once been destroyed and then has arisen with renewed life. Ruin from the skies descended upon it in the war; but it is once again showing its indestructability. One thing war has not touched—the glimmering beauty of Tokyo's mountain, Fujiyama. The city unfolds like a gorgeous fan to welcome the ships and to allow visitors their first glimpse of "No Two Such"—the name of Fuji as written in Chinese characters. As a native poet wrote of the lovely mountain: "One glance, and you would give your province; another and you would barter your kingdom."

THE city now known as Tokyo was founded in 1456, but under another name. For four hundred years it was called Yedo. In 1590 it became the capital of the Shoguns, powerful feudal lords who really ruled Japan, while the emperors lived at Kioto. It was not until 1868, when the Shogunate was overthrown and the modern Japanese empire was established, that the city's name was changed to Tokyo and it became the sole capital. In 1940 Tokyo was the third largest city in the world, surpassed only by New York and London. It was, and is still, an important industrial city, and through its seaport, Yokohama, at the entrance to Tokyo Bay, it has access to all the seas of the world. The city has long been a curious mixture of the modern West and the ancient East. There are broad, paved streets, gas and electric light, a modern water supply system, streetcars and even a subway; but there are many more narrow, winding streets, large areas of paper-and-matchwood houses, and other reminders of the days of the Shoguns.

Every city set up by the hand of man possesses its distinctive smell. An ungrudging and enthusiastic liberality characterizes the smells on some of the canals in Tokyo. Were Tokyo more compact, and could one get a bird's-eye view of it, it would bear some likeness to Venice or Bangkok, for canals cross and recross it. Only the fine sea breeze, the "saving grace of the city," minimizes to some extent the mingled odors of dampness, soap, fish,

pickled radish and other less pleasant substances which assail the noses of natives and visitors.

Then there are the crowds, and with them comes the noise that only an oriental city could produce; the sound of thousands of wooden clogs, or *getas*, beating their tattoo on the pavements. It somehow suggests perpetual motion, like a river rattling the pebbles along its banks—a noise not unmusical, but unforgettable. It becomes the background for the piles of glowing silks, the superb materials spread out for the great ladies of the town; it goes with the endless displays of pottery; it sounds natural in the flower shops, because you remember that you have heard the same sound on the paved walks of the public parks and gardens.

The *riki* is still the dominant vehicle in native Tokyo, for manpower is even today cheaper than gasoline. In the roadways the "hai-hai" of the jinrikisha bearers accents the honk of motor horns; the patter of the bearers' padded stockings beats a rhythm to the hum of automobile engines. The rikisha man removes his pudding hat and mops his head with his towel as he lowers the shafts of the rikisha for a moment's rest. Then he is off and away again.

There are also bicycles — apparently thousands of them, whizzing in all directions, their riders often carrying bundles and even three-tiered trays of bowls of soup. There seems to be nothing that can not be carried by a Tokyo cyclist, and

PHILIP GENDREAU

WINDOW SHOPPING ON THE GINZA

The Ginza is the Fifth Avenue, or Rue de la Paix, of Tokyo. Though Japanese are fast adopting Western dress, the picturesque kimono is by no means out of fashion.

these men ride as if they were part of their machines.

The Ginza is Tokyo's great shopping center and promenade. Everyone goes there, to see and be seen, or perhaps to spend a pleasant hour loitering before the windows of the tempting shops. The foreign visitor goes to the Ginza again and again, to buy some fruit for breakfast, or a fine cultured pearl, or yards of silken damask or a bit of old carved ivory. Whatever his purchases, the traveler will bring away also a store of kaleidoscopic impressions. There is no better way to observe a cross section of Tokyo life than to stroll along the Ginza.

Tokyo after Dark

To all but the initiated, Tokyo after dark is a big, dusky village, and to some visitors it is even a dull one. To hobnob for hours with a few boon companions over a tiny pot of weak, sugarless tea, while puffing a tobacco pipe with an incredibly tiny bowl seems to fill the men of Tokyo with boundless content.

They have also Napoleon's ability to sleep anywhere, in any position and at any time. Before World War II young men loved to clatter along the streets in their wooden clogs, singing, utterly unconcerned with the rest of the multitude. Now the joyous singing is gone. The long years of war and more than six years of occupation have turned the thoughts of all—but especially of the young—to stern realities. There is wonder about what the future will hold for the individual. There is dissention, even among close friends, on such subjects as politics and foreign relations. In more respects than one Japan is standing at the crossroads of her national life; and nowhere is this fact more apparent than in Tokyo.

The city is full of cafés, always crowded. In former days prosperous men gave geisha parties, rather solemn affairs at which geisha—professional entertainers—danced their ceremonial dances. *Sukiyaki,* the main dish, was customarily prepared by the host, who, with his guests, sat on the floor. Warmed *sake,* a wine made from rice and served in thimble-sized cups, punctuated the mouthfuls of *suki-yaki*.

Today there is very little of this sort of entertainment. The cafés are crowded, their principal patrons being *mobos* and *mogas*. The Japanese love to abbreviate. *Mobo* is the abbreviation for modern boy and *moga* for modern girl. These Westernized young people, with their modern clothes and freedom of manner, are an interesting proof of the influence that Europe and America—especially America—have had upon the younger generation in Japan.

The loveliest and most characteristic thing about Tokyo is its gardens, both public and private. Somehow the smoke and noise and odor of the city do not penetrate the gardens, which look unchanged by time. The beauty-loving people of Tokyo are seized with a species of flower-madness. The blossoming of the plum trees, harbingers of spring, begin the flower season, and man, woman and child hasten to the gardens to drink in this loveliness. Then there are the iris, and of

PIX

AN ATTRACTIVE CAR of the Tokyo subway. It is on a branch line that was opened in 1954.

AMERICAN PRESIDENT LINES

THE MARUNOUCHI DISTRICT, the commercial heart of Japan's capital city. The imposing buildings—banks, offices—face the moat that surrounds the Imperial Palace grounds.

PIX

APPLES, POTATOES, WHITE RADISHES—the choice of produce is rather limited but the housewife shops with great care. Little stores like this are everywhere in Tokyo.

A DINNER PARTY IN JAPANESE STYLE

These ladies of Japan show us how dinner is served in their homes. Dressed in Kimonos, they sit or kneel on the floor before low tables. Some of the dinner service has a modern and Western appearance, but the rice bowls and chopsticks are in keeping with the Japanese setting. Sukiaki is a favorite dish, a mixture of meat and vegetables. Tea, of course, is the beverage. In all likelihood, a fish course is also served.

course, the wistaria and cherry blossoms.

The real glory of a cherry in blossom is when you see it like a white mist—there is only a suggestion of pink. Behind the cherry trees, giving a somber background that sets off their shining delicacy, are splendid pines and yews, so dark a green as to be almost black. The Japanese have a saying: "As the warrior is king of men, so the cherry tree is first among flowers."

To the blossoming cherry branch add a flower of verse! One may often see a young girl, her black hair brushed until it shines like a wet coal, attaching a poem to a tree so that those who come to enjoy the flowers may also read her work.

Although, as we have said, much of Tokyo was destroyed in the war, one may still catch glimpses here and there of cool gardens. There are bits of lovely moss-grown walls with wistaria-veiled arbors; garden pools, lush with iris standing waist-high, or

crowded with lotus cups. In the more open spaces are seen the masses of the flame-like azaleas, and always the curious, crooked dwarf pines. A sense of peace and tranquility steals over the sojourner

THE SHOE STORE IS OPEN

A shoe vendor spreads his wares on a clean cloth, and he is ready for business. As we see, the stock here is limited to sandals, and does not show us other forms of Japanese footwear, such as wooden clogs.

369

PIX

TWO THEATERS and a movie auditorium are housed in the Nichigeki Theater Building.

in a perfect garden, even one that has suffered from wartime neglect. The gardens are the last stronghold of the feudal aristocracy—also, perhaps, the last strongholds of the ancient beauty of the capital.

If one wanders about Tokyo one may come suddenly on winding, narrow passageways that lead in and out among quiet houses, past gateways through which can be glimpsed lovely miniature gardens, and tea houses. At night one may be kept awake, listening to the deep, thrilling tones of the drums spreading their triple warning of fire throughout the city. Fire has always been a hazard in the wood-and-paper cities of Japan. The winds of Tokyo, described as "propitious for kite flying," are also propitious for spreading fire. At one time in the city's history, fire was called the Flower of Yedo. In the old days fires occurred almost every day in winter and spring, when the winds are high. In

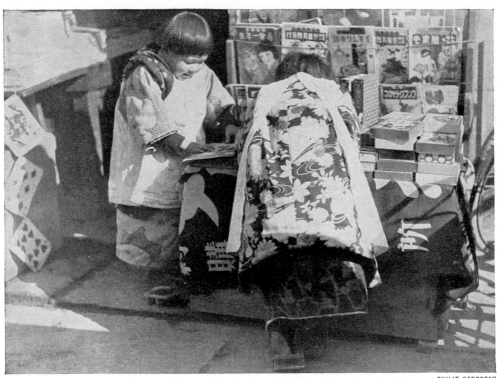

PHILIP GENDREAU

A BOOK AND GAMES STALL enthralls two little girls. They are dressed for cold weather in padded clothing. White aprons help to keep the youngsters' gay kimonos clean.

GEISHA GIRLS DANCE IN FOREST SCENE

Philip Gendreau, N.Y.

The name geisha means "a person of pleasing accomplishments," and was given to the professional dancing and singing girls of Japan. The training of the true Geisha or singing girl began often as early as her seventh year, and her period of service was only terminated by marriage. It is possible that the many changes in postwar Japan may bring an end to this ancient Japanese custom.

1601 and again in 1657 flames swept over Yedo, reducing the entire city to ashes.

As recently as one hundred years ago the arsonists, if caught, were crucified; but even this draconic measure of fire prevention does not seem to have done much good. Today the people are learning elementary precautions against fire; but until the buildings are constructed of materials less flimsy than paper and thin wood, danger will be ever present.

In 1923 more than half Tokyo's buildings were destroyed by the earthquakes and the fire that followed. More than 150,000 people perished, and, partly because of the country's poverty, it took nearly seven years for the city to be completely restored. In 1942 General Doolittle's bombers heralded a new kind of destruction, in the first dramatic air raid over Japan in April of that year. The city was bombed many times in the later years of the war and roughly three-fourths of its area was in ruins at the time of the surrender. The biggest burned-out patch straddles the important Ueno railroad station. The imperial palace, hidden within walled acres of gardens and lakes, groves and pavilions, was so damaged as to be uninhabitable, and when war ended it was found that the emperor had been living for some time in a building designed for an air raid shelter. Beautiful as it was, this palace will be missed less than almost any of the other Tokyo targets, for scarcely any of Tokyo's millions of inhabitants had ever seen beyond the outer walls of the imperial domain.

Perhaps the most significant change that the war has brought to Tokyo is the revolutionary change in the relationship between the people and their emperor. He is no longer a sacred symbol kept aloof from the people who were governed in his name. Instead, as the link between the democratic conquerors and the Japanese people, he is quite likely to be seen driving or walking about the streets of the city just as the American president and the British kings have been doing for centuries. It is difficult for the western mind to realize what an important move in the direction of democracy this has been. It remains to be seen how the people of Japan will react to this opportunity for self-rule. The regime inaugurated under General MacArthur may find a solid, permanent foundation among the Japanese masses.

The re-birth of Tokyo is both actual and inevitable. It is a matter of concern to many nations, especially to those whose lands border on the Pacific Ocean.

JAPANESE SURRENDER ON BOARD U.S.S. MISSOURI

Four years of violent warfare, which began at Pearl Harbor, came to a decisive end in this ceremony on board the mighty battleship U.S.S. Missouri, at anchor in Tokyo Bay. The warship served as a stage for the surrender, in which, for the first time in her more than 2000-year history, the Land of the Rising Sun capitulated to an enemy, and lost her chance for world conquest.

THE LAND OF THE MORNING CALM

Korea, One of the World's Oldest Kingdoms

The name the Japanese gave Korea long ago—Land of the Morning Calm—has always had a rather bitter irony. Strife has devastated the peninsula many times in the past, and never more so than in the middle of the twentieth century. Though the conflict of the early 1950's was not labeled "war" officially, it brought Korea to world attention as never before. Communist aggression was stopped but the unhappy little country was left divided as it had been since the end of World War II. Regarding conditions in communist North Korea, the outside world knows very little. South Korea, with funds from abroad, has been slowly pulling itself out of the chaos left by war. The peninsula remains, however, a subject of controversy between the communist world and the West.

KOREA (Chosen) is a peninsular tableland, about as large as the mainland of Japan, that extends southward from Manchuria, between the two naval bases of Vladivostok and Port Arthur. Viewed from the deck of a steamer cruising up the east coast, it is seen that an unbroken chain of rocky mountains runs down this side. Islands dot the shores. Some of these islands rise several hundred feet above the blue of the sea and are lush with vegetation. The largest island, Quelpart, south of Korea, has an old volcanic crater rising to a height of over six thousand feet. Traces of its former activity can be seen in the quantities of pumice stone which are found all over the island.

Korean history can definitely be traced for over three thousand years. It was founded about 1100 B.C. by a Chinese statesman, Ki-tze (now a legendary hero), who settled at Ping-yang. For centuries a high degree of civilization existed, a Korean language developed, and movable type was used in printing years before the Gutenberg discovery. Japanese settlers came, but also Japanese corsairs who raided the coast towns.

But the ancient kingdom did not enjoy unbroken peace. The Mongol, Kublai Khan, repeatedly invaded the territory. Then in 1419 a Yi ruler determined to destroy the Japanese pirates and fitted out a Korean fleet with a view to attacking the island of Tsushima, which was their stronghold. Though he failed of his objective he did later establish trade relations with Japan through the Daimio who ruled the island.

At the end of the sixteenth century a Japanese ruler, Hideyoshi, tried to capture Korea as one move in his advance on China. He took city after city, till at last the Koreans appealed for aid to the Chinese. Though the Japanese were driven out, they left the country in ruins, took many Korean craftsmen home with them as prisoners, and Korea found herself vassal to China. She deteriorated rapidly under this state of affairs.

The Koreans now forbade strangers to land on their shores, they successively repelled France and the United States of America and persecuted Christian missionaries with their converts. But on the advice of the Chinese statesman Li Hung Chang, Korea finally established trade relations with Japan, the United States, and other countries.

Now it happened that China had, about a generation previously, lost two huge provinces in the northeast to Russia: she was therefore the more reluctant to lose her hold on Korea and in 1894 China and Japan went to war over this key territory. The Chinese were defeated and agreed to recognize the independence of Korea.

Japan had by now secured a foothold on the mainland of Asia. This Russia found distasteful and compelled her to abandon. Russia, in the meantime, was advancing into northern China. Taking advantage of ill-feeling between certain Japanese officials and the Korean king, Russia secured valuable concessions in

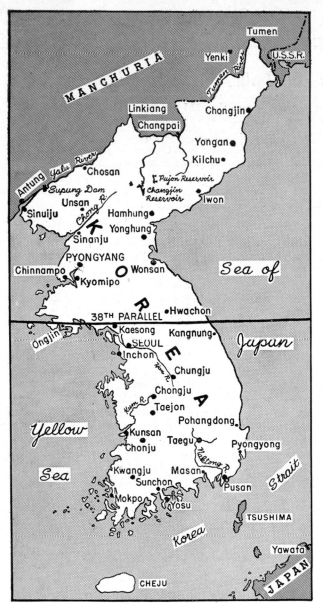

KOREA, THE ANCIENT CHOSEN

ished friendly relations with Korea and in 1910 Japan annexed the country under its ancient name of Chosen. But while the Japanese did much to further material progress, the Koreans deeply resented attempts to force the Japanese language and institutions on them.

Following the ouster of the Japanese government in 1945, the country was occupied jointly by United States and Russian forces. It was decided that Korea, once a kingdom, should have a free and independent democratic form of government.

However, rival factions disputed for control of the country. In May of 1948, two elections were held. The first took place in Soviet-occupied northern Korea and resulted in the formation of a communist form of People's Republic. The second election, in southern Korea, named the Korean Republic. The second election was recognized by the United Nations. Later, the Korean Republic adopted a constitution which also was recognized by the UN. The events that followed are discussed later on in this article.

The climate of Korea is dry and bracing in spring and fall though there is abundant rain in summer. It is never extremely hot or cold. Korea escapes the floods, droughts and typhoons that so often bring disaster to China and Japan; and there are no destructive earthquakes. The light sandy loam of the river plains produces two crops a year.

Land is easy to procure. Any native may become a farmer; he has only to reclaim and cultivate unoccupied land, and in three years the land becomes his own. His agricultural implements, however,

timber, ports and fisheries. As a result, in 1904 Japan declared war on the Tsar and by the next year had driven Russia out of Korea. By a treaty between the two warring countries, Korea was promised autonomy, while Russia surrendered to Japan the disputed foothold on the mainland and at Port Arthur.

The Marquis (later Prince) Ito as Japanese Resident-General now estab-

HOPEFUL KOREANS REBUILD THEIR HOME, NEAR CHINJU

Sixty per cent of the city of Chinju and its suburbs had been destroyed when the United Nations forces recaptured it in 1950. Chinju is in the South Keisho Province, in the cotton-growing region of Korea. It is only fifty-five miles from the seaport of Pusan. In the background is a typical Korean roof, with up-curved gables and up-curved ridgepole.

PHOTOS, UNATIONS

NO IDLE HANDS HERE

A South Korean farmer spreads wheat grains on a mat to dry in the sun. He will plant them in late October after the rice crop has been harvested. While the northern section of Korea endures extremes of heat and cold, the south, tempered by ocean breezes, allows a long season for agriculture. The valley of the Naktong River is able to produce two crops a year.

PUBLIC NEWSPAPERS ON AN OPEN-AIR BULLETIN BOARD

Even under normal conditions, newspapers and radios are still scarce in Korea; and most of the people get their news of local happenings and world events from public newspapers such as these, which serve hundreds. The wall notices are one indication of the fact that many more Koreans have been learning to read (and to write) in recent years.

jungle, but the thief lived to boast of his ride. Many such superstitious stories about the tiger are related in Korea.

The basic religions of Korea have been Confucianism, Animism (the belief that all natural objects have souls) and Buddhism. However, all of these faiths have been declining, particularly since 1945, as has ancestor worship. In 1948, it was estimated that almost 700,000 Koreans were Christians. In the past most religious observances were concerned with the propitiation of wicked demons. To keep these away, large sums were paid to professional sorceresses, of whom, at the end of the nineteenth century, there were

UNATIONS

BEATING CLOTHES WITH A STICK TO MAKE THEM SNOW-WHITE

For hundreds of years, while Korea was still a kingdom and forbiddingly remote from the world, the people wore white or pale blue clothing. Even today, when it would seem to be a hopeless task to keep garments immaculate, many Koreans still cling to the old costume. But as long as a Korean housewife has a clear stream nearby and a stick, she will attack dirt with vigor.

over one thousand. The Christian religion was introduced to Korea in the eighteenth century by a Roman Catholic priest and for some time was hotly resisted; converts were persecuted and priests tortured and killed. Since 1882, however, the teaching of the Christian religion has been allowed and, more recently, even encouraged.

The Koreans are taller than the Japanese, well made, with oval faces, high cheek bones and narrow eyes. The usual dress of the men is a plain white cotton robe, simply made. No needles or thread are used in the construction of Korean clothing: it is cut out and stuck together with glue. When washed it is simply unstuck, dried and stuck together again.

Summer undershirts of laborers are of airy, woven rattan. Stockings are of cotton wadding. Korean men wear curious little sailor hats perched on the tops of their heads, unless they are undergoing their three years of mourning for a parent. In that case they appear in mourning-hats with brims that rest on their shoulders. Korean gentlemen almost universally carry fans, and often they ride on palanquins made to rest on one central wheel to relieve the coolies of their weight.

Korean women pluck their eyebrows and redden their lips, but are kept in considerable seclusion. They marry very young and are considered successes when they have brought sons into the world. They are then called "the mother of" so-and-so.

A Korean wedding is strange; the couple do not see each other until the ceremony. When the bride is first led into the presence of her husband her eyes are sealed up and she does not speak. Even after marriage the Korean woman must be silent for a long time.

The one-story houses are made of mud and beams, and usually thatched. The floors are made of dried mud, which is stamped down and covered with oiled paper. The making of oiled paper is a large industry in Korea, for the windows

WIDE WORLD

JUST ANOTHER DISPLACED PERSON—WITH NO PLACE TO GO!

Trudging along a rocky road, a refugee carries with him all that he has left in the world—a pitifully small load—on his own back and tied to his pony. He may find shelter for a night; but his land is so blasted from years of warfare that he can have little hope of a bright future. Elsewhere in the world, too, oppression still creates a tragic toll of exiles.

KOREAN FARMERS LABOR LONG AND HARD WITH PRIMITIVE METHODS

This scene in the village of Kamjyun-ri, not far from the port city of Pusan, shows a Korean peasant woman drying red peppers in the sun. Korea is largely an agricultural country, rice being its most important crop. Barley, wheat and other grains, tobacco and cotton are also cultivated. Deep-sea fishing is a gainful calling of many on the eastern coast.

of the houses are also made of it and the same material is used as a lining for clothing. Koreans like "kimshee," a combination of turnips and sauerkraut; also a certain kind of seaweed cooked in oil, and occasionally, dog flesh served with a peppery relish. The rich drink honey water flavored with orange peel and ginger.

Seoul, the chief city, was founded by Emperor Yi Taejo as Hanyang (Fortress of the Han) in 1392, and it was the capital of the Korean rulers until Japan an-

nexed the country in 1910. On August 15, 1948, Seoul was made the capital of the Republic of Korea.

The city lies in a small valley, on the banks of the Han River, hemmed in by granite mountains, none more than 3,000 feet high. As Seoul is only a few miles south of the 38th parallel, the dividing line between North and South Korea, the city was a main objective in the invasion that began in June 1950. Battle lines have crossed it several times, the chief bridge across the Han has been destroyed, and today Seoul is a melancholy ruin.

Long ago it was completely surrounded by a wall, pierced by eight gates. One of these was called the Gate of Elevated Humanity and another the Gate of Bright Amiability. Until 1950 sections of this wall remained. Within the city there was another wall, enclosing the five hundred acres of ground on which the royal palace stood.

Among several ancient temples there was an elaborately carved marble pagoda, dating from the thirteenth century, and

a bell tower containing a bronze bell dated 1468. This bell had an especially lovely tone, which the Koreans explained by the following fable. The emperor ordered a bell-maker to fashion, on pain of death, a bell with a clear tone. Although the artisan tried, he was unable to do this until his daughter, who had a beautiful voice, flung herself into the molten metal from which the huge tongue was to be cast. The bell used to be rung at sunset and at dawn. At sunset all the men had to come indoors, for then it was the women's time to enjoy the open air.

UNATIONS

KOREA'S GREATEST HOPE FOR THE FUTURE IS HER CHILDREN

These youngsters are playing around an ancient stone image in the village of Mi A Ri, near the city of Seoul. They are as fascinated by wild flowers as children are everywhere, and they welcome the summer in spite of the searing sun. This portion of west central Korea is circled by low mountains; its summers are hot and humid, and its winters are severe.

The recent history of Korea is a far cry from legends or a serene evening stroll. Though the Koreans had to yield to the might of Japan in 1910, they never gave up hope of independence. In 1919 there was a rebellion, which the Japanese put down with great cruelty. A few Koreans escaped to other countries, partly to secure an education and also to enlist the sympathy of the outside world in Korea's plight.

With Japan's defeat at the end of World War II, she was stripped of all her acquired territory, including Korea. For a time, Russian forces occupied Korea north of the 38th parallel (which divides the country practically in the middle), and United States forces the area south of it. Though these forces were later withdrawn, the parallel continued to divide the country politically. Two independent governments were established: the Korean People's Republic, in the north; and the Republic of Korea, in the south.

North Korea, led by Communists, came into the Soviet sphere of influence, while South Korea had strong ties with the Western powers. Friction developed between North and South Korea and burst into flame when North Korean forces crossed the parallel on June 25, 1950. The United Nations (Russia was boycotting the Security Council at the time) considered this a clear case of aggression and called on member nations to help South Korea. Most of the forces involved in the conflict that followed have come from the United States.

By October of 1950, UN troops had reached the Yalu River, the boundary between North Korea and Manchuria, and hope arose in the Western world that the North Koreans were about to be defeated. Instead, Chinese Communist soldiers appeared in ever increasing numbers and began to push the UN forces back. By the late spring of 1951, however, the tide had turned again. On July 27, 1953, three years of war ended with the signing of a truce at Panmunjom. Fighting ceased immediately.

To this extent, one of the aims of the United Nations had been achieved —to drive the aggressors north of the parallel; but to establish a "free, independent and democratic Korea" still presented many difficulties. The Koreans will need help for some time to come.

KOREA: FACTS AND FIGURES

THE COUNTRY

A peninsula in Northeastern Asia bounded on the north by Manchuria and Siberia, on the east by the Sea of Japan, on the south by the Korea Strait and on the west by the Yellow Sea. Korea includes many islands along the south and west coasts. The area is 85,266 square miles and the population is 25,120,174 (1944).

GOVERNMENT

The government is divided. The communistic "People's Republic" set up in North Korea on May 1, 1948, is not recognized in the south, where a Constitution of the Korean Republic was adopted July 12, 1948, and its first president elected under UN supervision July 20, 1948.

COMMERCE AND INDUSTRIES

The country is almost entirely agricultural, with rice, barley, wheat, beans, and grains the chief crops. Cattle of good quality are raised and whale fishing pursued. Silkworm-raising is carried on. Gold, copper, iron and coal are abundant. The principal exports are rice, beans, peas, and pulse, hides, cattle, silk, cocoons and gold, and the imports include cotton goods, silk goods, machinery, kerosene oil, grass cloth, sugar and coal.

COMMUNICATIONS

Interior transport is by pack-horse, oxen, rail, motor cars and by river. Before the outbreak of the Korean war in 1950, there were 1,676 miles of railway in operation. Length of telegraph line was 5,496 miles and telephone line, 5,991 miles.

RELIGION AND EDUCATION

A large number still follow ancestor worship and Confucianism. There are also Buddhists and Christians. There are technical schools, industrial schools, a university in Seoul, and 18 special colleges. An adult-education campaign against illiteracy has been launched in South Korea.

CHIEF TOWNS

Population, 1946: Seoul, capital of South Korea, 1,141,766; Pusan, 400,156; Taegu, 269,113; Inchon, 215,784. The city of Pyengyang, capital of North Korea, had a population of 285,965 in 1940. Later figures are unavailable.

COLOR PLATES IN VOLUME IV

AFGHANISTAN: PAGE
Glacier on Chitral Border 9
Fruit from Kandahar 12
Woman Collecting Wood 13
Stone Watch Tower 16
Mountainous Kafiristan 17

BHUTAN:
Royal Palace 125
Maharaja and Councilors 132
Reincarnation of Buddha 133
Dharm Rájá 136

CEYLON:
Rice Fields 170
Tea Garden 171
Tamil Dancers 174
Tamil Girls 175
Native Boats on a River 178
Image of Buddha 179
Devil Dancer 182
Sinhalese Girl 183

CHINA:
The Great Wall 250
Monastery on Pu Tu Island 251
Priest of Pu Tu 254
Holy Man 255
Yangtze Kiang 258
Highway to Kalgan 259
Shanghai Man 262
Chinese Actor 263
Temple in Ningpo 266
Street of Kiukiang 267
Bride and Bridegroom 270
Grandmother and Grandson 271
Canal in Sungkiang 274
Pagoda at Soochow 275
Barren Mountain Slopes 278
Walls of Liaoyang 279
Hall of Classics, Peking 330
Entrance to Imperial Palace 331

INDIA, REPUBLIC OF:
Pearl Palace, Gwalior 20
Daulatabad Fortress 21
Maratha Horseman 24
Pearl Mosque, Delhi 26
Old-Time Executioner 27
Shah Jehan Palace, Delhi 30
Pearl Mosque, Delhi 31
Jama Masjid, Ahmadabad 34
Open-Air Temple 35
Great Mosque, Delhi 38
Cenotaph at Alwar 39
Dancing Girls 41
Hall of Private Audience 44

INDIA, REPUBLIC OF (continued):   PAGE
Taj Mahal, Agra 45
Bijapur Ruins 48–49
Jain Temples, Kathiawar 52
Hindu Temple, Sriringam 53
Ghurka Woman 56
Hindu Temple, Gujarat 57
Buddh Gaya Temple, Bihar 60
Kutb Minar Tower 61
Banaras 64–65
Jama Masjid Courtyard, Delhi 68
Golden Temple, Amritsar 69

INDOCHINA:
Emperor of Annam 214
Cambodia's King 215

JAPAN:
Sacred Isle of Miyajima 334
Fuji the Peerless 335
Two Japanese Maidens 338
Under the Cherry Trees 339
Temple Gate at Miyajima 342
Temple Garden, Kyoto 343
Buddhist Priest 346
Friendly Greetings 347
Gardens of Hori-Kiri 350
Girls and Babies 351
New Year's Customs 354
Wistaria Garden 355
Yasaka Pagoda, Kyoto 358
Japanese Garden 359

PAKISTAN:
Dancers 72
Fruit-Seller 90
Washing in River 91
Musicians and Dancers 94
Sikhs 95
Pathans 98
Ivory-Carver 99

THAILAND:
Bangkok 202
Houses on Piles 203
Outside the Royal Palace 206
Siamese Drama 207
Elephants 210
Buddhist Temple 211

TIBET:
Devil Dancer 121
Na-Chung Monastery 124
The Potala, Lhasa 128–29

ARCTIC
OCEAN
Ellesmere I.
GREENLAND
Baffin
Bay
Bank I.
Victoria
I.
Baffin
I.
ASIA
Bering Strait
Yukon
River
Mackenzie
River
Great Bear
Lake
Great Slave
Lake
Davis
Strait
Hudson
Bay
Bering
Sea
ROCKY
R. Nelson
L. Winnipeg
Aleutian Islands
Vancouver
Island
NORTH
Great
Lakes
St. Lawrence R.
Newfoundland
Columbia R.
Missouri R.
MTS.
AMERICA
APPALACHIAN MTS.
Azores
ATLANTIC
Colo. R.
Rio
Grande
Miss.
Bermuda I.
Gulf of
Mexico
Bahama Is.
West
Indies
Cuba
Hawaii
Islands
CENTRAL
AMERICA
Caribbean
Sea
OCEAN
PACIFIC
Panama
Canal
Orinoco R.
Gilbert Is.
EQUATOR
Amazon
River
Phoenix Is.
Solomon Is.
Marquesas Is.
ANDES
SOUTH
Madeira R.
São
R.
Francisco
Society Is.
New
Hebrides
OCEAN
AMERICA
New
Caledonia
Fiji Is.
Tuamotu
Archipelago
MTS.
Paraná R.
NEW
ZEALAND
Falkland
Islands
Strait of Magellan
Cape Horn
Drake Strait
ANTARCTIC
CIRCLE
Weddell
Sea